TRUTH AND INNOCENCE VINDICATED

John Owen

Vintage Puritan Series
GLH Publishing
LOUISVILLE, KY

Sourced from *The Works of John Owen*, Vol. XIII.
Edited by William Goold. Johnstone & Hunter, London, 1852.

Republished by GLH Publishing, 2020.

ISBN:
 Paperback 978-1-64863-018-7
 Epub 978-1-64863-019-4

CONTENTS

Prefatory Note. 1
A Survey of a Discourse Concerning Ecclesiastical Polity...........4
A Survey of the First Chapter...45
A Survey of the Second Chapter...92
A Survey of the Third Chapter..127
A Survey of the Fourth Chapter..143
A Survey of the Fifth Chapter 145
A Survey of the Sixth Chapter...155

PREFATORY NOTE.

SAMUEL PARKER, author of the "Discourse of Ecclesiastical Polity, and of the Power of the Magistrate in Matters of Religion," to which Owen supplied the following answer, was a noted character in his day. When a student in Wadham College, Oxford, he was a Puritan of the strictest fashion; but as worldly advancement was his ruling motive, he changed his views, and recommended himself to the Court by his abject subserviency to its arbitrary measures. He was made Bishop of Oxford in 1686, and when the Fellows of Magdalen College distinguished themselves by their magnanimous resistance to the encroachment on their privileges attempted by the Crown, and Hough, who had obtained their almost unanimous suffrages to the vacant office of President, had been forcibly ejected, Parker was thrust, upon them, as a fit tool for promoting the despotic and popish views of James II. It was natural that such a man should harbour the deepest malice against Nonconformists, — a malice in which the usual rancour of apostasy mingled as an ingredient of especial bitterness.

We refer to the Life of Owen, vol. i., p. 88, for an account of the controversy to which Parker's book gave rise, and for a just appreciation of the merits of Owen's work in reply to it. Besides Owen's work, several anonymous answers to Parker appeared, under such titles as the following:— "Insolence and Impudence Triumphant; Envy and Fury Enthroned; The Mirror of Malice and Madness," etc., 1670; "Toleration Discussed in Two Dialogues," 1670; "Animadversions on a New Book entitled Ecclesiastical Polity," 1670; and, "A Free Inquiry into the Causes of that very great Esteem the Nonconformists are in with their Followers," 1673.

Parker in 1671 replied to Owen, in "A Defense and Continuation of the Ecclesiastical Polity," and in a preface to Bishop Bramhall's "Vindication of the Episcopal Clergy," written in a characteristic strain of mingled ribaldry and bombast. In 1672, Marvell published his famous "Rehearsal Transprosed." Marvell was immediately assailed in a host of pamphlets:— "The Transproser Rehearsed;" "Rosemary and Bayes;" "Gregory Father Greybeard with his Vizor off;" "A Common-place Book out of the Rehearsal Transprosed;" "S'too him Bayes," etc. Parker's own pamphlet in reply to him bore the title, "A Reproof to the Rehearsal Transprosed, in a Discourse to its Author."

The genius of Marvell, however, carried all before him in the second part of his work, published in 1673. The title of it, with the exception of an oath prefixed to the threat quoted in it, is subjoined, as an illustration of the intensity of feeling excited by the dispute, and of the dread which the friends of Parker entertained for the keen weapons of the puritan wit:— "The Rehearsal Transprosed, the second part: occasioned by two letters; the first printed by a nameless author, entitled 'A Reproof,' etc.; the second left for me at a friend's house, dated November 3, 1673, subscribed 'J. G.,' and concluding with these words, 'If thou darest to print any lie or libel against Dr Parker, ... I will cut thy throat.'" Marvell, undeterred by these profane threats and ravings, dealt such a blow to his main opponent as made him the laughing-stock of every circle, and compelled him for a time to hide his shame in rural obscurity.

Owen in the following work confines himself to a refutation of the slavish and extravagant notions respecting magistratical authority and the royal prerogative which the minion of the Court had not shrunk from propounding. The work is a complete magazine of sound argumentation on such questions as the power of the magistrate, the rights of conscience, and the iniquity of persecution. If Marvell had the credit of silencing Parker in a torrent of caustic ridicule, which, though not untainted with the coarseness of the age, has rendered his "Rehearsal" a source of interest and amusement to many who, taking no interest in ecclesiastical disputes, have been drawn to the perusal of it simply by its literary merit, still we may claim for Owen the praise of establishing, on a basis of able argument, the rights and privileges of which such abettors of arbitrary power as Parker sought to deprive their countrymen. Owen writes in that spirit of calm self-possession and dignity which never under any provocations deserted him, and, compared with the "Rehearsal Transprosed," his treatise will be accounted dull. Frequently, however, he brightens and relieves the tenor of his reasonings by strokes of effective sarcasm, which it may be questioned if even the genius of Marvell has surpassed. Parker's views are ludicrously reduced to an absurdity by the supposition of an edict for the settlement of religion, drawn up according to his own principles, and almost in his own words. See page 382. And again, after showing that Parker virtually claimed for the civil magistrate an authority which God only possesses over the conscience, Owen alludes to the preposterous argument that the magistrate should now inflict penalties for errors in religion, in room of what the excommunicated suffered in the days of the apostles at the hands of the devil, p. 406. This work,'" he remarks, in a sally of exquisite humour, "the devil now ceasing to attend unto, he would have the magistrate to take upon him to supply his place and office, by punishments of his own appointment and infliction: and so at last, to be sure of giving him full measure, he hath ascribed two extremes unto him about religion, — namely to act the part of God and the devil!" For an estimate of the more solid qualities and general merits of the following work, the reader is again commended to the critique on it, in the "Life of Owen." — ED.

A SURVEY OF A DISCOURSE CONCERNING ECCLESIASTICAL POLITY.

REVIEW OF THE PREFACE.

AMONG the many disadvantages which those who plead in any sense for liberty of conscience are exposed unto, it is not the least that in their arguings and pleas they are enforced to admit a supposition that those whom they plead for are indeed really mistaken in their apprehensions about the matters concerning which they yet desire to be indulged in their practice: for unless they will give place to such a supposition, or if they will rigidly contend that what they plead in the behalf of is absolutely the truth, and that obedience thereunto is the direct will and command of God, there remains no proper field for the debate about indulgence to be managed in; for things acknowledged to be such are not capable of an indulgence, properly so called, because the utmost liberty that is necessary unto them is their right and due in strict justice and law. Men, therefore, in such discourses, speak not to the nature of the things themselves, but to the apprehensions of them with whom they have to do. But yet against this disadvantage every party which plead for themselves are relieved by that secret reserve that they have in the persuasion of the truth and goodness of what they profess, and desire to be indulged in the practice of; and this, also, as occasion doth offer itself, and in defence of themselves from the charge of their adversaries, they openly contend and avow. Neither was it judged formerly that there was any way to deprive them of this reserve and relief but by a direct and particular debate of the matters specially in difference, carried on unto their conviction by evidence of truth, managed from the common principles of it. But after trial made, this way to convince men of their errors and mistakes, who stand in need of indulgence with respect unto the outward administration of the powers that they are under, is found, as it should seem, tedious, unreasonable, and ineffectual. A new way, therefore, to this purpose is fixed on, and it is earnestly pleaded that there needs no other argument or medium to prove men to be mistaken in their apprehensions, and to miscarry in their practice of religious duties, than that at any time or in any place they stand in need of indulgence. To dissent, at all adventures, is a crime, and he whom others persecute, tacitly at least, confesseth himself guilty; for it is said that the law of the magistrate being the sole rule of obedience in religious worship, their non-compliance with any law by him established, evidencing itself in their desire of exemption, is a sufficient conviction, yea, a self-acknowledgment, not only of their errors and mistakes in what they apprehend of their duty in these things, and of their miscarriages in what they practice, but also that themselves are persons turbulent and seditious, in withdrawing obedience from the laws which are justly imposed on them. With what restrictions and limitations, or whether with any or no, these assertions are maintained, we shall afterward inquire.

The management of this plea (if I greatly mistake him not) is one of the principal designs of the author of that discourse, a brief survey whereof is here proposed. The principle which he proceeds herein upon himself, it seems, knew to be novel and uncouth, and therefore thought it incumbent on him that both the manner of its handling, and the other principles that he judged meet to associate with it or annex unto it, should be of the same kind and complexion. This design hath at length produced us this discourse; which, of what use it may prove to the church of God, what tendency it may have to retrieve or promote love and peace among Christians, I know not. This I know, that it hath filled many persons of all sorts, with manifold surprisals, and some with amazement. I have, therefore, on sundry considerations, prevailed with myself, much against my inclinations, for the sake of truth and peace, to spend a few hours in the examination of the principal parts and seeming pillars of the whole fabric. And this I was in my own mind the more easily induced unto, because there is no concernment either of the church or state in the things here under debate, unless it be that they should be vindicated from having any concern in the things and opinions here pleaded and argued. For as to the present church, if the principles and reasonings here maintained and managed are agreeable unto her sentiments, and allowed by her, yet there can be no offence given in their examination, because she hath nowhere yet declared them so to be. And the truth is, if they are once owned and espoused by her, to the ends for which they are asserted, as the Christians of old triumphed in the thoughts of him who first engaged in ways of violence against them among the nations in the world, so the Nonconformists will have no small relief to their minds in their sufferings, when they understand these to be the avowed principles and grounds on which they are to be persecuted and destroyed. And for the power of ecclesiastical jurisdiction belonging to the kings of this nation, as it hath been claimed and exercised by them in all ages since the establishment of Christian religion among us, as it is declared in the laws, statutes, and customs of the kingdom, and prescribed unto an acknowledgment in the oaths of allegiance and supremacy, it hath not the least concern in the matter here in question; yea, it is allowed, acknowledged, and pleaded for, by those whom this author designs to oppose. Whatever, then, shall be spoken of this subject, it is but a bare ventilation of private opinions, and those such as which, if one doctor's judgment may advance into the reputation of probability, so that some may venture to act upon them, yet are they not so far thereby secured as to have sanctuary given them even from private men's examinations. Herein, then, I suppose, a liberty may be exercised without just offence to any; and our disquisition after the truth of the principles and theorems that will come under consideration may be harmlessly accompanied with a moderate plea in the behalf of their innocency who are invidiously traduced, contemptuously reproached, unduly charged and calumniated, beyond, I am sure, any ordinary examples or precedents, among men of any sort, rank, degree, difference, or profession in the world. Yea, this seems to be called for by the light and law of nature, and to be useful, yea, needful to public tranquillity, beyond what in this present hasty review shall be attempted.

For the author of this discourse, he is to me utterly unknown; neither do I intend either to make any inquiry after him, or hastily to fix a credit unto any reports concerning either who he is or of what consideration in the world. I am not concerned to know what, it seems, he was concerned to conceal. Nor do I use to consider reasons, arguments, or writings under a relation to any persons; which contributes nothing to their worth or signification. Besides, I know how deceitful reports are in such matters, and no way doubt but that they will betray persons of an over-easy credulity into those mistakes about the writer of this survey which he is resolved to avoid with reference to the author of the discourse itself. Only, the character that in the entrance of it he gives of himself, and such other intimations of his principles as he is pleased to communicate, I suppose he will be willing we should take notice of, and that we may do so without offence.

Thus, in the entrance of his preface, he tells us that he is "a person of such a tame and softly humour, and so cold a complexion, that he thinks himself scarce capable of hot and passionate impressions," though I suppose he avow himself, p. 4, to be chafed into some heat and briskness with that evenness and steadiness of expression which we shall be farther accustomed unto. But in what here he avers of himself, he seems to have the advantage of our Lord Jesus Christ, who, upon less provocations than he hath undertaken the consideration of (for the Pharisees with whom he had to deal were gentlemen, he tells us, unto those with whom himself hath to do), as he saith, "fell into a hot fit of zeal, yea, into a height of impatience, which made him act with a seeming fury and transport of passion," p. 7. And if that be indeed his temper which he commends in himself, he seems to me to be obliged for it unto his constitution and complexion, as he speaks, and not to his age, seeing his juvenile expressions and confidence will not allow us to think that he suffers under any defervescency of spirit by his years. The philosopher tells us that old men, in matters dubious and weighty, are not over-forward to be positive, but ready to cry, ἴσως καὶ τάχα, perhaps, and it may be so; and this δι' ἐμπειρίαν, because they have experience of the uncertainty of things in this world; as, indeed, those who know what entanglements all human affairs are attended withal, what appearing causes and probable reasons are to be considered and examined about them, and how all rational determinations are guided and influenced by unforeseen emergencies and occasions, will not be over-forward to pronounce absolutely and peremptorily about the disposal of important affairs. But, as the same author informs us, Οἱ νέοι εἰδέναι πάντα οἴονται καὶ διϊσχυρίζονται, "Young men suppose that they know all things, and are vehement in their asseverations:" from which frame proceeded all those dogmatical assertions of what is politic and impolitic in princes, of what will establish or ruin governments, with the contempt of the conceptions of others about things conducing to public peace and tranquillity, which so frequently occur in our author. This makes him smile at as serious consultations for the furtherance of the welfare and prosperity of this nation as, it may be, in any age or juncture of time have been upon the wheel, preface, p. 48. These considerations made it seem to me that, in an ordinary course, he hath time enough before him to improve the notions he hath here blessed the world with a discovery of, if, upon second thoughts, he be equally enamoured of them unto what now he seems to be.

I could, indeed, have desired that he had given us a more clear account of that religion which in his judgment he doth most approve. His commendation of the church of England sufficiently manifesteth his interest to lie therein, and that, in pursuit of his own principles, he doth outwardly observe the institutions and prescriptions of it; but the scheme he hath given us of religion, or religious duties, — wherein there is mention neither of sin nor a Redeemer, without which no man can entertain any one true notion of Christian religion, — would rather bespeak him a philosopher than a Christian. It is not unlikely but that he will pretend he was treating of religion as religion in general, without an application of it to this or that in particular; but to speak of religion as it is among men in this world, or ever was since the fall of Adam, without a supposition of sin, and the way of a relief from the event of it mentioned, is to talk of chimeras, — things that neither are, ever were, or will be. On the other hand, the profit and advantage of his design falls clearly on the papal interest; for whereas it is framed and contrived for the advantage, security, and unquestionableness of absolute compliers with the present possessors of power, it is evident that, in the state of Europe, the advantage lies incomparably on that hand. But these things are not our concernment. The designs which he manageth in his discourse, the subject-matter of it, the manner how he treats those with whom he hath to do, and deports himself therein, are by himself exposed to the judgment of all, and are here to be taken into some examination. Now, because we have in his preface a perfect representation of the things last mentioned throughout the whole, I shall, in the first place, take a general view and prospect of it.

And here I must have regard to the judgment of others. I confess, for my own part, I do not find myself at all concerned in those invectives, tart and upbraiding expressions, those sharp and twinging satires against his adversaries, which he avoweth or rather boasteth himself to have used. If this unparalleled heap of revilings, scoffings, despiteful reproaches, sarcasms, scornful, contemptuous expressions, false criminations, with frequent intimations of sanguinary affections towards them, do please his fancy and express his morality to his own satisfaction, I shall never complain that he hath used his liberty, and do presume that he judgeth it not meet that it should be restrained. It is far from my purpose to return him any answer in the like manner to these things; to do it

"— opus est mangone perito
Qui Smithfieldensi polleat eloquio."

Yet some instances of prodigious excesses in this kind will, in our process, be reflected on; and it may be the repetition of them may mae an appearance, unto some less considerate readers, of a little harshness in some passages of this return. But as nothing of that nature in the least is intended, — nothing that might provoke the author in his own spirit, were he capable of any "hot impressions," nothing to disadvantage him in his reputation or esteem, — so what is spoken, being duly weighed, will be found to have nothing sharp or unpleasant in it, but what is unavoidably infused into it from the discourse itself, in its approach unto it to make a representation of it.

It is of more concernment to consider with what frame and temper of spirit he manageth his whole cause and debate; and this is such as that a man who knows nothing of him but what he learns from this discourse would suppose that he hath been some great commander

"In campis Gurgustidoniis,
Ubi Bombamachides Cluninstarydisarchides
Erat imperator summus; Neptuni nepos,"
[Plaut. Mil. I. i. 13,]

associate unto him who with his breath blew away and scattered all the legions of his enemies, as the wind doth leaves in autumn.

Such confidence in himself and his own strength; such contempt of all his adversaries, as persons "silly, ignorant, illiterate;" such boastings of his achievements, with such a face and appearance of scorning all that shall rise up against him; such expressions "animi gladiatorii," doth he march withal as no man, sure, will be willing to stand in his way, unless he think himself to have lived, at least quietly, long enough. Only, some things there are which I cannot but admire in his undertaking and management of it; as, first, that such a man of arms and art as he is should harness himself with so much preparation, and enter the lists with so much pomp and glow, to combat such pitiful, poor, baffled ignoramuses as he hath chosen to contend withal, especially considering that he knew he had them bound hand and foot, and cast under his stroke at his pleasure. Methinks it had more become him to have sought out some giant in reason and learning, that might have given him at least "par animo periculum," as Alexander said in his conflict with Porus, a danger big enough to exercise his courage, though through mistake it should, in the issue, have proved but a windmill. Again; I know not whence it is, nor by what rules of errantry it may be warranted, that, being to conflict with such pitiful triflers, he should, before he come near to touch them, thunder out such terrible words, and load them with so many reproaches and contemptuous revilings; as if he designed to scare them out of the lists, that there might be no trial of his strength nor exercise of his skill.

But leaving him to his own choice and liberty in these matters, I am yet persuaded that if he knew how little his adversaries esteem themselves concerned in or worsted by his revilings, how small advantage he hath brought unto the cause managed by him, with what severity of censures, that I say not indignation, his proceedings herein are reflected on by persons sober and learned, who have any respect to modesty or sobriety, or any reverence for the things of God as debated among men, he would abate somewhat of that self-delight and satisfaction which he seems to take in his achievement.

Neither is it in the matter of *dissent* alone from the established forms of worship that this author and some others endeavour, by their revilings and scoffings, to expose Nonconformists to scorn and violence, but a semblance at least is made of the like reflections on their whole profession of the gospel and their worship of God; yea, these are the special subjects of those swelling words of contempt, those sarcastical, invidious representations of what they oppose, which they seem to place their confidence of success in. But what do they think to effect by this course of procedure? Do they suppose that by crying out, "canting phrases, silly nonsense, metaphors," they shall shame the Nonconformists out of the profession of the gospel, or make them forego the course of their ministry, or alienate one soul from the truth taught and professed amongst them? They know how their predecessors in the faith thereof have been formerly entertained in the world. St Paul himself, falling among the gentlemen philosophers of those days, was termed by them σπερμολόγος, a "babbler," or one that *canted*, his doctrine despised as silly and foolish, and his phrases pretended to be unintelligible. These things move not the Nonconformists, unless it be to a compassion for them whom they see to press their wits and parts to so wretched an employment. If they have any thing to charge on them with respect to gospel truths, — as, that they own, teach, preach, or publish, any doctrines or opinions that are not agreeable thereunto and to the doctrine of the ancient and late (reformed) churches, let them come forth, if they are men of learning, reading, and ingenuity, and, in ways used and approved from the beginning of Christianity for such ends and purposes, endeavour their confutation and conviction; — let them, I say, with the skill and confidence of men, and according to all the rules of method and art, state the matters in difference between themselves and their adversaries, confirm their own judgments with such reasons and arguments as they think pleadable in their behalf, and oppose the opinions they condemn with testimonies and reasons suited to their eversion. The course at present steered and engaged in, to carp at phrases, expressions, manners of the declaration of men's conceptions, collected from, or falsely fathered upon, particular persons, thence intimated to be common to the whole party of Nonconformists (the greatest guilt of some whereof, it may be, is only their too near approach to the expressions used in the Scripture to the same purpose, and the evidence of their being educed from thence), is unmanly, unbecoming persons of any philosophic generosity, much more Christians and ministers; nay, some of the things or sayings reflected on and carped at by a late author are such as those who have used or asserted them dare modestly challenge him, in their defence, to make good his charge in a personal conference, — provided it may be scholastical or logical, not dramatic or romantic. And surely were it not for their confidence in that tame and patient humour which this author so tramples upon, p. 15, they could not but fear that some or other, by these disingenuous proceedings, might be provoked to a recrimination, and to give in a charge against the cursed oaths, debaucheries, profaneness, various immoralities, and sottish ignorance, that are openly and notoriously known to have taken up their residence among some of those persons, whom the railleries of this and some other authors are designed to countenance and secure.

Because we may not concern ourselves again in things of this nature, let us take an instance or two of the manner of the dealing of our author with the Nonconformists, and those as to their preaching and praying, which of all things they are principally maligned about. For their preaching, he thus sets it out, p. 75: "Whoever among them can invent any new language presently sets up for a man of new discoveries; and he that lights upon the prettiest nonsense is thought by the ignorant rabble to unfold new gospel mysteries; and thus is the nation shattered into infinite factions with senseless and fantastic phrases: and the most fatal miscarriage of them all lies in abusing Scripture expressions, not only without but in contradiction to their sense; so that had we but an act of parliament to abridge preachers the use of fulsome and luscious metaphors, it might perhaps be an effectual cure of all our present distempers. Let not the reader smile at the oddness of the proposal; for were men obliged to speak sense as well as truth, all the swelling mysteries of fanaticism would then sink into flat and empty nonsense, and they would be ashamed of such jejune and ridiculous stuff as their admired and most profound notions would appear to be." Certainly there are few who read these expressions that can retain themselves from smiling at the pitiful, fantastic souls that are here characterized, or from loathing their way of preaching here represented. But yet if any should, by a surprisal, indulge themselves herein, and one should seriously inquire what it is that stirred those humours in them, it may be they could scarce return a rational account of their commotions; for when they have done their utmost to countenance themselves in their scorn and derision, they have nothing but the bare assertions of this author for the proof of what is here charged on those whom they deride. And how if these things are most of them, if not all of them, absolutely false? how if he be not able to prove any of them by any considerable avowed instance? how if all the things intended, whether they be so or no as here represented, depend merely on the judgment and fancy of this author, and it should prove in the issue that they are no such rules, measures, or standards of men's rational expressions of their conceptions, but that they may be justly appealed from? And how if sundry things so odiously here expressed be proved to have been sober truths, declared in words of wisdom and sobriety? what if the things condemned as "fulsome metaphors" prove to be scriptural expressions of gospel mysteries? what if the principal doctrines of the gospel, about the grace of God, the mediation of Christ, of faith, justification, gospel obedience, communion with God, and union with Christ, are esteemed and stigmatized by some as "swelling mysteries of fanaticism," and the whole work of our redemption by the blood of Christ, as expressed in the Scripture, be deemed metaphorical? In brief, what if all this discourse concerning the preachings of Nonconformists be, as unto the sense of the words he used, false, and the crimes in them injuriously charged upon them? what if the metaphors they are charged with are no other but their expression of gospel mysteries, "not in the words which man's wisdom teacheth, but which the Holy Ghost teacheth, comparing spiritual things with spiritual? As these things may and will be made evident when particulars shall be instanced in, so when, I say, these things are discovered and laid open, there will be a composure, possibly, of those affections and disdainful thoughts which those swelling words may have moved in weak and inexperienced minds. It may be, also, it will appear that, upon a due consideration, there will be little subject-matter remaining to be enacted in that law or act of parliament which he moves for; unless it be from that uncouth motion, that men may be "obliged to speak sense as well as truth," seeing hitherto it hath been supposed that every proposition that is either true or false hath a proper and determined sense; and if sense it have not, it can be neither. I shall only crave leave to say, that as to the doctrines which they preach, and the manner of their preaching, or the way of expressing those doctrines or truths which they believe and teach, the Nonconformists appeal from the rash, false, and invidious charge of this author, to the judgment of all learned, judicious, and pious men in the world; and are ready to defend them against himself, and whosoever he shall take to be his patrons or his associates, before any equal, competent, and impartial tribunal under heaven. It is far from me to undertake the absolute defence of any party of men, or of any man because he is of any party whatever, much less shall I do so of all the individual persons of any party, and least of all as to all their expressions, private opinions, and peculiar ways of declaring them, which too much abound among persons of all sorts. I know there is no party but have weak men belonging to it, nor any men amongst them but have their weaknesses, failings, and mistakes; and if there are none such in the church of England, — I mean those that universally comply with all the observances at present used therein, — I am sure enough that there are so amongst all other parties that dissent from it. But such as these are not principally intended in these aspersions, nor would their adversaries much rejoice to have them known to be and esteemed of all what they are. But it is others whom they aim to expose unto contempt; and in the behalf of them, not the mistakes, misapprehensions, or undue expressions of any private persons, these things are pleaded.

But let us see if their prayers meet with any better entertainment. An account of his thoughts about them he gives us, p. 19: "It is the most solemn strain of their devotion, to vilify themselves with large confessions of the heinousest and most aggravated sins. They will freely acknowledge their offences against all the commands, and that with the foulest and most enhancing circumstances; they can rake together and confess their injustice, uncleanness, and extortion, and all the publican and harlot sins in the world: in brief, in all their confessions they stick not to charge themselves with such large catalogues of sin, and to amass together such a heap of impieties, as would make up the completest character of lewdness and villany; and if their consciences do really arraign them of all those crimes whereof they so familiarly indict themselves, there are no such guilty and unpardonable wretches as they. So, then, their confessions are either true or false. If false, then they fool and trifle with the

Almighty; if true, then I could easily tell them the fittest place to say their prayers in."

I confess this passage, at its first perusal, surprised me with some amazement. It was unexpected to me that he who designed all along to charge his adversaries with Pharisaism, and to render them like unto them, should instance in *their confession of sin* in their prayers, when it is even a *characteristical note* of the Pharisees that in their prayers they made no confession of sin at all; but it was far more strange to me that any man durst undertake the reproaching of poor sinners with the deepest acknowledgment of their sins before the holy God that they are capable to conceive or utter. Is this, thought I, the spirit of the men with whom the Nonconformists do contend, and upon whose instance alone they suffer? Are these their apprehensions concerning God, sin, themselves, and others? Is this the spirit wherewith the children of the church are acted? Are these things suited to the principles, doctrines, practices, of the church of England? Such reproaches and reflections, indeed, might have been justly expected from those poor deluded souls who dream themselves perfect and free from sin; but to meet with such a treaty from them who say or sing, "O God, the father of heaven, have mercy upon us, miserable sinners," at least three times a-week, was some surprisal. However, I am sure the Nonconformists need return no other answer, to them who reproach them for vilifying themselves in their confessions to God, but that of David to Michal, "It is before the Lord; and we will yet be more vile than thus, and will be base in our own sight." Our author makes no small stir with the pretended censures of some whom he opposes, — namely, that they should "esteem themselves and their party to be the elect of God, all others to be reprobates, — themselves and theirs to be godly, and all others ungodly;" wherein I am satisfied that he unduly chargeth those whom he intends to reflect upon. However, I am none of them. I do not judge any party to be all the elect of God, or all the elect of God to be confined unto any party. I judge no man living to be a reprobate, though I doubt not but that there are living men in that condition. I confine not holiness or godliness to any party, — not to the church of England, nor to any of those who dissent from it; but am persuaded that in all societies of Christians that are under heaven that hold the Head, there are some really fearing God, working righteousness, and accepted with him. But yet neither my own judgment nor the reflections of this author can restrain me from professing that I fear that he who can thus trample upon men, scoff at and deride them for the deepest confessions of their sins before God which they are capable of making, is scarce either well acquainted with the holiness of God, the evil of sin, or the deceitfulness of his own heart, or did not in his so doing take them into sufficient consideration. The church of England itself requires its children to "acknowledge their manifold sins and wickednesses, which from time to time they have grievously committed by thought, word, and deed, against the divine Majesty;" and what in general others can confess more, I know not. If men that are, through the light of God's Spirit and grace, brought to an acquaintance with the deceitful workings of sin in their own hearts and the hearts of others, considering aright the terror of the Lord, and the manifold aggravations wherewith all their sins are attended, do more particularly express these things before and to the Lord, when indeed nor they nor any other can declare the thousandth part of the vileness and unworthiness of sin and sinners on the account thereof, shall they be now despised for it, and judged to be men meet to be hanged? If this author had but seriously perused the confessions of Austin, and considered how he traces his sin from his nature in the womb, through the cradle, into the whole course of his life, with his marvellous and truly ingenuous acknowledgments and aggravations of it, perhaps the reverence of so great a name might have caused him to suspend this rash, and I fear impious discourse.

For the particular instances wherewith he would countenance his sentiments and censures in this matter, there is no difficulty in their removal. Our Lord Jesus Christ hath taught us to call the most secret workings of sin in the heart, though resisted, though controlled and never suffered to bring forth, by the names of those sins which they lie in a tendency unto; and men in their confessions respect more the pravity of their natures and the inward working and actings of sin than the outward perpetrations of it, wherein perhaps they may have little concernment in the world: as Job, who pleaded his uprightness, integrity, and righteousness against the charge of all his friends, yet when he came to deal with God, he could take that prospect of his nature and heart as to vilify himself before him, yea, to "abhor himself in dust and ashes."

Again; ministers, who are the mouths of the congregation to God, may and ought to acknowledge, not only the sins whereof themselves are personally guilty, but those also which they judge may be upon any of the congregation. This assuming of the persons of them to whom they speak, or in whose name they speak, is usual even to the sacred writers themselves. So speaks the apostle Peter, 1 Epist. iv. 3, "For the time past of our lives may suffice us to have wrought the will of the Gentiles, when we walked in lasciviousness, lusts, excess of wine, revellings, banquetings, and abominable idolatries." He puts himself amongst them, although the time past of his life, in particular, was remote enough from being spent in the manner there described; and so it may be with ministers when they confess the sins of the whole congregation. And the dilemma of this author about the truth or falsehood of these confessions will fall as heavy on St Paul as on any Nonconformist in the world; for besides the acknowledgment that he makes of the former sins of his life, when he was "injurious, a blasphemer, and persecutor" (which sins I pray God deliver others from), and the secret working of indwelling sin, which he cries out in his present condition to be freed from, he also, when an apostle, professeth himself the "chiefest of sinners." Now, this was either true or it was not: if it was not true, God was mocked; if it were, our author could have directed him to the fittest place to have made his acknowledgments in. What thinks he of the confessions of Ezra, of Daniel, and others, in the name of the whole people of God; of David concerning himself, whose self-abasements before the Lord, acknowledgments of the guilt of sin in all its aggravations and effects, far exceed any thing that Nonconformists are able to express?

As to his instances of the confession of "injustice, uncleanness, and extortion," it may be, as to the first and last, he would be put to it to make it good by express particulars; and I wish it be not found that some have need to confess them who cry at present they are not of these publicans. Uncleanness seems to bear the worst sound, and to lead the mind to the worst apprehensions of all the rest; but it is God with whom men have to do in their confessions, and before him, "What is man, that he should be clean? and he that is born of a woman, that he should be righteous? Behold, he putteth no trust in his saints; yea, the heavens are not clean in his sight. How much more abominable and filthy is man, who drinketh iniquity like water," Job xv. 14–16. And the whole church of God in their confession cry out, "We are all as an unclean thing, and all our righteousnesses are as filthy rags," Isa. lxiv. 6. There is a pollution of flesh and spirit which we are still to be cleansing ourselves from whilst we are in this world.

But to what purpose is it to contend about these things? I look upon this discourse of our author as a signal instance of the power of prejudice and passions over the minds of men: for, setting aside the consideration of a present influence from them, I cannot believe that any one that professeth the religion taught by Jesus Christ and contained in the Scripture can be so ignorant of the terror of the Lord; so unaccustomed to thoughts of his infinite purity, severity, and holiness; such a stranger to the accuracy, spirituality, and universality of the law; so unacquainted with the sin of nature, and the hidden deceitful workings of it in the hearts, minds, and affections of men; so senseless of the great guilt of the least sin, and the manifold inexpressible aggravations wherewith it is attended; so unexercised to that self-abasement and abhorrency which becomes poor sinners in their approaches to the holy God, when they consider what they are in themselves; so disrespective of the price of redemption that was paid for our sins, and the mysterious way of cleansing our souls from them by the blood of the Son of God, — as to revile, despise, and scoff at men for the deepest humblings of their souls before God, in the most searching and expressive acknowledgments of their sins, that they do or can make at any time.

The like account may be given of all the charges that this author manageth against the men of his indignation; but I shall return at present to the preface under consideration.

In the entrance of his discourse, being, as it seems, conscious to himself of a strange and wild intemperance of speech in reviling his adversaries, which he had either used or intended so to do, he pleads sundry things in his excuse or for his justification. Hereof the first is his zeal for the reformation of the church of England, and the settlement thereof with its forms and institutions. These, he saith, are "countenanced by the best and purest times of Christianity, and established by the fundamental laws of this land" (which yet, as to the things in contest between him and Nonconformists, I greatly doubt of, as not believing any fundamental law of this land to be of so late a date). To see this "opposed by a wild and fanatic rabble, rifled by folly and ignorance, on slender and frivolous pretences, so often and so shamefully baffled, yet again revived by the pride and ignorance of a few peevish, ignorant, and malapert preachers, brain-sick people" (all which gentle and peaceable expressions are crowded together in the compass of a few lines), is that which hath "chafed him into this heat and briskness." If this be not to deal with gainsayers in a "spirit of meekness;" if herein there be not an observation of the rules of speaking evil of no man, despising no man, of not saying "Raca" to our brother, or calling of him "fool;" if here be not a discovery how remote he is from self-conceit, elation of mind, and the like immoralities, — we must make inquiry after such things elsewhere: for, in this whole ensuing treatise, we shall scarce meet with any thing more tending to our satisfaction. For the plea itself made use of, those whom he so tramples on do highly honour the reformation of the church of England, and bless God for it continually, as that which hath had a signal tendency unto his glory, and usefulness to the souls of men. That as to the outward rites of worship and discipline contested about, it was in all things conformed unto the great rule of them, our author doth not pretend; nor can he procure it in those things, whatever he says, any "countenance from the best and purest times of Christianity." That it was every way perfect in its first edition, I suppose will not be affirmed; nor, considering the posture of affairs at the time of its framing, both in other nations and in our own, was it like it should so be. We may rather admire that so much was then done according to the will of God, than that there was no more. Whatever is wanting in it, the fault is not to be cast on the first reformers, who went as far as well in those days could be expected from them. Whether others who have succeeded in their place and room have since discharged their duty in perfecting what was so happily begun is "sub judice," and there will abide after this author and I have done writing. That as to the things mentioned, it never had an absolute quiet possession or admittance in this nation, — that a constant and no inconsiderable suffrage hath, from first to last, been given in against it, — cannot be denied; and for any "savage worrying" or "rifling of it" at present, no man is so barbarous as to give the least countenance to any such thing. That which is intended in these exclamations [explanations?] is only a desire that those who cannot comply with it as now established, in the matters of discipline and worship before mentioned, may not merely for that cause be worried and destroyed, as many have already been.

Again, the chief glory of the English Reformation consisted in the purity of its doctrine, then first restored to the nation. This, as it is expressed in the articles of religion, and in the publicly-authorized writings of the bishops and chief divines of the church of England, is, as was said, the glory of the English Reformation. And it is somewhat strange to me, that whilst one writes against *original sin*, another preaches up *justification by works*, and scoffs at *the imputation of the righteousness of Christ* to them that believe; yea, whilst some can openly dispute against the *doctrine of the Trinity*, the *Deity of Christ*, and *the Holy Ghost*; whilst instances may be collected of some men's impeaching all the articles almost throughout, — there should be no reflection in the least on these things. Only those who dissent from some outward methods of worship must be made the object of all this wrath and indignation.

"Quis tulerit Gracchos de seditione querentes?"
[Juv., ii. 24.]

Some men's guilt in this nature might rather mind them of pulling the beam out of their own eyes than to act with such fury to pull out the eyes of others for the motes which they think they espy in them. But hence is occasion given to pour out such a storm of fury, conveyed by words of as great reproach and scorn as the invention of any man, I think, could suggest, as is not lightly to be met withal. Might our author be prevailed with to mind the old rule, "Mitte male loqui, dic rem ipsam," these things might certainly be debated with less scandal, less mutual offences and provocations.

Another account of the reasons of his intemperance in these reproaches, supplying him with an opportunity to increase them in number and weight, he gives us, pp. 6, 7 of his preface; which, because it may well be esteemed a summary representation of his way and manner of arguing in his whole discourse, I shall transcribe: —

"I know," says he, "but one single instance in which zeal, or a high indignation, is just and warrantable, and that is when it vents itself against the arrogance of haughty, peevish, and sullen religionists, that, under higher pretences of godliness, supplant all principles of civility and good-nature; that strip religion of its outside, to make it a covering for spite and malice; that adorn their peevishness with a mark of piety, and shroud their ill-nature under the demure pretences of godly zeal, and stroke and applaud themselves as the only darlings and favourites of Heaven; and, with a scornful pride, disdain all the residue of mankind as a rout of worthless and unregenerate reprobates. Thus, the only hot fit of zeal we find our Saviour in was kindled by an indignation against the pride and insolence of the Jews, when he whipped the buyers and sellers out of the outward court of the temple; for though they bore a blind and superstitious reverence towards that part of it that was peculiar to their own worship, yet as for the outward court, the place where the Gentiles and proselytes worshipped, that was so unclean and unhallowed that they thought it could not be profaned by being turned into an exchange of usury. Now, this insolent contempt of the Gentiles, and impudent conceit of their own holiness, provoked the mild spirit of our blessed Saviour to such an height of impatience and indignation as made him, with a seeming fury and transport of passion, whip the tradesmen thence, and overthrow their tables."

What truth, candour, or conscience, hath been attended unto in the insolent reproaches here heaped up against his adversaries is left to the judgment of God and all impartial men; yea, let judgment be made and sentence be passed according to the ways, course of life, conversation, usefulness amongst men, readiness to serve the common concerns of mankind, in exercising loving-kindness in the earth, of those who are thus injuriously traduced, compared with any in the approbation and commendation of [those by] whom they are covered with these reproaches, and there lives not that person who may not be admitted to pronounce concerning the equity and righteousness, or iniquity, of these intemperances. However, it is nothing with them with whom he hath to do to be judged in man's day; they stand at the judgment-seat of Christ, and have not so learned him as to relieve themselves by false or fierce recriminations. The measure of the covering provided for all these excesses of unbridled passion is that alone which is now to be taken. The case expressed, it seems, is the only single instance in which zeal is "just and warrantable." How our author came to be assured thereof, I know not; sure I am that it doth neither comprise in it, nor hath any aspect on, the ground, occasion, or nature of the zeal of Phinehas, or of Nehemiah, or of David, or of Joshua, and, least of all, of our Saviour, as we shall see. He must needs be thought to be over-intent upon his present occasion, when he forgot not one or two, but indeed all instances of just and warrantable zeal that are given us in the only sacred repository of them.

For what concerns the example of our blessed Saviour, particularly insisted on, I wish he had offended one way only in the report he makes of it; for let any sober man judge, in the first place, whether those expressions he useth, of the "hot fit of zeal" that he was in, of the "height of impatience" that he was provoked unto, the "seeming fury and transport of passion" that he acted withal, do become that reverence and adoration of the Son of God which ought to possess the hearts and guide the tongues and writings of men that profess his name. But whatever other men's apprehensions may be, as it is not improbable but that some will exercise severity in their reflections on these expressions, for my part, I shall entertain no other thoughts but that our author, being engaged in the composition of an invective declamation, and aiming at a grandeur of words, yea, to fill it up with tragical expressions, could not restrain his pen from some extravagant excess when the Lord Christ himself came in his way to be spoken of.

However, it will be said the instance is pertinently alleged, and the occasion of the exercise of the zeal of our blessed Saviour is duly represented. It may be some will think so; but the truth is, there are scarce more lines than mistakes in the whole discourse to this purpose. What *court* it was of the temple wherein the action remembered was performed is not here particularly determined; only it is said to be the "outward court, wherein the Gentiles and proselytes worshipped, in opposition to that which was peculiar to the worship of the Jews." Now, of old, from the first erection of the temple, there were two courts belonging unto it, and no more: the inward court, wherein were the *brazen altar*, with all those utensils of worship which the priests made use of in their sacred offices; and the outward court, whither the people assembled, as for other devotions, so to behold the priests exercising their function, and to be in a readiness to bring in their own especial sacrifices, upon which account they were admitted to the altar itself. Into this outward court, which was a dedicated part of the temple, all Gentiles who were proselytes of righteousness, — that is, who, being circumcised, had taken upon them the observation of the law of Moses, and thereby joined themselves to the people of God, — were admitted, as all the Jewish writers agree. And these were all the courts that were at first sanctified, and were in use when the words were spoken by the prophet which are applied to the action of our Saviour, — namely, "My house shall be called a house of prayer, but ye have made it a den of thieves." Afterward, in the days of the Herodians, another court was added, by the immuring of the remainder of the hill, whereinto a promiscuous entrance was granted unto all people. It was, therefore, the ancient outward court whereinto the Jews thought that Paul had brought Trophimus the Ephesian, whom they knew to be uncircumcised. I confess some expositors think that it was this latter area from whence the Lord Christ cast out the buyers and sellers, but their conjecture seems to be altogether groundless; for neither was that court ever absolutely called "the temple," nor was it esteemed sacred, but common or profane, nor was it in being when the prophet used the words mentioned concerning the temple. It was, therefore, the other ancient outward court, common to the Jews and proselytes of the Gentiles, that is intended; for as there the salt and wood were stored that were daily used in their sacrifices, so the covetous priests, knowing that many who came up to offer were wont to buy the beasts they sacrificed at Jerusalem, to prevent the charge and labour of bringing them from far, to further, as they pretended, their accommodation, appropriated a market to themselves in this court, and added a trade in money, relating it may be thereunto, and other things, for their advantage. Hence the Lord Christ twice drove them, once at the beginning, and once at the end of his ministry in the flesh; not with "a seeming transport of fury," but with that evidence of the presence of God with him, and majesty of God upon him, that it is usually reckoned amongst one of the miracles that he wrought, considering the state of all things at that time amongst the Jews. And the reason why he did this, and the occasion of the exercise of his zeal, is so express in the Scripture, as I cannot but admire at the invention of our author, who could find out another reason and occasion of it;

for it is said directly that he did it because of their wicked profanation of the house of God, contrary to his express institution and command. Of a regard to the Jews' "contempt of the Gentiles" there is not one word, not the least intimation; nor was there in this matter the least occasion of any such thing.

These things are not pleaded in the least to give countenance to any in their proud, supercilious censures and contempt of others; wherein if any person living have outdone our author, or shall endeavour so to do, he will not fail, I think, to carry away the prize in this unworthy contest. Nor is it to apologize for them whom he charges with extravagancies and excesses in this kind. I have no more to say in their behalf but that, as far as I know, they are falsely accused and calumniated, though I will not be accountable for the expressions of every weak and impertinent person. Where men, indeed, sin openly in all manner of transgressions against the law and gospel; where a spirit of enmity to holiness and obedience unto God discovers and acts itself constantly on all occasions; in a word, where men wear sin's livery, — some are not afraid to think them sin's servants. But as to that elation of mind in self-conceit wherewith they are charged, their contempt of other men upon the account of party, which he imputes unto them, I must expect other proofs than the bare assertion of this author before I join with him in the management of his accusations. And no other answer shall I return to the ensuing leaves, fraught with bitter reproaches, invectives, sarcasms, far enough distant from truth and all sobriety; nor shall I, though in their just and necessary vindication, make mention of any of those things which might represent them persons of another complexion. If this author will give those whom he probably most aims to load with these aspersions leave to confess themselves poor and miserable sinners in the sight of God, willing to bear his indignation against whom they have sinned, and to undergo quietly the severest rebukes and revilings of men, in that they know not but that they have a providential permissive commission from God so to deal with them; and add thereunto that they yet hope to be saved by Jesus Christ, and in that hope endeavour to give up themselves in obedience to all his commands, — it contains that description of them which they shall always, and in all conditions, endeavour to answer. But I have only given these remarks upon the preceding discourse to discover upon what feeble grounds our author builds for his own justification in his present engagement.

Page 13 of his preface, he declares his *original design* in writing this discourse, — which was to "represent to the world the lamentable folly and silliness of those men's religion with whom he had to do;" which he farther expresses and pursues with such a lurry[1] of virulent reproaches as I think is not to be paralleled in any leaves but some others of the same hand; and in the close thereof he supposeth he hath evinced that, in comparison of them, "the most insolent of the Pharisees were gentlemen, and the most savage of the Americans philosophers." I must confess myself an utter stranger unto that generous disposition and philosophic nobleness of mind which vent themselves in such revengeful, scornful wrath, expressed in such rude and barbarous railings, against any sort of men whatever, as that here manifested in, and those here used by this author. If this be a just delineation and character of the spirit of a gentleman, a due portraiture of the mind and affections of a philosopher, I know not who will be ambitious to be esteemed either the one or the other. But what measures men now make of gentility I know not. Truly noble generosity of spirit was heretofore esteemed to consist in nothing more than remoteness from such pedantic severities against, and contemptuous reproaches of, persons under all manner of disadvantages, yea, impossibilities to manage their own just vindication; as are here exercised and expressed in this discourse; and the principal pretended attainment of the old philosophy was a sedateness of mind, and a freedom from turbulent passions and affections under the greatest provocations: which if they are here manifested by our author, they will give the greater countenance unto the character which he gives of others, the judgment and determination whereof is left unto all impartial readers.

But in this *main design* he professeth himself prevented by "the late learned and ingenious discourse, The Friendly De-

---

[1] A word occurring more than once in Owen's writings, though not noticed in such dictionaries as those of Webster and Richardson. It seems to mean "a disturbance, or tumult." See Halliwell's "Dictionary of Archaic and Provincial Words," where he quotes Cotton using the word in this sense. — Ed.

bate;"[2] which, to manifest, it may be, that his rhetorical faculty is not confined to invectives, he spendeth some pages in the splendid encomiums of. There is no doubt, I suppose, but that the author of that discourse will, on the next occasion, requite his panegyric, and return him his commendations for his own achievements with advantage. They are like enough to agree, like those of the poet:—

"Discedo Alcæus puncto illius, ille meo quis?
Quis nisi Callimachus?"
[Hor. Ep., ii. 2, 99.]

For the present, his account of the excellencies and successes of that discourse minds me of the dialogue between Pyrgopolynices and Artotrogus:—

Pyrg. Ecquid meministi? *Art.* Memini; centum in Ciliciâ,
Et quinquaginta centum Sycolatron dæ,
Triginta Sardi, sexaginta Macedones,
Sunt homines tu quos occidisti uno die.
Pyrg. Quanta isthæc hominum summa est?
Art. Septem millia.
Pyrg. Tantum esse oportet; rectè rationem tenes.
Art. At nullos habeo scriptos, sic memini tamen."
[Plaut. Mil. Glor., i. 1, 42.]

Although the particular instances he gives of the man's successes are prodigiously ridiculous, yet the casting up of the sum-total to the completing of his victory sinks them all out of consideration. And such is the account we have here of the Friendly Debate. This and that it hath effected; which though unduly asserted as to the particular instances, yet altogether

---

2   The work to which Owen refers is entitled, "A Friendly Debate between a Conformist and a Nonconformist, in two parts," London, 1669. It is understood to have been written by Dr Simon Patrick, who was afterwards successively Bishop of Chichester and of Ely. He died in 1691, and his memory is still respected for his Paraphrase and Critical Commentaries on the books of the Old Testament, and other works of a theological and devotional character. The "Debate" was resented by the Nonconformists as harsh and unjust in its strictures; and even on the other side, the eminent Judge Hale wrote to Baxter in strong disapproval of it. — ED.

comes short of that absolute victory and triumph which are ascribed unto it. But I suppose that, upon due consideration, men's glorying in those discourses will be but as the crackling of thorns in the fire, — noise and smoke, without any real and solid use or satisfaction. The great design of the author, as is apparent unto all, was to render the sentiments and the expressions of his adversaries ridiculous, and thereby to expose their persons to contempt and scorn.

"Egregiam verò laudem et spolia ampla!
[Æn., iv. 93.]

And to this end his way of writing by dialogues is exceedingly suited and accommodated; for although ingenious and learned men, such as Plato and Cicero, have handled matters of the greatest importance in that way of writing, candidly proposing the opinions and arguments of adverse parties in the persons of the dialogists, and sometimes used that method to make their design of instruction more easy and perspicuous, yet it cannot be denied that advantages may be taken from this way of writing to represent both persons, opinions, and practices, invidiously and contemptuously, above any other way; and therefore it hath been principally used by men who have had that design. And I know nothing in the skillful contrivance of dialogues, which is boasted of here with respect unto the Friendly Debate, as also by the author of it in his preface to one of his worthy volumes, that should free the way of writing itself from being supposed to be peculiarly accommodated to the ends mentioned. Nor will these authors charge them with want of skill and art in composing of their dialogues, who have designed nothing in them but to render things uncouth and persons ridiculous, with whom themselves were, in worth and honesty: no way to be compared.

An instance hereof we have in the case of Socrates. Sundry in the city being weary of him, for his uprightness, integrity, and continual pressing of them to courses of the like nature; some, also, being in an especial manner incensed at him and provoked by him; amongst them they contrived his ruin. That they might effect this design, they procured Aristophanes to write a dialogue, his comedy, which he entitled Νεφέλαι, "The Clouds;" wherein Socrates is introduced and personated, talking at as contemptible and ridiculous a rate as any one can represent the

Nonconformists to do, and yet withal to commend himself as the only man considerable amongst them. Without some such preparation of the people's minds, his enemies thought it impossible to obtain his persecution and destruction. And they failed not in their projection. Aristophanes, being poor, witty, and, as is supposed, hired to this work, lays out the utmost of his endeavours so to frame and order his dialogues, with such elegancy of words and composure of his verses, with such a semblance of relating the words and expressing the manner of Socrates, as might leave an impression on the minds of the people. And the success of it was no way inferior to that of the Friendly Debate; for though at first the people were somewhat surprised with seeing such a person so traduced, yet they were after a while so pleased and tickled with the ridiculous representation of him and his philosophy, wherein there was much of appearance and nothing of truths, that they could make no end of applauding the author of the Dialogues. And though this was the known design of that poet, yet that his dialogues were absurd and inartificial I suppose will not be affirmed, seeing few were ever more skilfully contrived. Having got this advantage of exposing him to public contempts his provoked malicious adversaries began openly to manage their accusation against him. The principal crime laid to his charge was *nonconformity*, or that he did not comply with the religion which the supreme magistrate had enacted; or, as they then phrased it, "he esteemed not them to be gods whom the city so esteemed." By these means, and through these advantages, they ceased not until they had destroyed the best and wisest person that ever that city bred in its heathen condition, and whereof they quickly repented themselves. The reader may see the whole story exactly related in Ælian., lib. ii.; Var. Histor., cap. 13. Much of it also may be collected from the Apologies of Xenophon and Plato in behalf of Socrates, as also Plutarch's Discourse concerning his Genius. To this purpose have dialogues very artificially written been used, and are absolutely the most accommodate of all sorts of writing unto such a design. Hence Lucian, who aimed particularly to render the things which he disliked ridiculous and contemptible, used no other kind of writing; and I think his Dialogues will be allowed to be artificial, though sundry of them have no other design but to cast contempt on persons and opinions better than himself and his own. And this way of dealing with adversaries in points of faith, opinion, and judgment, hath hitherto been esteemed fitter for the stage than a serious disquisition after truth, or confutation of error. Did those who admire their own achievements in this way of process but consider how easy a thing it is for any one, deposing that respect to truth, modesty, sobriety, and Christianity, which ought to accompany us in all that we do, to expose the persons and opinions of men, by false, partial, undue representations, to scorn and contempt, they would perhaps cease to glory in their fancied success. It is a facile thing to take the wisest man living, and after he is lime-twigged with ink and paper, and gagged with a quill, so that he can neither move nor speak, to clap a fool's coat on his back, and turn him out to be laughed at in the streets. The Stoics were not the most contemptible sort of philosophers of old, nor will be thought so by those who profess their religion to consist in morality only, and yet the Roman orator, in his pleading for Muræna, finding it his present interest to cast some disreputation upon Cato, his adversary in that cause, who was addicted to that sect, so represented their dogmas that he put the whole assembly into a fit of laughter; whereunto Cato only replied, that he made others laugh, but was himself ridiculous. And, it may be, some will find it to fall out not much otherwise with themselves by that time the whole account of their undertaking is well cast up.

Besides, do these men not know that if others would employ themselves in a work of the like kind, by way of retortion and recrimination, that they would find real matter, amongst some whom they would have esteemed sacred, for an ordinary ingenuity to exercise itself upon unto their disadvantage? But what would be the issue of such proceedings? who would be gainers by it? Every thing that is professed among them that own religion, all ways and means of their profession, being by their mutual reflections of this kind rendered ridiculous, what remains but that men fly to the sanctuary of atheism to preserve themselves from being scoffed at and despised as fools? On this account alone I would advise the author of our late Debates to surcease proceeding in the same kind, lest a provocation unto a retaliation should befall any of those who are so foully aspersed.

But, as I said, what will be the end of these things, namely, of mutual virulent reflections upon one another? Shall this "sword devour for ever? and will it not be bitterness in the latter end?" for, as he said of old of persons contending with revilings,—

Ἔστι γὰρ ἀμφοτέροισιν ὀνείδεα μυθήσασθαι
Πολλὰ μάλ'· οὐδ' ἂν νηῦς ἑκατόζυγος ἄχθος ἄροιτο.
Στρεπτὴ δὲ γλῶσσ' ἐστὶ βροτῶν, πολέες δ' ἔνι μῦθοι,
Παντοῖοι· ἐπέων δὲ πολὺς νομὸς ἔνθα καὶ ἔνθα.
Ὁπποῖόν κ' εἴπῃσθα ἔπος, τοῖόν κ' ἐπακούσαις.
[Il., xx. 246–250]

Great store there are of such words and expressions on every hand, and every provoked person, if he will not bind his passion to a rule of sobriety and temperance, may at his pleasure take out and use what he supposeth for his turn. And let not men please themselves with imagining that it is not as easy, though perhaps not so safe, for others to use towards themselves haughty and contemptuous expressions, as it is for them to use them towards others. But shall this wrath never be allayed? Is this the way to restore peace, quietness, and satisfaction to the minds of men? Is it meet to use her language in this nation concerning the present differences about religion:—

"Nullus amor populis, nec fœdera sunto.
Littora littoribus contraria, fluctibus undas
Imprecor, arma armis: pugnent ipsique nepotes!"
[Æn., iv. 624–628.]

Is agreement in all other things, all love and forbearance, unless there be a centring in the same opinions absolutely, become criminal, yea detestable? Will this way of proceeding compose and satisfy the minds of men? If there be no other way for a *coalescence* in love and unity, in the bond of peace, but either that the Nonconformists do depose and change in a moment, as it were, their thoughts, apprehensions, and judgments, about the things in difference amongst us, which they cannot, which is not in their power to do; or that in the presence, and with a peculiar respect unto the eye and regard of God, they will act contrary unto them, which they ought not, which they dare not, no not upon the present instruction,— the state of these things is somewhat deplorable.

That alone which, in the discourses mentioned, seemeth to me of any consideration, if it have any thing of truth to give it countenance, is, that the Nonconformists, under pretence of preaching *mysteries and grace*, do neglect the pressing of *moral duties*, which are of near and indispensable concernment unto men in all their relations and actions, and without which religion is but a pretence and covering for vice and sin. A crime this is, unquestionably, of the highest nature, if true, and such as might justly render the whole profession of those who are guilty of it suspected. And this is again renewed by our author, who, to charge home upon the Nonconformists, reports the saying of Flacius Illyricus, a Lutheran, who died a hundred years ago, namely, that "bona opera sunt perniciosa ad salutem;" though I do not remember that any such thing was maintained by Illyricus, though it was so by Amsdorfius against Georgius Major. But is it not strange how any man can assume to himself and swallow so much confidence as is needful to the management of this charge? The books and treatises published by men of the persuasion traduced, their daily preaching, witnessed unto by multitudes, of all sorts of people, the open avowing of their duty in this matter, their principles concerning sin, duty, holiness, virtue, righteousness, and honesty, do all of them proclaim the blackness of this calumny, and sink it, with those who have taken, or are able to take, any sober cognizance of these things, utterly beneath all consideration. Moral duties they do esteem, commend, count as necessary in religion as any men that live under heaven. It is true, they say that on a supposition of that performance whereof they are capable without the assistance of the grace and Spirit of God, though they may be good in their own nature and useful to mankind, yet they are not available unto the salvation of the souls of men; and herein they can prove that they have the concurrent suffrage of all known churches in the world, both those of old and these at present. They say, moreover, that for men to rest upon their performances of these moral duties for their justification before God, is but to set up their own righteousness through an ignorance of the righteousness of God, for we are freely justified by his grace; neither yet are they sensible of any opposition to this assertion.

For their own discharge of the work of the ministry, they endeavour to take their rule, pattern, and instruction, from the precepts, directions, and examples of them who were first commissioned unto that work, even the apostles of our Lord Jesus Christ, recorded in the Scripture, that they might be used and improved unto that end. By them are they taught to endeavour the declaring unto men all the counsel of God concerning his grace, their obedience, and salvation; and having the word of reconciliation committed unto them, they do pray their bearers "in Christ's stead to be reconciled unto God." To this end do they declare the "unsearchable riches of Christ," and comparatively determine to know nothing in this world but "Christ and him crucified," — whereby their preaching becometh principally the word or doctrine of the cross, which by experience they find to be a "stumbling-block" unto some, and "foolishness" unto others; by all means endeavouring to make known "what is the riches of the glory of the mystery of God in Christ, reconciling the world unto himself;" praying withal for their hearers, that "the God of our Lord Jesus Christ, the Father of glory, would give unto them the spirit of wisdom and revelation in the knowledge of him," that "the eyes of their understanding being enlightened," they may learn to know "what is the hope of his calling, and what the riches of the glory of his inheritance in the saints." And in these things are they "not ashamed of the gospel of Christ, which is the power of God unto salvation."

By this dispensation of the gospel do they endeavour to ingenerate in the hearts and souls of men "repentance toward God, and faith toward our Lord Jesus Christ." To prepare them also hereunto they cease not, by the preaching of the law, to make known to men "the terror of the Lord," to convince them of the nature of sin, of their own lost and ruined condition by reason of it, through its guilt, as both original in their natures and actual in their lives; that they may be stirred up to "flee from the wrath to come," and to" lay hold on eternal life." And thus, as God is pleased to succeed them, do they endeavour to lay the great foundation, Jesus Christ, in the hearts of their hearers, and to bring them to an interest in him by believing. In the farther pursuit of the work committed unto them, they endeavour more and more to declare unto, and instruct their hearers in, all the mysteries and saving truths of the gospel; to the end that, by the knowledge of them, they may be wrought unto obedience, and brought to conformity to Christ, — which is the end of their declaration. And in the pursuit of their duty there is nothing more that they insist upon, as far as ever I could observe, than an endeavour to convince men that that faith or profession that doth not manifest itself, which is not justified by works, which doth not purify the heart within, that is not fruitful in universal obedience to all the commands of God, is vain and unprofitable; letting them know that though we are saved by grace, yet we are the "workmanship of God, created in Christ Jesus unto good works, which he hath before ordained that we should walk in them," — a neglect whereof doth uncontrollably evict men of hypocrisy and falseness in their profession: that, therefore, these things, in those that are adult, are indispensably necessary to salvation. Hence do they esteem it their duty continually to press upon their hearers the constant observance and doing of "whatsoever things are honest, whatsoever things are just, whatsoever things are pure, whatsoever things are lovely, whatsoever things are of good report;" letting them know that those who are called to a participation of the grace of the gospel have more, higher, stronger obligations upon them to righteousness, integrity, honesty, usefulness amongst men, in all moral duties, throughout all relations, conditions, and capacities, than any others whatever.

For any man to pretend, to write, [to] plead that this they do not, but indeed do discountenance morality and the duties of it, is to take a liberty of saying what he pleases for his own purpose, when thousands are ready from the highest experience to contradict him. And if this false supposition should prove the soul that animates any discourses, let men never so passionately admire them and expatiate in the commendation of them, I know some that will not be their rivals in their ecstasies. For the other things which those books are mostly filled withal, setting aside frivolous, trifling exceptions about modes of carriage and common phrases of speech, altogether unworthy the review or perusal of a serious person, they consist of such exceptions against expressions, sayings, occasional reflections on texts of Scripture, invectives, and impertinent calling over of things past and bygone, as the merit of the cause under contest is no way concerned in. And if any one would engage in so unhandsome an employment as to collect such fond speeches, futilous expressions, ridiculous expositions of Scripture, smutty passages, weak and impertinent discourses, yea, profane scurrilities, which some others, whom for their honour's sake and other reasons I shall not name, have in their sermons and discourses about sacred things been guilty of, he might provide matter enough for a score of such dialogues as the Friendly Debates are composed of.

But to return: that the advantages mentioned are somewhat peculiar unto dialogues, we have a sufficient evidence in this, that our author having another special design, he chose another way of writing suited thereunto. He professeth that he hath neither hope nor expectation to convince his adversaries of their crimes or mistakes, nor doth endeavour any such thing. Nor did he merely project to render them contemptible and ridiculous (which to have effected, the writing of dialogues in his management would have been most accommodate); but his purpose was to expose them to persecution, or to the severity of penal laws from the magistrates, and if possible, it may be, to popular rage and fury. The voice of his whole discourse is the same with that of the Jews concerning St Paul, "Away with such fellows from the earth, for it is not fit that they should live." Such an account of his thoughts he gives us, p. 253. Saith he, "The only cause of all our troubles and disturbances" (which what they are he knows not nor can declare), "is the inflexible perverseness of about a hundred proud, ignorant, and seditious preachers; against whom if the severity of the laws were particularly levelled, how easy would it be," etc.

"Macte novâ virtute puer: sic itur ad astra."
[Æn., ix. 641.]

But I hope it will appear, before the close of this discourse, that our author is far from deserving the reputation of infallible in his polities, whatever he may be thought to do in his divinity. It is sufficiently known how he is mistaken in his calculation of the numbers of those whom he designs to brand with the blackest marks of infamy, and whom he exposeth in his desires to the severities of law for their ruin. I am sure it is probable that there are more than a hundred of those whom he intends, who may say unto him as Gregory of Nazianzum introduceth his father speaking to himself,

"Nondum tot sunt anni tui, quot jam in sacris nobis sunt
  peracti victimis,"

who have been longer in the ministry than he in the world. But suppose there were but a hundred of them, he knows, or may know, when there was such a disparity in the numbers of them that contested about religion, that it was said of them, "All the world against Athanasius, and Athanasius against the world," who yet was in the right against them all, as they must acknowledge who frequently say or sing his "Quicunque vult."

But how came he so well acquainted with them all and every one as to pronounce of them that they are "proud, ignorant, and seditious?" Allow him the liberty, — which I see he will take whether we allow it him or no, — to call whom he pleaseth "seditious," upon the account of real or supposed principles not compliant with his thoughts and apprehensions, yet that men are "proud and ignorant," how he can prove but by particular instances from his own acquaintance with them, I know not. And if he should be allowed to be a competent judge of knowledge and ignorance in the whole compass of wisdom and science, — which, it may be, some will except against, — yet unless he had personally conversed with them all, or were able to give sufficient instances of their ignorance from actings, writings, or expressions of their own, he would scarce be able to give a tolerable account of the honesty of this his peremptory censure. And surely this must needs be looked on as a lovely, gentle, and philosophic humour, to judge all men proud and ignorant who are not of our minds in all things, and on that ground alone.

But yet, let them be as ignorant as can be fancied, this will not determine the difference between them and their adversaries. One unlearned Paphnutius[3] in the Council of Nice stopped all the learned fathers, when they were precipitately casting the church into a snare; and others, as unlearned as he, may honestly attempt the same at any time. And for our author's projection for the obtaining of quiet by severe dealings with these men in an especial manner, one of the same nature failed in the instance mentioned; for when Athanasius stood almost by himself in the eastern empire for a profession in religion which the supreme magistrate and the generality of the clergy condemned, it was thought the levelling of severity in particular against him would bring all to a composure. To this purpose, after they had again and again charged him to be proud and seditious, they vigorously engaged in his prosecution, according to the projection here proposed, and sought him near all the world over, but

---

3   See Cave's Lives of the Fathers; Life of Athanasius sec. Iii. 2. — ED.

to no purpose at all, as the event discovered; for the truth which he professed having left its root in the hearts of multitudes of the people, on the first opportunity they returned again to the open avowing of it.

But to return from this digression: this being the design of our author, not so much to expose his adversaries to common contempt and laughter as to ruin and destruction, he diverted from the beaten path of dialogues, and betook himself unto that of rhetorical invective declamations; which is peculiarly suited to carry on and promote such a design. I shall, therefore, here leave him for the present, following the triumphal chariot of his friend, singing, "Io triumphe!" and casting reflections upon the captives that he drags after him at his chariot wheels; which will doubtless supply his imagination with a pleasing entertainment, until he shall awake out of his dream, and find all the pageantry that his fancy hath erected round about him to vanish and disappear.

His next attempt is upon *atheists*, wherein I have no concern, nor his principal adversaries, the Nonconformists. For my part, I have had this advantage by my own obscurity and small consideration in the world, as never to converse with any persons that did or durst question the being or providence of God, either really or in pretence. By common reports and published discourses, I find that there are not a few in these days who, either out of pride and ostentation or in a real compliance with their own darkness and ignorance, do boldly venture to dispute the things which we adore; and, if I am not greatly misinformed, a charge of this prodigious licentiousness and impiety may, from pregnant instances, be brought near the doors of some who on other occasions declaim against it. For practical atheism, the matter seems to be unquestionable; many live as though they believed neither God nor devil in the world but themselves. With neither sort am I concerned to treat at present, nor shall I examine the invectives of our author against them, though I greatly doubt whether ever such a kind of defence of the being of God was written by any man before him. If a man would make a judgment upon the genius and the way of his discourse, he might possibly be tempted to fear that it is persons rather than things that are the object of his indignation; and it may be the fate of some to suffer under the infamy of atheism, as it is thought Diagoras did of old, not for denying the Deity, nor for any absurd conceptions of mind concerning it, but for deriding and contemning them who, without any interest in or sense of religion, did foolishly, in idolatrous instances, make a pretence of it in the world. But whatever wickedness or miscarriages of this nature our author hath observed, his zeal against them were greatly to be commended, but that it is not in that only instance wherein he allows of the exercise of that virtue. Let it, then, be his anger or indignation, or what he pleases, that he may not miss of his due praises and commendation. Only I must say, that I question whether to charge persons inclined to atheism with profaning Jonson and Fletcher, as well as the holy Scriptures, be a way of proceeding probably suited to their conviction or reduction.

It seems, also, that those who are here chastised do vent their atheism in scoffing, drollery, and jesting, and such like contemptible efforts of wit, that may take for a while amongst little and unlearned people, and immediately evaporate. I am more afraid of those who, under pretences of sober reason, do vent and maintain opinions and principles that have a direct tendency to give an open admission unto atheism in the minds of men, than of such fooleries. When others' fury and raving cruelties succeeded not, he alone prevailed "qui solus accessit sobrius ad perdendam rempublicam." One principle contended for as rational and true, which, if admitted, will insensibly seduce the mind unto and justify a practice ending in atheism, is more to be feared than ten thousand jests and scoffs against religion, which, me-thinks, amongst men of any tolerable sobriety, should easily be buried under contempt and scorn. And our author may do well to consider whether he hath not, unwittingly I presume, in some instances, so expressed and demeaned himself as to give no small advantage to those corrupt inclinations unto atheism which abound in the hearts of men. Are not men taught here to keep the liberty of their minds and judgments to themselves, whilst they practice that which they approve not nor can do so? which is directly to act against the light and conviction of conscience. And yet an associate of his in his present design, in a modest and free conference, tells us that "there is not a wider step to atheism than to do any thing against conscience;" and informs his friend that "dissent out of grounds that appear to any founded on the will of God is conscience." But against such a conscience, the light, judgment, and conviction of it, are men here taught to practise; and thereby, in the judgment of that author, are instructed unto atheism! And, indeed, if once men find themselves at liberty to practice contrary to what is prescribed unto them in the name and authority of God, as all things are which conscience requires, it is not long that they will retain any regard of him or reverence unto him. It hath hitherto been the judgment of all who have inquired into these things, that the great concern of the glory of God in the world, the interest of kings and rulers, of all governments whatever, the good and welfare of private persons, lies in nothing more than in preserving conscience from being debauched in the conducting principles of it, and in keeping up its due respect to the immediate sovereignty of God over it in all things. Neither ever was there a more horrid attempt upon the truth of the gospel, all common morality, and the good of mankind, than that which some of late years or ages have been engaged in, by suggesting, in their casuistical writings, such principles for the guidance of the consciences of men as in sundry particular instances might set them free, as to practice, from the direct and immediately influencing authority of God in his word. And yet I doubt not but it may be made evident that all their principles in conjunction are scarce of so pernicious a tendency as this one general theorem, that men may lawfully act in the worship of God, or otherwise, against the light, dictates, or convictions of their own consciences. Exempt conscience from an absolute, immediate, entire, universal dependence on the authority, will, and judgment of God, according to what conceptions it hath of them, and you disturb the whole harmony of divine providence in the government of the world, and break the first link of that great chain whereon all religion and government in the world do depend. Teach men to be like Naaman the Syrian, to believe only in the God of Israel, and to worship him according to his appointment, by his own choice and from a sense of duty, yet also to bow in the house of Rimmon, contrary to his light and conviction, out of compliance with his master; or, with the men of Samaria, to fear the Lord but to worship their idols, — and they will not fail, at one time or other, rather to seek after rest in restless atheism than to live in a perpetual conflict with themselves, or to cherish an everlasting sedition in their own bosoms.

I shall not much reflect upon those expressions which our author is pleased to vent his indignation by, such as "religious rage and fury, religions villany, religious lunacies, serious and conscientious villanies, wildness of godly madness, men led by the Spirit of God to disturb the public peace, the world filled with a buzz and noise of the Divine Spirit, sanctified fury, sanctified barbarism, pious villanies, godly disobedience, sullen and cross-grained godliness," with innumerable others of the like kind; which, although perhaps he may countenance himself in the use of, from the tacit respect that he hath to the persons whom he intends to vilify and reproach, yet in themselves, and to others who have not the same apprehensions of their occasion, they tend to nothing but to beget a scorn and derision of all religion and the profession of it, — a humour which will not find where to rest or fix itself, until it come to be swallowed up in the abyss of atheism.

We are at length arrived at the last act of this tragical preface; and as in our progress we have rather heard a great noise and bluster than really encountered either true difficulty or danger, so now I confess that weariness of conversing with so many various sounds of the same signification, the sum of all being "knaves, villains, fools," will carry me through the remainder, of it with some more than ordinary precipitation, as grudging an addition in this kind of employment to those few minutes wherein the preceding remarks were written or dictated.

There are two or three heads which the remainder of this prefatory discourse may be reduced unto: First, a magnificent proclamation of his own achievements, — what he hath proved, what he hath done, especially in representing the "inconsistence of liberty of conscience with the first and fundamental laws of government." And I am content that he please himself with his own apprehensions, like him who admired at the marvellous feats performed in an empty theatre; for it may be that, upon examination, it will be found that there is scarce in his whole discourse any one argument offered that hath the least seeming cogency towards such an end. Whether you take "liberty of conscience" for liberty of judgment, which himself confesseth uncontrollable, or liberty of practice upon indulgence, which he seems to oppose, an impartial reader will, I doubt, be so far from finding the conclusion mentioned to be evinced, as he will scarcely be able to satisfy himself that there are any premises that have a tendency thereunto. But I suppose he must extremely want an employment who will design himself a business in endeavouring to dispossess him of his self-pleasing imagination. Yea, he seems not to have pleaded his own cause absurdly at Athens, who, giving the city the news of a victory when they had received a fatal defeat, affirmed that public thanks were due to him for affording them two days of mirth and jollity before the tidings came of their ill success, which was more than they were ever likely to see again in their lives! And there being as much satisfaction in a fancied as a real success, though useless and failing, we shall leave our author in the highest contentment that thoughts of this nature can afford him. However, it may not be amiss to mind him of that good old counsel, "Let not him that girdeth on his armour boast himself as he that putteth it off."

Another part of his oration is, to decry the folly of that brutish apprehension, that men can possibly live peaceably and quietly if they enjoy the liberty of their consciences; where he fears not to affirm that it is more eligible to tolerate the highest debaucheries than liberty for men to worship God according to what they apprehend he requires! whence some severe persons would be too apt, it may be, to make a conjecture of his own inclinations, for it is evident that he is not absolutely insensible of self-interest in what he doth or writes. But the contrary to what he asserts being a truth at this day written with the beams of the sun in many nations of Europe, let envy, malice, fear, and revenge suggest what they please otherwise, and the nature of the thing itself denied being built upon the best, greatest, and surest foundations and warranty that mankind hath to build on or trust unto for their peace and security, I know not why its denial was here ventured at, unless it were to embrace an opportunity once more to give vent to the remainders of his indignation by revilings and reproaches, which I had hoped had been now exhausted.

But these things are but collateral to his principal design in this close of his declamation, and this is, the removal of an objection, that "liberty of conscience would conduce much to the improvement of trade in the nation." It is known that many persons of great wisdom and experience, and who, as it is probable, have had more time to consider the state and proper interest of this nation, and have spent more pains in the weighing of all things conducing thereunto, than our author hath done, are of this mind and judgment. But he at once strikes them and their reasons dumb by drawing out his Gorgon's head, that he hath proved it inconsistent with government, and so it must needs be a foolish and silly thing to talk of its usefulness to trade. "Verum, ad populum phaleras." If great blustering words, dogmatical assertions, uncouth, unproved principles, accompanied with a pretence of contempt and scorn of all exceptions and oppositions to what is said, with the persons of them that make them, may be esteemed proofs, our author can prove what he pleaseth, and he is to be thought to have proved whatever he affirms himself so to have done. If sober reason, experience, arguments derived from commonly-acknowledged principles of truth, if a confirmation of deductions from such principles by confessed and commonly approved instances, are necessary to make up convincing proofs in matters of this nature and importance, we are yet to seek for them, notwithstanding any thing that hath been offered by this author, or, as far as I can conjecture, is likely so to be. In the meantime, I acknowledge many parts of his discourse to be singularly remarkable. His insinuation "that the affairs of the kingdom are not in a fixed and established condition, that we are distracted amongst ourselves with a strange variety of jealousies and animosities," and such like expressions, as, if divulged in a book printed without licence, would, and that justly, be looked on as seditious, are the foundations that he proceedeth upon. Now, as I am confident that there is very little ground, or none at all, for these insinuations, so the public disposing of the minds of men to fears, suspicions, and apprehensions of unseen dangers by such means, becomes them only who care not what disadvantage they cast others, nay, their rulers under, so they may compass and secure their own private ends and concerns.

But yet, not content to have expressed his own real or pretended apprehensions, he proceeds to manifest his scorn of those, or his smiling at them, who "with mighty projects labour for the improvement of trade;" which the council appointed, as I take it, by his majesty, thence denominated, is more concerned in than the Nonconformists, and may do well upon this information, finding themselves liable to scorn, to desist from such a useless and contemptible employment. They may now know that to erect and encourage trading combinations is only to build so many nests of faction and sedition; for he says, "There is not any sort of people so inclinable to seditious practices as the trading part of a nation," and that "their pride and arrogance naturally increase with the improvement of their stock." Besides, "the fanatic party," as he says, "live in these greater societies, and it is a very odd and preposterous folly to design the enriching of that sort of people; for wealth doth but only pamper and encourage their presumption, and he is a very silly man, and understands nothing of the follies, passions, and inclinations of human nature, who sees not that there is no creature so ungovernable as a wealthy fanatic."

It cannot be denied but that this modern policy runs contrary to the principles and experience of former ages. To preserve industrious men in a peaceable way of improving their own interests, whereby they might partake, in their own and family concerns, of the good and advantages of government, hath been by the weak and silly men of former generations esteemed the most rational way of inducing their minds unto peaceable thoughts and resolutions; for as the wealth of men increaseth, so do their desires and endeavours after all things and ways whereby it may be secured, that so they may not have spent their labour and the vigour of their spirits, with reference unto their own good and that of their posterity, in vain. Yea, most men are found to be of Issachar's temper, who, when he saw that "rest was good, and the land pleasant," wherein his own advantages lay, "bowed his shoulder to bear, and became a servant unto tribute." "Fortes" and "miseri" have heretofore been only feared, and not such as found satisfaction to their desires in the increases and successes of their endeavours. And as Cæsar said he feared not those fat and corpulent persons, Antony and Dolabella, but those pale and lean discontented ones, Brutus and Cassius, so men have been thought to be far less dangerous or to be suspected in government who are well clothed with their own wealth and concerns, than such as have nothing but themselves to lose, and, by reason of their straits and distresses, do scarce judge them worth the keeping.

And hath this gentleman really considered what the meaning of that word "trade" is, and what is the concernment of this nation in it? or is he so fond of his own notions and apprehensions as to judge it meet that the vital spirits and blood of the kingdom should be offered in sacrifice unto them? Solomon tells us that the "profit of the earth is for all, and the king himself is served by the field;" and we may truly in England say the same of trade. All men know what respect unto it there is in the revenues of the crown, and how much they are concerned in its growth and promotion. The rents of all, from the highest to the lowest that have an interest in the soil, are regulated by it, and rise and fall with it; nor is there any possibility to keep them up to their present proportion and standard, much less to advance them, without the continuance of trade in its present condition at least, nay, without a steady endeavour for its increase, furtherance, and promotion. Noblemen and gentlemen must be contented to eat their own beef and mutton at home if trade decay; to keep up their ancient and present splendour, they will find no way or means. Corporations are known to be the most considerable and significant bodies of the common people, and herein lies their being and bread. To diminish or discountenance their trade is to starve them, and discourage all honest industry in the world. It was a sad desolation that not long since befell the great city by fire; yet, through the good providence of God, under the peaceable government of his majesty, it is rising out of its ashes with a new signal beauty and lustre. But that consumption and devastation of it which the pursuit of this counsel will inevitably produce would prove fatal and irreparable. And as the interests of all the several parts of the commonwealth do depend on the trade of the people amongst ourselves, so the honour, power, and security of the whole, in reference unto foreign nations, are resolved also into the same principles: for as our soil is but small in comparison of some of our neighbours', and the numbers of our people no way to be compared with theirs, so if we should forego the advantages of trade, for which we have opportunities, and unto which the people of this nation have inclinations above any country or nation in the world, we should quickly find how unequal the competition between them and us would be; for even our naval force, which is the honour of the king, the security of his kingdoms, the terror of his enemies, oweth its rise and continuance unto that preparation of persons employed therein which is made by the trade of the nation. And if the counsel of this author should be followed, to suspend all thoughts of the supportment, encouragement, and furtherance of trade, until all men, by the severities of penalties, should be induced to a uniformity in religion, I doubt not but our envious neighbours would as readily discern the concernment of their malice and ill-will therein as Hannibal did his in the action of the Roman general, who, at the battle of Cannæ, according to their usual discipline (but fatally at that time misapplied), caused, in the great distress of the army, his horsemen to alight and fight on foot, not considering the advantage of his great and politic enemy as things then stood; who immediately said, "I had rather he had delivered them all bound unto me," though he knew there was enough done to secure his victory.

A SURVEY OF THE FIRST CHAPTER

Inconsistent expressions of Parker in regard to the power of the magistrate and the rights of conscience — The design of his discourse to prove the magistrate's authority to govern the consciences of his subjects in affairs of religion — This doctrine inconsistent with British law — Ascribes more power to the magistrate than to Christ — Contrary to the history of the royal prerogative — Alleged necessity of the principle to public peace and order — Evils alleged to spring from liberty of conscience — The principle of Parker no real preventive to these evils — Various pleas refuted.[4]

THE author of this discourse seems, in this first chapter, to design the stating of the controversy which he intendeth to pursue and handle (as he expresseth himself, p. 11); as also, to lay down the main foundations of his ensuing superstructure. Nothing could be more regularly projected, nor more suited to the satisfaction of ingenious inquirers into the matters under debate; for those who have any design in reading beyond a present divertisement of their minds or entertainment of their fancies, desire nothing more than to have the subject-matter which they exercise their thoughts about clearly and distinctly proposed, that a true judgment may be made concerning what men say and whereof they do affirm. But I fear our author hath fallen under the misadventure of a failure in these projections, at least as unto that certainty, clearness, and perspicuity in the declaration of his conceptions and expression of his assertions and principles, without which all other ornaments of speech, in matters of moment, are of no use or consideration. His language is good and proper; his periods of speech laboured, full, and even;

---

4 No contents to the different sections of this treatise appear in the previous editions. We have prefixed a brief table of them to each section, as far as possible in the words of our author. — ED.

his expressions poignant towards his adversaries, and, singly taken, appearing to be very significative and expressive of his mind. But I know not how it is come to pass that, what either [whether?] through his own defect as to a due comprehension of the notions whose management he hath undertaken, or out of a design to cloud and obscure his sentiments, and to take the advantage of loose, declamatory expressions, it is very hard, if possible, to gather from what he hath written either what is the true state of the controversy proposed to discussion, or what is the precise, determinate sense of those words wherein he proposeth the principles that he proceeds upon.

Thus, in the title of the book he asserts "the power of the magistrate over the consciences of men;" elsewhere [he] confines "the whole work and duty of conscience to the inward thoughts and persuasions of the mind, over which the magistrate hath no power at all." "Conscience itself," he sometimes says, "is every man's opinion;" sometimes he calls it an "imperious faculty;" — which surely are not the same. Sometimes he pleads for "the uncontrollable power of magistrates over religion and the consciences of men;" sometimes asserts their "ecclesiastical jurisdiction" as the same thing, and seemingly all that he intends; — whereas, I suppose, no man ever yet defined "ecclesiastical jurisdiction" to be "an uncontrollable power over religion and the consciences of men." The magistrate's "power over religion" he asserts frequently, and denieth outward worship to be any part of religion, and at last pleads upon the matter only for his power over outward worship. Every *particular virtue* he affirms to be such, because it is "a resemblance and imitation of some of the divine attributes;" yet [he] also teacheth that there may be more virtues, or new ones that were not so, and that to be virtue in one place which is not so in another. Sometimes he pleads that the magistrate hath power to impose "any religion on the consciences of his subjects that doth not countenance vice or disgrace the Deity," and then anon pleads for it in indifferent things and circumstances of outward worship only. Also, that the magistrate may" oblige his subjects' consciences" to the performance of moral duties, and other duties in religious worship, under penalties, and yet "punisheth none for their crime and guilt, but for the example of others. And many other instances of the like nature may be given.

Now, whatever dress of words these things may be set off withal, they savour rankly of crude and undigested notions, not reduced unto such a consistency in his mind as to suffer him to speak evenly, steadily, and constantly to them. Upon the whole matter, it may not be unmeetly said of his discourses, what Tully said of Rullus's oration about the agrarian law: "Concionem...advocari jubet: summâ cum expectatione concurritur. Explicat orationem sanè longam, et verbis valdè bonis. Unum erat quod mihi vitiosum videbatur, quod tantâ ex frequentitâ inveniri nemo potuit, qui intelligere posset, quid diceret. Hoc ille utrum insidiarum causâ fecerit, an hoc genere eloquentiæ delectetur, nescio. Tamen, siqui acutiores in concione steterunt, de lege agraria nescio quid voluisse eum dicere, suspicabantur." [De Lege Agr., ii. 5] Many good words it is composed of, many sharp reflections are made on others, a great appearance there is of reason; but besides that it is plain that he treats of the Nonconformists and the magistrate's power, and would have this latter exercised about the punishment or destruction of the former (which almost every page expresseth), it is very hard to gather what is the case he speaks unto, or what are the principles he proceeds upon.

The entrance of his discourse is designed to give an account of the great difficulty which he intends to assail, of the controversy that he will handle and debate, and of the difference which he will compose. Here, if anywhere, accuracy, perspicuity, and a clear, distinct direction of the minds of the reader unto a certain just apprehension of the matter in question and difference, ought to be expected; for if the foundation of discourses of this nature be laid in terms general, ambiguous, loose, rhetorical, and flourishing, giving no particular, determinate sense of the controversy (for so this is called by our author), all that ensues in the pursuit of what is so laid down must needs be of the same complexion. And such appears to be the declamatory entrance of this chapter; for instead of laying a solid foundation to erect his superstructure upon, the author seems in it only to have built a castle in the air, that makes a goodly appearance and show, but is of no validity or use. Can he suppose that any man is the wiser or the more intelligent, in the difference about liberty of conscience, the power and duty of magistrates in granting or denying an indulgence unto the exercise of it, by reading an elegant parabolical discourse of "two supreme powers, the magistrate and conscience, contesting for sovereignty, in and about" no man knows what? What conscience is, what liberty of conscience, what it is pleaded for to extend unto, who are concerned in it, whether its plea be resolved absolutely into its own nature and constitution, or into that respect which it hath to another common rule of the minds and conceptions of men in and about the worship of God, is not declared; nor is it easily discernible what he allows and approves of in his own discourse, and what he introduceth to reflect upon, and so reject. Page 5, he tells us that "conscience is subject and accountable to God alone, that it owns no superior but the Lord of consciences;" and, p. 7, "that those who make it accountable to none but God alone do in effect usurp their prince's crown, defy his authority, and acknowledge no governor but themselves"! If it be pleaded that, in the first place, not what is, but what is unduly pretended, is declared, his words may be as well so expounded in all his ascriptions unto magistrates also, — namely, that it is not with them as he asserts, but only it is unduly pretended so to be, — as to any thing that appears in the discourse. The distinct consideration of the principles of conscience and the outward exercise of it can alone here give any show of relief. But as no distinction of that nature doth as yet appear, and, if rested on, ought to have been produced by any one who understood himself, and intended not to deceive or entangle others, so when it is brought on the stage, its inconsistency to serve the end designed shall be evinced. But that a plea for the consciences of private men (submitting themselves freely and willingly to the supreme power and government of magistrates in all things belonging to public peace and tranquillity) to have liberty to express their obedience unto God in the exercise of his outward worship, should receive such a tragical description, of a "rival supreme power set up against the magistrate, to the usurpation of his crown and dignity," is a new way of stating controversies, whether in divinity or policy, which this author judgeth conducing to his design and purpose; and I shall say no more but that those who delight in such a way of writing, and do receive light and satisfaction thereby, do seem to be exercised in a logic that I was never acquainted withal, and which I shall not now inquire after.

What seems to be of real difficulty in this matter, which is so rhetorically exaggerated, our blessed Saviour hath stated and determined in one word. "Give," saith he, "unto Cæsar the things that are Cæsar's, and to God the things that are God's;" and this he did when he gave his disciples command not only to think, judge, and believe according to what he should propose and reveal unto them, but also to observe and do in outward practices whatever he should command them. As he requires all subjection unto the magistrate in things of his proper cognizance, — that is, all things necessary to public peace and tranquillity in this world, the great end of his authority; so he asserts also that there are things of God which are to be observed and practised, even all and every one of his own commands, in a neglect whereof, on any pretence or account, we give not unto God that which is his. And he doubted not but that these things, these distinct respects to God and man, were exceedingly well consistent, and together directive to the same end of public good. Wherefore, passing through the flourishes of this frontispiece with the highest unconcernment, we may enter the fabric itself, where, possibly, we may find him declaring directly what it is that he asserts in this matter and contendeth for; and this he doth, p. 10: "And, therefore, it is the design of this discourse, by a fair and impartial debate, to compose all these differences, and adjust all these quarrels and contentions, and settle things upon their true and proper foundations; first, by proving it to be absolutely necessary to the peace and government of the world, that the supreme magistrate of every commonwealth should be vested with a power to govern and conduct the consciences of subjects in affairs of religion."

I am sure our author will not be surprised, if, after he hath reported the whole party whom he opposeth as a company of "silly, foolish, illiterate persons," one of them should so far acknowledge his own stupidity as to profess that, after the consideration of this declaration of his intention and mind, he is yet to seek for the direct and determinate sense of his words, and for the principle that he designs the confirmation of. I doubt not but that the magistrate hath all that power which is absolutely necessary for the preservation of public peace and tranquillity in the world; but if men may be allowed to fancy what they please to be necessary unto that end, and thence to make their own measures of that power which is to be ascribed unto him, no man knows what bounds will be fixed unto that ocean wherein the leviathans they have framed in their imaginations may sport themselves. Some will, perhaps, think it necessary to this purpose that the magistrate should have power to declare and determine whether there be a God or no; Whether, if there be, it be necessary he should be worshipped or no; whether any religion be needful in, or useful to, the world; and if there be, then to determine what all subjects shall believe and practice from first to last in the whole of it. And our author hopes that some are of this mind. Others may confine it to lesser things, according as their own interest doth call upon them so to do, though they are not able to assign a clear distinction between what is subjected unto him and what may plead an exemption from his authority. He, indeed, who is the fountain and original of all power hath both assigned its proper end, and fully suited it to the attainment thereof; and if the noise of men's lusts, passions, and interests, were but a little silenced, we should quickly hear the harmonious consenting voice of human nature itself declaring the just proportion that is between the grant of power and its end, and undeniably expressing it in all the instances of it: for as the principle of rule and subjection is natural to us, concreated with us, and indispensably necessary to human society, in all the distinctions it is capable of, and the relations whence those distinctions arise; so nature itself, duly attended unto, will not fail, by the reason of things, to direct us unto all that is essential unto it and necessary unto its end. Arbitrary fictions of ends of government, and what is necessary thereunto, influenced by present interest, and arising from circumstances confined to one place, time, or nation, are not to be imposed on the nature of government itself, which hath nothing belonging unto it but what inseparably accompanieth mankind as sociable.

But to let this pass; the authority here particularly asserted is a "power in the supreme magistrate to govern and guide the consciences of his subjects in affairs of religion." Let any man duly consider these expressions, and if he be satisfied by them as to the sense of the controversy under debate, I shall acknowledge that he is wiser than I, — which is very easy for any one to be. What are the "affairs of religion" here intended, all or some; whether in religion or about it; what are the "consciences of men," and how exercised about these things; what it is to "govern and conduct" them; with what "power," by what means, this may be done, — I am at a loss, for aught that yet is here declared. There is a guidance, conduct, yea, government of the consciences of men, by instructions and directions, in a due proposal of rational and spiritual motives, for those ends, such as is that which is vested in and exercised by the guides of the church, and that in subjection to and dependence on Christ alone, as hath been hitherto apprehended, though some now seem to have a mind to change their master, and to take up "præsente Numine," who may be of more advantage to them. That the magistrate hath also power so to govern and conduct the consciences of his subjects in his way of administration, — that is, by ordering them to be taught, instructed, and guided in their duty, — I know none that doth deny: so did Jehoshaphat, 2 Chron. xvii. 7–9. But it seems to be a government and guidance of another nature that is here intended. To deliver ourselves, therefore, from the deceit and entanglement of these general expressions, and that we may know what to speak unto, we must seek for a declaration of their sense and importance from what is elsewhere, in their pursuit, affirmed and explained by their author.

His general assertion is, as was observed, "That the magistrate hath power over the consciences of his subjects in religion," as appears in the title of his book; here, p. 10, that power is said to be "to govern and conduct their consciences in religious affairs;" p. 13, that "religion is subject to his dominion, as well as all other affairs of state;" p. 27, that "it is a sovereignty over men's consciences in matters of religion, and this universal, absolute, and uncontrollable." Matters of religion are as uncontrollably subject to the supreme power as all other civil concerns: "He may, if he please, reserve the exercise of the priesthood to himself," p. 32; — that is, what now in religion corresponds unto the ancient priesthood, as the ordering bishops and priests, administering sacraments, and the like; as the Papists in Queen Elizabeth's time did commonly report, in their usual manner, that it was done by a woman amongst us, by a fiction of such principles as begin, it seems, now to be owned. That if this "power of the government of religion be not universal and unlimited, it is useless," p. 35; that this "power is not derived from Christ, nor any grant of his, but is antecedent to his coming, or any power given unto him or granted by him," p. 40. "Magistrates have a power to make that a particular of the divine law which God had not made so," p. 80, and "to introduce new duties in the most important parts of religion: so that there is a public conscience, which men are in things of a public concern (relating to the worship of God) to attend unto, and not to their own; and if there be any sin in the command, he that imposed it shall answer for it, and not I, whose whole duty it is to obey," p. 308. Hence, the command of "authority will warrant obedience, and obedience will hallow my actions and excuse me from sin," ibid. Hence it follows, that whatever the magistrate commands in religion, his authority doth so immediately affect the consciences of men that they are bound to observe it, on the pain of the greatest sin and punishment; and he may appoint and command whatever he pleaseth in religion, "that doth not either countenance vice or disgrace the Deity," p. 85. And many other expressions are there of the general assertion before laid down.

This, therefore, seems to me, and to the most impartial considerations of this discourse that I could bring unto it, to be the doctrine or opinion proposed and advanced for the quieting and composing of the great tumults described in its entrance, — namely, that the supreme magistrate in every nation hath power to order and appoint what religion his subjects shall profess and observe, or what he pleaseth in religion, as to the worship of God required in it, provided that he" enjoineth nothing that doth countenance vice or disgrace the Deity;" and thereby binds their consciences to profess and observe that which is by him so appointed (and nothing else are they to observe), making it their duty in conscience so to do, and the highest crime or sin to do any thing to the contrary, and that whatever the precise truth in these matters be, or whatever be the apprehensions of their own consciences concerning them. Now, if our author can produce any law, usage, or custom of this kingdom, any statute or act of parliament, any authentic record, any acts or declarations of our kings, any publicly-authorized writing, before or since the Reformation, declaring, asserting, or otherwise approving, the power and authority described to belong unto, to be claimed or exercised by, the kings of this nation, I will faithfully promise him never to write one word against it, although I am sure I shall never be of that mind. And, if I mistake not, in a transient reflection on these principles, compared with those which the church of England hath formerly pleaded against them who opposed her constitutions, they are utterly by them cast out of all consideration; and this one notion is advanced in the room of all the foundations which, for so many years, her defenders (as wise and as learned as this author) have been building upon. But this is not my concernment to examine; I shall leave it unto them whose it is, and whose it will be made appear to be, if we are again necessitated to engage in this dispute.

For the present be it granted that it is the duty and in the power of every supreme magistrate to order and determine what religion, what way, what modes in religion, shall be allowed, publicly owned, and countenanced, and by public revenue maintained in his dominions; — that is, this is allowed with respect to all pretensions of other sovereigns, or of his own subjects. With respect unto God, it is his truth alone, the religion by him revealed, and the worship by him appointed, that he can so allow or establish. The rule that holds in private persons with respect to the public magistrate holds in him with respect unto God. "Illud possumus quod jure possumus." It is also agreed that no men, no individual person, no order or society of men, are, either in their persons or any of their outward concerns, exempted, or may be so, on the account of religion, from his power and jurisdiction; nor any causes that are liable unto a legal, political disposal and determination. It is also freely acknowledged that whatever such a magistrate cloth determine about the observances of religion, and under what penalties soever, his subjects are bound to observe what he doth so command and appoint, unless by general or especial rules their consciences are obliged to a dissent or contrary observation, by the authority of God and his word. In this case they are to keep their souls entire in their spiritual subjection unto God, and quietly and peaceably to bear the troubles and inconveniences which on the account thereof may befall them, without the least withdrawing of their obedience from the magistrate. And in this state of things, as there is no necessity or appearance of it that any man should be brought into such a condition as wherein sin on the one hand or the other cannot be avoided, so that state of things will probably occur in the world, as it hath done in all ages hitherto, that men may be necessitated to sin or suffer.

To wind up the state of this controversy, we say, that antecedent to the consideration of the power of the magistrate, and all the influence that it hath upon men or their consciences, there is a superior determination of what is true, what false in religion, what right and what wrong in the worship of God, wherein the guidance of the consciences of men doth principally depend, and whereinto it is ultimately resolved. This gives an obligation or liberty unto them antecedent unto the imposition of the magistrate of whose commands, and our actual obedience unto them in these things, it is the rule and measure. And I think there is no principle, no common presumption of nature, nor dictate of reason, more evident, known, or confessed than this, that whatever God commands us, in his worship or otherwise, that we are to do; and whatever he forbids us, that we are not to do, be the things themselves in our eye great or small.

Neither is there any difference, in these things, with respect unto the way or manner of the declaration of the will of God. Whether it be by *innate common light* or by revelation, all is one; the authority and will of God in all is to be observed. Yea, in command of God, made known by revelation (the way which is most contended about), may suspend, as to any particular instance, the greatest command that we are obliged unto by the law of nature in reference unto one another; as it did in the precept given to Abraham for the sacrificing of his son. And we shall find our author himself setting up the supremacy of conscience in opposition unto and competition with that of the magistrate (though with no great self-consistency), ascribing the pre-eminence and prevalency in obligation unto that of conscience, and that in the principal and most important duties of religion and human life. Such are all those moral virtues which have in their nature a resemblance of the divine perfections, wherein he placeth the substance of religion. With respect unto these, he so setteth up the throne of conscience as to affirm that if any thing be commanded by the magistrate against them, "to disobey him is no sin, but a duty." And we shall find the case to be the same in matters of mere revelation; for what God commands, that he commands, by what way soever that command be made known to us; and there is no consideration that can add any thing to the obligatory power and efficacy of infinite authority. So that where the will of God is the formal reason of our obedience, it is all one how or by what means it is discovered unto us. Whatever we are instructed in by innate reason or by revelation, the reason why we are bound by it is neither the one nor the other, but the authority of God in both.

But we must return unto the consideration of the sentiments of our author in this matter, as before laid down. The authority ascribed to the civil magistrate being as hath been expressed, it will be very hard for any one to distinguish between it and the sovereignty that the Lord Christ himself hath in and over his church; yea, if there be any advantage on either side, or a comparative pre-eminence, it will be found to be cast upon that of the magistrate. Is the Lord Christ the lord of the souls and consciences of men? hath he dominion over them, to rule them in the things of the worship of God? — it is so with the magistrate also; he hath a universal power over the consciences of his subjects." Doth the Lord Christ require his disciples to do and observe in the worship of God whatever he commanded them? — so also may the magistrate, "the rule and conduct of conscience in these matters belonging unto him," provided that he command nothing that may "countenance vice or disgrace the Deity;" which, with reverence be it spoken, our Lord Jesus Christ himself, not only on the account of the perfection and rectitude of his own nature, but also of his commission from the Father, could not do. Is the authority of Christ the formal reason making obedience necessary to his commands and precepts? — so is the authority of the magistrate in reference unto what he requires. Do men, therefore, sin if they neglect the observance of the commands of Christ in the worship of God, because of his immediate authority so to command them binding their consciences? — so do men sin if they omit or neglect to do what the magistrate requires in the worship of God, because of his authority, without any farther respect. Hath the Lord Christ instituted two sacraments in the worship of God, that is, "outward visible signs," or symbols, of inward invisible or spiritual grace?" — the magistrate, if he please, may institute and appoint twenty under the name of "significant ceremonies," that is, "outward visible signs of inward spiritual grace," which alone is the significancy contended about. Hath the magistrate this his authority in and over religion and the consciences of men from Jesus Christ? No more than Christ hath his authority from the magistrate, for he holds it by the law of nature, antecedent to the promise and coming of Christ. Might Christ in his own person administer the holy things of the church of God? Not in the church of the Jews, for he "sprang of the tribe of Judah, concerning which nothing was spoken as to the priesthood;" only he might in that of the gospel, but hath judged meet to commit the actual administration of them to others. So it is with the magistrate also.

Thus far, then, Christ and the magistrate seem to stand on even or equal terms. But there are two things remaining that absolutely turn the scale, and cast the advantage on the magistrate's side; for, first, Men may do and practice many things in the worship of God which the Lord Christ hath nowhere nor by any means required. Yea, to think that his word, or the revelation of his mind and will therein, is "the sole and adequate rule of religious worship," is reported as an "opinion foolish, absurd, and impious, and destructive of all government." If this be not supposed, not only the whole design of our author in this book is defeated, but our whole controversy also is composed and at an end. But, on the other hand, no man must do or practice any thing in that way but what is prescribed, appointed, and commanded by the magistrate, upon pain of sin, schism, rebellion, and all that follow thereon. To leave this unasserted is all that the Nonconformists would desire in order unto peace. Comprehension and indulgence would ensue thereon. Here, I think, the magistrate hath the advantage. But that which follows will make it yet more evident; for, secondly, Suppose the magistrate require any thing to be done and observed in the worship of God, and the Lord Christ require the quite contrary in a man's own apprehension, so that he is as well satisfied in his apprehension of his mind as he can be of any thing that is proposed to his faith and conscience in the word of God; in this case he is to obey the magistrate, and not Christ, as far as I can learn, unless all confusion and disorder be admitted an entrance into the world. Yea, but this seems directly contrary to that rule of the apostles, which hath such an evidence and power of rational conviction attending it, that they refer it to the judgment of their adversaries, and those persons of as perverse, corrupt minds and prejudicate engagements against them and their cause as ever lived in the world, — namely, "Whether it be right to obey God or man, judge ye." But we are told that "this holds only in greater matters," the logic (by the way) of which distinction is as strange as its divinity; for if the formal reason of the difference intimated arise from the comparison between the authority of God and man, it holds equally as to all things, small or great, that they may be oppositely concerned in. Besides, who shall judge what is small or what is great in things of this nature? "Cave ne titubes." Grant but the least judgment to private men themselves in this matter, and the whole fabric tumbles. If the magistrate be judge of what is great and of what is little, we are still where we were, without hope of delivery. And this, to me, is a notable instance of the pre-eminence of the magistrate above Christ in this matter. Some of the old Irish have a proverbial speech amongst them, "That if Christ had not been Christ when he was Christ, Patrick had been Christ," but it seems now, that taking it for granted that he was Christ, yet we have another that is so also, that is lord over the souls and consciences of men; and what can be said more of him "who sits in the temple of God, and shows himself to be God?"

As we formerly said, Nonconformists, who are unacquainted with the mysteries of things of this nature, must needs desire to know whether these be the avowed principles of the church of England, or whether they are only inventions to serve a present turn of the pursuit of some men's designs. Are all the old pleas of the *"jus divinum" of episcopacy, of example and direction apostolical, of a parity of reason between the condition of the church whilst under extraordinary officers and whilst under ordinary, of the power of the church to appoint ceremonies* for decency and order, *of the consistency of Christian liberty with the necessary practice of indifferent things, of the pattern of the churches of old*, which (whether duly or otherwise we do not now determine) have been insisted on in this cause, swallowed all up in this abyss of magistratical omnipotency, which plainly renders them useless and unprofitable? How unhappy hath it been that the Christian world was not sooner blessed with this great discovery of the only way and means of putting a final end unto all religious contests! that he should not until now appear,

"Qui genus humanum ingenio superavit, et omnesPræstinx-
  it, stellas exortus ut ætherius sol!"
          [Lucret. of Epicurus, iii. 1056.]

But every age produceth not a Columbus. Many indeed have been the disputes of learned men about the power of magistrates in and concerning religion. With us it is stated in the recorded actings of our sovereign princes, in the oath of supremacy, and the acts of parliament concerning it, with other authentic writings explanatory thereof. Some have denied him any concern herein; our author is none of them, but rather is like the frenetic gentleman, who, when he was accused, in former days, for denying the corporeal presence of Christ in the sacrament, replied, in his own defence, that he "believed him to be present, booted and spurred as he rode to Capernaum." He hath brought him booted and spurred, yea, armed cap-a-pie, into the church of God, and given all power into his hands, to dispose of the worship of God according to his own will and pleasure; and that not with respect unto outward order only, but with direct obligation upon the consciences of men.

But, doubtless, it is the wisdom of sovereign princes to beware of this sort of enemies, — persons who, to promote their own interest, make ascriptions of such things unto them as they cannot accept of without the utmost hazard of the displeasure of God. Is it meet that, to satisfy the desires of any, they should invade the prerogative of God, or set themselves down at his right hand, in the throne of his only-begotten Son? I confess they are no way concerned in what others, for their advantage' sake, as they suppose, will ascribe unto them, which they may sufficiently disown by scorn and silence; nor can their sin involve them in any guilt. It was not the vain acclamation of the multitude unto Herod, "The voice of a god, and not of a man," but his own arrogant satisfaction in that blasphemous assignation of divine glory to him, that exposed him to the judgment and vengeance of God. When the princes of Israel found, by the answer of the Reubenites, that they had not transgressed against the law of God's worship in adding unto it or altering of it, which they knew would have been a provocation not to have been passed over without a recompense of revenge, they replied unto them, "Now ye have delivered the children of Israel out of the hand of the LORD;" and it is to be desired that all the princes of the Israel of God in the world, all Christian potentates, would diligently watch against giving admission unto any such insinuations as would deliver them into the hand of the Lord.

For my own part, such is my ignorance that I know not that any magistrate from the foundation of the world, unless it were Nebuchadnezzar, Caius Caligula, Domitian, and persons like to them, ever claimed, or pretended to exercise, the power here assigned unto them. The instances of the laws and edicts of Constantine in the matters of religion and the worship of God, of Theodosius and Gratian, Arcadius, Marcian, and other emperors of the east, remaining in the Code and Novels; the Capitular of the western emperors, and laws of Gothish kings; the right of ecclesiastical jurisdiction inherent in the imperial crown of this nation, and occasionally exercised in all ages, — are of no concernment in this matter: for no man denies but that it is the duty of the supreme magistrate to protect and further the true religion and right worship of God, by all ways and means suited and appointed of God thereunto. To encourage the professors thereof, to protect them from wrong and violence, to secure them in the performance of their duties, is doubtless incumbent on them. Whatever, under pretence of religion, brings actual disturbance unto the peace of mankind, they may coerce and restrain. When religion, as established in any nation by law, doth or may interest the professors of it, or guides in it, in any privileges, advantages, or secular emoluments, which are subject and liable, as all human concerns, to doubts, controversies, and litigious contests, in their security and disposal, all these things depend merely and solely on the power of the magistrate, by whose authority they are originally granted, and by whose jurisdictive power both the persons vested with them and themselves are disposable. But for an absolute power over the consciences of men, to bind or oblige them formally thereby to do whatever they shall require in the worship of God, so as to make it their sin, deserving eternal damnation, not so to do, without any consideration whether the things are true or false, according to the mind of God or otherwise, yea, though they are apprehended by them who are so obliged to practice them to be contrary to the will of God, — that this hath hitherto been claimed by any magistrate, unless such as those before mentioned, I am yet to seek. And the case is the same with respect unto them who are not satisfied that what is so prescribed unto them will be accepted with God; for whereas, in all that men do in the worship of God, they ought to be fully persuaded of its acceptableness to God in their own minds, seeing "whatsoever is not of faith is sin," he that "doubteth" is in a very little better capacity to serve God on such injunctions than he who apprehendeth them to be directly contrary to his mind.

If an edict were drawn up for the settlement of religion and religious worship in any Christian nation, according to the principles and directions before laid down, it may be there would be no great strife in the world by whom it should be first owned and espoused; for it must be of this importance: —

"Whereas we have a universal and absolute power over the consciences of all our subjects in things appertaining to the worship of God, so that, if we please, we can introduce new duties, never yet heard of, in the most important parts of religion (p. 80), and may impose on them, in the practice of religion and divine worship, what we please, so that, in our judgment, it do not countenance vice nor disgrace the Deity (p. 85): and whereas this power is naturally inherent in us; not given or granted unto us by Jesus Christ, but belonged to us or our predecessors before ever he was born; nor is expressed in the Scripture, but rather supposed; and this being such as that we ourselves, if we would, whether we be man or woman" (here France must be excepted by virtue of the Salique law, though the whole project be principally calculated for that meridian), "might exercise the special offices and duties of religion in our own person, especially that of the priesthood, though we are pleased to transfer the exercise of it unto others: and whereas all our prescriptions, impositions, and injunctions, in these things, do immediately affect and bind the consciences of our subjects, because they are ours, whether they be right or wrong, true or false, so long as in our judgment they neither, as was said, countenance vice nor disgrace the Deity, we do enact and ordain as followeth:"

(Here, if you please, you may intersert the scheme of religion given us by our author in his second chapter, and add unto it, "That because sacrifices were a way found out by honest men of old to express their gratitude unto God thereby, so great and necessary a part of our religious duty, it be enjoined that the use of them be again revived, seeing there is nothing in them that offends against the bounds prescribed to the power to be expressed, and that men in all places do offer up bulls and goats, sheep and fowls, to God," with as many other institutions of the like nature as shall be thought meet.) Hereunto add, —

"Now, our express will and pleasure is, that every man may and do think and judge what he pleaseth concerning the things enjoined and enacted by us; for what have we to do with their thoughts and judgments? They are under the empire and dominion of conscience, which we cannot invade if we would. They may, if they please, judge them inconvenient, foolish, absurd, yea, contrary to the mind, will, and law of God. Our only intention, will, and pleasure is, to bind them to the constant observation and practice of them, and that under the penalties of hanging and damnation." I know not any expression in such an impious and futilous edict that may not be warranted out of the principles of this discourse, the main parts of it being composed out of the words and phrases of it, and those used, to the best of my understanding, in the sense fixed to them by our author.

Now, as was said before, I suppose Christian princes will not be earnest in their contests who shall first own the authority intimated, and express it in a suitable exercise; and if any one of them should put forth his hand unto it, he will find that

— "Furiarum maxima juxta
Accubat, et manibus prohibet contingere mensas." —
[Æn., vi. 605.]

There is one who lays an antecedent claim to a sole interest in this power, and that bottomed on other manner of pretensions than any which as yet have been pleaded in their behalf; for the power and authority here ascribed unto princes is none other but that which is claimed by the pope of Rome, with some few enlargements, and appropriated unto him by his canonists and courtiers. Only here "the old gentleman" (as he is called by our author) hath the advantage, in that, beside the precedency of his claim, it being entered on record at least six or seven hundred years before any proctor or advocate appeared in the behalf of princes, he hath forestalled them all in the pretence of infallibility: which, doubtless, is a matter of singular use in the exercise of the power contended about; for some men are so peevish as to think that thus to deal with religion and the consciences of men belongs to none but him who is absolutely, yea, essentially so, — that is, infallible. For, as we have now often said (as, contrary to their design, men in haste oftentimes speak the same things over and over), as to all ecclesiastical jurisdiction over persons and causes ecclesiastical, and the sovereign disposal of all the civil and political concernments of religion, which is vested in the imperial crown of this nation, and by sundry acts of parliament is declared so to be, I shall be always ready to plead the right of our kings, and all Christian kings whatever, against the absurd pleas and pretences of the pope; so, as to this controversy between him and such princes as shall think meet to contend with him about it, concerning the power over the consciences of men before described, I shall not interpose myself in the scuffle, as being fully satisfied they are contending about that which belongs to neither of them.

But what reason is there why this power should not be extended unto the inward thoughts and apprehensions of men about the worship of God, as well as the expression of them in pure, spiritual acts of that worship? The power asserted, I presume, will be acknowledged to be from God, though I can scarce, meet with the communication and derivation of it from him in this discourse. But whereas it is granted on all hands that "the powers that be are of God," and that none can have authority over another unless it be originally "given him from above," I desire to be informed why the other part of the power mentioned, — namely, over the thoughts, judgments, and apprehensions of men, in the things of the worship of God, — should not be invested in the magistrate also; that so, he having declared what is to be believed, thought, and judged in such things, all men should be obliged so to believe, think, and judge: for this power God can give, and hath given it unto Jesus Christ. I presume it will be said that this was no way needful for the preservation of peace in human society, which is the end for which all this power is vested in the magistrate; for let men believe, think, and judge what they please, so long as their outward actings are or may be, overruled, there is no danger of any public disturbance. But this seems to be a mighty uneasy condition for mankind, — namely, to live continually in a contradiction between their judgments and their practices; which in this case is allowed to be incident unto them. Constantly to judge one way best and most according to the mind of God in his worship, and constantly to practice another, will, it is to be feared, prove like the conflicting of vehement vapours with their contrary qualities, that at one time or other will produce an earthquake. How, then, if men, weary of this perplexing, distorting condition of things in their minds, should be provoked to run to excesses and inordinate courses for their freedom and rest, such as our author excellently displays in all their hideous colours and appearances, and which are really pernicious to human policy and society? were it not much better that all these inconveniences had been prevented in the first instance, by taking care that the faith, thoughts, persuasions, and judgments of all subjects about the things of God, should be absolutely bound up unto the declared conceptions of their rulers in these matters? Let it not be pretended that this is impossible, and contrary to the natural liberty of the minds of men as rational creatures, guiding and determining themselves according to their own reason of things and understandings; for do but fix the declared will of the ruler in the room and place of divine revelation (which is no hard matter to do, which some actually do universally, and our author as to a great share and proportion), and the obligation sought after to prevent all inconveniences in government falls as full and directly upon the minds, thoughts, and judgments of men, as upon any of their outward actions. And this, for the substance of it, is now pleaded for, seeing it is pretended that in all things dubious, where men cannot satisfy themselves that it is the will of God that they should do a thing or no, the declaration of the magistrate determines not only their practice but their judgment also, and gives them that full persuasion of their minds which is indispensably required unto their acting in such things, and that faith which frees them from sin; for "he that doubteth is damned if he eat."

But it will be said that there will be no need hereof; for let men think and judge what they please, whilst they are convinced and satisfied that it is their duty not to practice any thing outwardly in religion but what is prescribed by their rulers, it is not possible that any public evil should ensue upon their mental conceptions only. We observed before that the condition described is exceedingly uneasy; which, I suppose, will not be denied by men who have seriously considered what it is either to judge or practice any thing that lies before them with reference unto the judgment of God. And that which should tie men up to rest perpetually in such a restless state is, as it seems, a mere conviction of their duty. They ought to be, and are supposed to be, convinced that it is their duty to maintain the liberty of their minds and judgments, but to submit in their outward practice universally to the laws of men that are over them; and this sense and conviction of duty is a sufficient security unto public tranquillity in all that contrariety and opposition of sentiments unto established religion and forms of worship that may be imagined. But if this be so, why will not the same conviction and sense of duty restrain them who do peaceably exercise the worship of God, according to the light and dictates of their consciences, from any actings whatever that may tend to the disturbance of the public peace? Duty, nakedly considered, is even, as such, the greatest obligation on the minds of men; and the great security of others in their actings ariseth from thence. But the more it is influenced and advantaged by outward considerations, the less it is assaulted and opposed by things grievous and perplexing in the way of the discharge of it, the more efficacious will be its operations on the minds of men, and the firmer will be the security unto others that thence ariseth. Now, these advantages lie absolutely on the part of them who practice, or are allowed so to do, according to their own light and persuasion in the worship of God, wherein they are at rest and full satisfaction of mind; and not on theirs who all their days are bound up to a perverse, distorted posture of mind and soul, in judging one thing to be best and most pleasing unto God, and practising of the contrary. Such a one is the man that, of all others, rulers have need, I think, to be most jealous of; for what security can be had of him who hath inured himself unto a continual contradiction between his faith and his practice? For my part, I should either expect no other measure from him in any other thing, nor ever judge that his profession and ways of acting are any sufficient indications of his mind (which takes away all security from mankind), or fear that his convictions of light and knowledge, as he apprehends, would, at one time or other, precipitate him into attempts of irregularity and violence, for his own relief.

— "Hic niger est, hunc tu Romane caveto."

It will be said, perhaps, that we need not look farther for the disturbance of public peace from them who practice outwardly any thing in the worship of God but what is prescribed, established, and enjoined, seeing that every such practice is such a disturbance itself. I say, this pretence is miserably ridiculous and contemptible, and contrary to the common experience of mankind. If this were so, the whole world for three hundred years lived in one continual disturbance and tumult upon the account of Christian religion, whose professors constantly practised and performed that in the worship of God which was so far from being established or approved by public authority, that it was proscribed and condemned under penalties of all sorts, pecuniary, corporeal, and sanguinary or capital; But we see no such matter ensued, nor the least disquietment unto the world, but what was given unto it by the rage of bloody persecutors, that introduced the first convulsions into the Roman empire, which were never well quieted, but ended in its dissolution. The experience, also, of the present and next preceding ages casts this frivolous exception out of consideration. And as such a practice, even against legal prohibitions, though it be by the transgression of a penal law, is yet in itself and [by] just consequence remote enough from any disturbance of government (unless we should suppose that every non-observance of a penal statute invalidates the government of a nation, which were to fix it upon such a foundation as will not afford it the steadiness of a weather-cock); so being allowed by way of exemption, it contains no invasion upon or intrusion into the rights of others, but, being accompanied with the abridgment of the privileges of none, or the neglect of any duty required to the good of the commonwealth, it is as consistent with, and may be as conducing to, public good and tranquillity, as any order of religious things in the world, as shall be elsewhere demonstrated.

It remains, therefore, that the only answer to this consideration is, that men who plead for indulgence and liberty of conscience in the worship of God, according to his word and the light which he hath given them therein, have indeed no conscience at all, and so are not to be believed as to what they profess against sinister and evil practices. This flail I know no fence against but this only, that they have as good and better grounds to suspect him to have no conscience at all who, upon unjust surmises, shall so injuriously charge them, as finding him in a direct transgression of the principal rules that conscience is to be guided and directed by, than he hath to pronounce such a judgment concerning them and their sincerity in what they profess. And whether such mutual censures tend not to the utter overthrow of all peace, love, and security amongst mankind, it is easy to determine. Certainly, it is the worst game in the world for the public, to have men bandying suspicions one against another, and thereon managing mutual charges of all that they do surmise, or what else they please to give the countenance of surmise unto.

I acknowledge the notion insisted on, — namely, "That whilst men reserve to themselves the freedom and liberty of judging what they please, or what seems good unto them, in matters of religion and the worship of God, they ought to esteem it their duty to practice in all things according to the prescription of their rulers, though every way contrary unto and inconsistent with their own judgments and persuasions, unless it be in things that countenance vice or disgrace the Deity" (whereof yet, it may be, it will not be thought meet that they themselves should judge for themselves and their own practice, seeing they may extend their conceptions about what doth so unto such minute instances as would frustrate the whole design), — is exceedingly accommodated to the corrupt lusts and affections of men, and suited to make provision for their security in this world by an exemption from the indispensable command of professing the truth communicated and known unto them; a sense of the obligation whereof hath hitherto exposed innumerable persons in all ages to great difficulties, dangers, and sufferings, yea, to death, the height and sum of all: for whereas men have been persuaded that "with the heart man believeth unto righteousness, and with the mouth confession is made unto salvation," the latter clause is in many cases hereby sufficiently superseded, and the troublesome duty seeming to be required in it is removed out of the way. It will not, it may be, be so easy to prove that in the religion of the Mohammedans there is any thing enjoined in practice that will directly fall under the limitations assigned unto the compliance with the commands of superiors contended for; and, therefore, let a man but retain his own apprehensions concerning Jesus Christ and the gospel, it may be lawful for him, yea, be his duty, to observe the worship enjoined by the law of Mohammed, if his lot fall to live under the power of the Grand Seignior or any sovereign prince of the same persuasion! But the case is clear in the religion of the Papists, which is under the protection of the greatest number of supreme magistrates in Europe. It will not be pretended, I suppose, by our author, that there is any thing in the confession of the church of Rome, or imposed by it on the practices of men, that directly gives countenance unto any immorality, especially as the sense of that term is by him stated; and it is no easy matter for ordinary men to prove and satisfy themselves that there is aught in their modes of worship of such a tendency as to cast disgrace upon the Deity, especially considering with how much learning and diligence the charge of any such miscarriage is endeavoured to be answered and removed, — all which pleas ought to be satisfied before a man can make sedately a determinate judgment of the contrary. Let, then, men's judgments be what they will in the matters of difference between Protestants and Papists, it is, on this hypothesis, the duty of all that live under the dominion of sovereign popish princes outwardly to comply with and practice that religious worship that is commanded by them and enjoined! The case is the same, also, as to the religion of the Jews!

Now, as this casts a reflection of incredible folly and inexpiable guilt upon all protestant martyrs, in casting away their own lives and disobeying the commands of their lawful sovereigns, so it exposeth all the Protestants in the world who are still in the same condition of subjection to the severe censures of impiety and rebellion, and must needs exasperate their rulers to pursue them to destruction, under pretence of unwarrantable obstinacy in them: for if we wholly take off the protection of conscience in this matter, and its subjection to the authority of God alone, there is no plea left to excuse dissenting Protestants from the guilt of such crimes as may make men justly cry out against them, as the Jews did against St Paul, "Away with such fellows from the earth; for it is not fit that they should live!" or, "Protestantes ad leones!" according to the old cry of the Pagans against the primitive Christians. But if this should prove to be a way of teaching and justifying the grossest hypocrisy and dissimulation that the nature of man is capable of, a means to cast off all regard unto the authority of God over the ways and lives of men, all the rhetoric in the world shall never persuade me that God hath so moulded and framed the order and state of human affairs that it should be any way needful to the preservation of public peace and tranquillity. Openness, plainness of heart, sincerity in our actions and professions, generous honesty, and a universal respect in all things to the supreme Rector of all, the great Possessor of heaven and earth, with an endeavour to comply with his present revealed mind and future judgment, are far better foundations for and ligaments of public peace and quietness. To make this the foundation of our political superstructure, that "divisum imperium cum Jove Cæsar habet," God hath immediate and sole power over the minds and inward thoughts of men, but the magistrate over the exercise of those thoughts, in things especially belonging to the worship of God, and in the same instances, seems not to prognosticate a stable or durable building. The prophet was not of that mind of old, who, in the name of God, blamed the people for willingly walking after the commandment of their ruler in concerns of worship not warranted by divine appointment; nor was Daniel so, who, notwithstanding the severe prohibition made against his praying in his house, continued to do so three times a day.

But besides all this, I do not see how this hypothesis is necessarily subservient to the principal design of the author, but it may be as well improved to quite distant, yea, contrary ends and purposes. His design, plainly, is to have one fabric of religion erected, one form of external worship enacted and prescribed, which all men should be compelled by penalties to the outward profession and observance of. These penalties he would have to be such as should not fail of their end, — namely, of taking away all professed dissent from his religious establishment; which, if it cannot be effected without the destruction and death of multitudes, they also are not to be forborne. Now, how this ensues from the forementioned principle I know not; for a supreme magistrate, finding that the minds of very many of his subjects are, in their judgments and persuasions, engaged in a dissent unto the religion established by him, or somewhat in it, or some part of it, especially in things of practical worship, though he should be persuaded that he hath so far a power over their consciences as to command them to practice contrary to their judgment, yet, knowing their minds and persuasions to be out of his reach and exempted from his jurisdiction, why may he not think it meet and conducing to public tranquillity and all the ends of his government, even the good of the whole community committed to his charge, rather to indulge them in the quiet and peaceable exercise of the worship of God according to their own light, than always to bind them up unto that unavoidable disquietment which will ensue upon the conflict in their minds between their judgments and their practices, if he should oblige them as is desired? Certainly, as in truth and reality, so according to this principle, he hath power so to do; for to fancy him [to have] such a power over the religion and consciences of his subjects as that he should be inevitably bound, on all occurrences, and in all conditions of affairs, to impose upon them the necessary observation of one form of worship, is that which would quickly expose him to inextricable troubles. And instances of all sorts might be multiplied to show the ridiculous folly of such a conception. Nay, it implies a perfect contradiction to what is disputed, before; for if he be obliged to settle and impose such a form on all, it must be because there was a necessity of somewhat antecedent to his imposition, whence his obligation to impose it did arise. And, on such a supposition, it is in vain to inquire after his liberty or his power in these things, seeing by his duty he is absolutely determined; and whatever that be which doth so determine him and put an obligation upon him, it doth indispensably do the same on his subjects also, which, as it is known, utterly excludes the authority pleaded for.

This principle, therefore, indeed asserts his liberty to do what he judgeth meet in these matters, but contains nothing in it to oblige him to judge that it may not be meet and most conducing unto all the ends of his government to indulge unto the consciences of men peaceable (especially if complying with him in all the fundamentals of the religion which himself professeth) the liberty of worshipping God according to what they apprehend of his own mind and will. And let an application of this principle be made to the present state of this nation, wherein there are so great multitudes of persons peaceable, and not unuseful unto public good, who dissent from the present establishment of outward worship, and have it not in their power either to change their judgments or to practice contrary unto them; and as it is in the power of the supreme magistrate to indulge them in their own way, so it will prove to be his interest, as he is the spring and centre of public peace and prosperity.

Neither doth it appear that, in this discourse, our author hath had any regard either to the real principles of the power of the magistrate as stated in this nation, or to his own, which are fictitious, but yet such as ought to be obligatory to himself. His principal assertion is, "That the supreme magistrate hath power to bind the consciences of men in matters of religion;" that is, by laws and edicts to that purpose. Now, the highest and most obligatory way of the supreme magistrate's speaking in England is by acts of parliament; it is therefore supposed that what is so declared in or about matters of religion should be obligatory to the conscience of this author; but yet quite otherwise, page 59, he sets himself to oppose and condemn a public law of the land, on no other ground than because it stood in his way, and seemed incompliant with his principles: for whereas the law of 2 and 3 Edward VI., which appointed two weekly days for abstinence from flesh, had been, amongst other reasons, prefaced with this, "That the king's subjects having now a more clear light of the gospel, through the infinite mercy of God" (such "canting" language was then therein used), "and thereby the king's majesty perceiving that one meat of itself was not more holy than another," etc., "yet considering that due abstinence was a means to virtue, and to subdue men's bodies to their souls and spirits," etc.; and it being after found (it should seem by a farther degree of light) that those expressions, meeting with the inveterate opinions of some newly brought out of Popery, had given countenance to them to teach or declare that something of religion was placed therein, thereon, by the law made 5 Eliz., adding another weekly day to be kept with the former for the same purpose, the former clause was omitted, and mention only made therein of the civil and politic reasons inducing the legislators thereunto, and withal a penalty of inflicting punishment on those who should affirm and maintain that there was any concernment of conscience and religion in that matter. This provision hath so distasted our author, that forgetting, it seems, his own design, he reproaches it with the title of "jejunium Cecilianum,"[5] and thinks it so far from obliging his conscience to acquiesce in the determination therein made, that he will not allow it to give law to his tongue or pen! But ("vexet censura columbas") it seems they are the fanatics only that are thus to be restrained.

Moreover, on occasion hereof, we might manifest how some other laws of this land do seem carefully to avoid that imposition on conscience which, against law and reason, he pleadeth for. For instance, in that of 21 Jac., touching usury, and the restraint of it unto the sum therein established, it was provided, "That no words in this act contained shall be construed or expounded to allow the practice of usury in point of religion and conscience." And why did not the supreme magistrate in that law determine and bind the consciences of men by a declaration of their duty in a point of religion, seeing whither way soever the determination had been made, neither would immorality have been countenanced nor the Deity disgraced? But, plainly, it is rather declared that he hath not Cognizance of such things with reference to the consciences of men, to oblige them or set them at liberty, but only power to determine what may be prac-

---

5   In allusion, doubtless, to Cecil, Lord Burleigh, the celebrated prime minister of Elizabeth. — ED.

tised in order to public profit and peace. And, therefore, the law would neither bind nor set at liberty the consciences of men in such cases; which is a work for the supreme Lawgiver only.

Neither, as it hath been before observed, do the principles here asserted and contended for either express or represent the supremacy of the kings of this nation in matters ecclesiastical, as it is stated and determined by themselves in parliament, but rather so as to give great offence and scandal to the religion here professed, and advantage to the adversaries thereof; for after there appeared some ambiguity in those words of the oath, enacted 1 Eliz., of "testifying the queen to be supreme governor, as well in all spiritual or ecclesiastical things or causes as in temporal," and many doubts and scruples had ensued thereon, as though there were assigned to her a power over the consciences of her subjects in spiritual things, or that she had a power herself to order and administer spiritual things, in Elizabeth it is enacted, by way of explanation, that the oaths aforesaid shall be expounded in such form as is set forth in the admonition annexed to the queen's injunctions, published in the first year of her reign; where, disclaiming the power of the ministry of divine offices in the church, or the power of the priesthood here by our author affixed to the supreme magistrate, her power and authority is declared to be a sovereignty over all manner of persons born within this realm, whether they be ecclesiastical or temporal, so that no foreign power hath, or ought to have, any superiority over them. And so is this supremacy stated in the articles, anno 1562, — namely, an authority to rule all estates and degrees committed to the charge of the supreme magistrate by God, whether they be ecclesiastical or temporal, and to restrain the stubborn or evil-doers. Of the things contended for by our author, — the authority of the priesthood, and power over the consciences of men in matters of religion, — there is not one word in our laws, but rather they are both of them rejected and condemned.

I have yet laid the least part of that load upon this principle, which, if it be farther pressed, it must expect to be burdened withal, and that from the common suffrage of Christians in all ages. But yet, that I may not transgress against the design of this short and hasty discourse, I shall proceed no farther in the pursuit of it, but take a little survey of what is here pleaded in its defence. Now, this is undertaken and pursued in the first chapter, with the two next ensuing, where an end is put to this plea: for if I understand any thing of his words and expressions, our author in the beginning of his fourth chapter cuts down all those gourds and wild vines that he had been planting in the three preceding; for he not only grants but disputes also for an obligation on the consciences of men antecedent and superior unto all human laws and their obligation! His words are as followeth, p. 115: "It is not because subjects are in any thing free from the authority of the supreme power on earth, but because they are subject to a superior in heaven, and they are only then excused from the duty of obedience to their sovereign when they cannot give it without rebellion against God: so that it is not originally any right of their own that exempts them from a subjection to the sovereign power in all things; but it is purely God's right of governing his own creatures that magistrates then invade when they make edicts to violate or control his laws. And those who will take off from the consciences of men all obligations antecedent to those of human laws, instead of making the power of princes supreme, absolute, and uncontrollable, they utterly enervate all their authority, and set their subjects at perfect liberty from all their commands."

I know no men that pretend to exemption from the obligation of human laws but only on this plea, that God by his law requires them to do otherwise; and if this be so, the authority of such laws as to the consciences of men is superseded, by the confession of this author. Allow, therefore, but the principles here expressed, — namely, that men have a superior Power over them in heaven, whose laws and the revelation of whose will concerning them is the supreme rule of their duty, whence an obligation is laid upon their consciences of doing whatever is commanded, or not doing what is forbidden by him, which is superior unto, and actually supersedes, all human commands and laws that interfere therewith, — and I see neither use of nor place for that power of magistrates over the consciences of men which is so earnestly contended for. And our author, also, in his ensuing discourse in that chapter, placeth all the security of government in the respect that the consciences of men have to the will and command of God, and which they profess to have; which in all these chapters he pleads to be a principle of all confusion! But it is the first chapter which alone we are now taking a view of.

The only argument therein insisted on to make good the ascription unto the magistrate of the power over religion and the consciences of men before described, is "the absolute and indispensable necessity of it unto public tranquillity; which is the principal and most important end of government." In the pursuit of this argument, sometimes, yea often, such expressions are used concerning the magistrate's power as, in a tolerable construction, declare it to be what no man denies nor will contend about: but it is necessary that they be interpreted according to the genius and tenor of the opinion contended for; and, accordingly, we will consider them. This alone, I say, is that which is here pleaded, or is given in as the subject of the ensuing discourse. But, after all, I think that he who shall set himself seriously to find out how any thing here spoken hath a direct and rational cogency towards the establishment of the conclusion before laid down will find himself engaged in no easy undertaking. We were told, I confess, at the entrance (so as that we may not complain of a surprisal) that we must expect to have invectives twisted with arguments, and some such thing seems here to be aimed at; but if a logical chemist come and make a separation of the elements of this composition, he will find, if I mistake not, a heap of the drossy invective, and scarce the least appearance of any argument ore. Instead of sober, rational arguing,

— "crimina rasis
Librat in antithetis;" —
Pers. i. 85,

great aggravations of men's miscarriages in the pursuit of the dictates of their consciences, either real or feigned, edged against and fiercely rejected upon those whom he makes his adversaries, and these the same for substance, repeated over and over in a great variety of well-placed words, take up the greatest part of his plea in this chapter, especially the beginning of it, wherein alone the controversy, as by himself stated, is concerned.

But if the power and authority over religion and the consciences of men here ascribed unto supreme magistrates be so indispensably necessary to the preservation of public tranquillity as is pretended, a man cannot but wonder how the world hath been in any age past kept in any tolerable peace and quietness, and how it is anywhere blessed with those ends of government at this day; for it will not be an easy task for our author, or any one else, to demonstrate that the power mentioned hath ever been either claimed or exercised by any supreme magistrate in Christendom, or that it is so at this day. The experience of past and present ages is, therefore, abundantly sufficient to defeat this pretence, which is sufficiently asserted, without the least appearance of proof or argument to give it countenance or confirmation, or they must be very charitable to hire, or ignorant in themselves, who will mistake invectives for arguments. The remembrance, indeed, of these severities I would willingly lay aside, especially because the very mention of them seems to express a higher sense of and regret concerning them than I am in the least subject unto, or something that looks like a design of retaliation; but as these things are far from my mind, so the continual returns that almost in every page I meet with of high and contemptuous reproaches will not allow that they be always passed by without any notice or remark.

It is, indeed, indispensably necessary that public peace and tranquillity be preserved; but that there is any thing in point of government necessary hereunto, but that God have all spiritual power over the consciences of men, and rulers political power over their actings, wherein public peace and tranquillity are concerned, the world hath not hitherto esteemed, nor do I expect to find it proved by this author. If these things will not preserve the public peace, it will not be kept if one should rise from the dead to persuade men unto their duty. The power of God over the consciences of men I suppose is acknowledged by all who own any such thing as conscience, or believe there is a God over all. That, also, in the exercise of this authority, he requires of men all that obedience unto rulers that is any way needful or expedient unto the preservation of the ends of their rule, is a truth standing firm on the same foundation of universal consent, derived from the law of creation; and his positive commands to that purpose have an evidence of his will in this matter not liable to exception or control. This conscience unto God our author confesseth (as we have observed in his fourth chapter) to be the great preservation and security of government and governors, with respect unto the ends mentioned; and if so, what becomes of all the pretences of disorder and confusion that will ensue unless this power over men's consciences be given to the magistrate, and taken as it were out of the hands of God? Nor is it to be supposed that men will be more true to their consciences, supposing the reiglement of them in the hand of men, than when they are granted to be in the hand and power of God; for both at present are supposed to require the same things. Certainly, where conscience respects authority, as it always doth, the more absolute and sovereign it apprehends the authority by which it is obliged, the greater and more firm will be the impression of the obligation upon it; and in that capacity of pre-eminence it must look upon the authority of God, compared with the authority of man. Here, then, lies the security of public peace and tranquillity, as it is backed by the authority of the magistrate, to see that all outward actions are suitable unto what conscience toward God doth in this matter openly and unquestionably require.

The pretence, indeed, is, that the placing of this authority over the consciences of men in the supreme ruler doth obviate and take away all grounds and occasions of any such actings on the account of religion as may tend unto public disturbance; for suppose conscience, in things concerning religion and the worship of God, subject to God alone, and the magistrate require such things to be observed in the one or the other as God hath not required, at least in the judgments and consciences of them of whom the things prescribed are required, and to forbid the things that God requires to be observed and done, in this case, it is said, they cannot or will not comply in active obedience with the commands of the magistrate. But, what if it so fall out? Doth it thence follow that such persons must needs rebel and be seditious, and disturb the public peace of the society whereof they are members? Wherefore is it that they do not do or observe what is required of them by the magistrate in religion or the worship of God, or that they do what he forbids? Is it not because of the authority of God over their minds and consciences in these things? and why should it be supposed that men will answer the obligations laid by God on their consciences in one thing and not in another, in the things of his worship and not of obedience unto civil power, concerning which his commands are as express and evident as they can be pretended to be in the things which they avow their obligation unto?

Experience is pretended to the contrary. It is said again and again that "men, under pretence of their consciences unto God in religion, have raised wars and tumults, and brought all things into confusion, in this kingdom and nation especially; and what will words avail against the evidence of so open an experience to the contrary?" But what if this also should prove a false and futilous pretence? Fierce and long wars have been in this nation of old, upon the various titles of persons pleading their right unto supreme government in the kingdom against one another; so also have there been about the civil rights and privileges of the subjects in the confusions commonly called "The barons' wars." The late troubles, disorders, and wars amongst us must bear the weight of this whole charge. But if any one will take the pains to review the public writings, declarations, treatises, whereby those tumults and wars were begun and carried on, he will easily discern that liberty of conscience in practice, or the exemption of it from the power of the magistrate, as to the rule and conduct of it, now ascribed unto him in the latitude, by sober persons defended or pleaded for, had neither place in nor influence into the beginnings of those troubles. And when such confusions are begun, no man can give assurance or conjecture where they shall end.

Authority, laws, privileges, and I know not what things, wherein private men, of whom alone we treat, have no pretence of interest, were pleaded in those affairs. He that would judge aright of these things must set aside all other considerations, and give his instance of the tumults and seditions that have ensued on the account of men's keeping their consciences entire for God alone, without any just plea or false pretence of authority, and the interest of men in the civil concerns of nations.

However, it cannot be pretended that *liberty of conscience* gave the least occasion unto any disorders in those days, for indeed there was none but only that of opinion and judgment, which our author placeth out of the magistrate's cognizance and dispose, and supposeth it is a thing wherein the public peace neither is nor can be concerned. It is well if it prove so; but this liberty of judgment, constantly pressed with a practice contrary to its own determinations, will, I fear, prove the most dangerous posture of the minds of men, in reference to public tranquillity, that they can be well disposed into. However, we may take a little nearer view of the certain remedy provided for all these evils by our author, and satisfy ourselves in some inquiries about it. Shall, then, according to this expedient, the supreme magistrate govern, rule, and oblige unto obedience the consciences of his subjects universally in all things in religion and the worship of God, so that, appoint what he please, forbid what he please, subjects are bound in conscience to observe them and yield obedience accordingly? His answer, as far as I can gather his meaning, is, that he may and must do so in all things, taking care that what he commands shall neither countenance vice nor disgrace the Deity; and then the subjects are obliged according to the inquiry. But there seems another limitation to be given to this power, p. 37, where he affirms that the "Lord Christ hath given severe injunctions to secure the obedience of men to all lawful superiors, except where they run directly cross to the interest of the gospel;" and elsewhere he seems to give the same privilege of exemption where a religion is introduced that is idolatrous or superstitious. I would, then, a little farther inquire, who shall judge whether the things commanded in religion and the worship of God be idolatrous and superstitious? whether they cross directly the interest of the gospel? whether they countenance vice and disgrace the Deity or no? To say that the magistrate is to judge and determine hereof is the highest foppery imaginable; for no magistrate, unless he be distracted, will enjoin such a religion to observance as he judgeth himself to fall under the [dis]qualifications mentioned, and when he hath done so declare that so they do, and yet require obedience unto them. Besides, if this judgment be solely committed unto him indeed, in the issue there neither is nor can be any question for a judgment to be passed upon in this matter, for his injunction doth quite render useless all disquisitions to that purpose. The judgment and determination hereof, therefore, is necessarily to be left unto the subjects from whom obedience is required. So it lies in the letter of the proposal; they must obey in all things but such; and, therefore, surely must judge what is such and what is not. Now, who shall fix bounds to what they will judge to fall under one or other of these limitations? If they determine, according to the best light they have, that the religious observances enjoined by the magistrate do directly cross the interest of the gospel, they are absolved by our author from any obligation in conscience to their observation; and so we are just as before, and this great engine for public tranquillity vanisheth into air and smoke.

Thus this author himself, in way of objection, supposeth a case of a magistrate enjoining, as was said, a religion superstitious and idolatrous. This he acknowledgeth to be an inconvenience, yet such as is far beneath the mischiefs that ensue upon the exemption of the consciences of men in religion from the power of the magistrate! which I confess I cannot but admire at, and can give reasons why I do so admire it, which also may be given in due season. But what, then, is to be done in this case? He answers, "It is to be borne." True, but how? Is it to be so borne as to practice and observe the things so enjoined, though superstitious and idolatrous? Though his words are dubious, yet I suppose he will not plainly say so, nor can he, unless he will teach men to cast off all respect unto the authority of God, and open such a door to atheism as his rhetorical, prefatory invective will not be able to shut. The bearing, then, intended, must be by patient suffering in a refusal to practice what is so commanded, and observing the contrary commands of God. But why in this case ought they to suffer quietly for refusing a compliance with what is commanded, and for their observance of the contrary precepts of the gospel? Why, they must do so because of the command of God, obliging their consciences unto obedience to the magistrate in all things wherein the public peace is concerned; and so that is absolutely secured. Is it not evident to him that hath but half an eye that we are come about again where we were before? Let this be applied to all the concernments of religion and religious worship, and there will arise, with respect unto them, the same security which in this case is deemed sufficient, and all that human affairs are capable of; for if in greater matters men may refuse to act according to the magistrate's command, out of a sense of the authority of God obliging them to the contrary, and yet their civil peaceableness and obedience be absolutely secured from the respect of their consciences to the command of God requiring it, why should it not be admitted that they may and will have the same respect to that command when they dissent from the magistrate's constitution in lesser things, on the same account of the authority of God requiring the contrary of them? Shall we suppose that they will cast off the authority of God requiring their obedience, on the account of their dissatisfaction in lesser things of the magistrate's appointment when they will not do so for all the violence that may be offered unto them in things of greater and higher importance? The principle, therefore, asserted is as useless as it is false, and partakes sufficiently of both these properties to render it inconsiderable and contemptible; and he that can reconcile these things among themselves or make them useful to the author's design will achieve what I dare not aspire unto.

I know not any thing that remains in the first chapter deserving our farther consideration; what seems to be of real importance, or to have any aspect towards the cause in hand, may undergo some brief remarks, and so leave us at liberty to a farther progress. In general, a supposition is laid down, and it is so vehemently asserted as is evident that it is accompanied with a desire that it should be taken for granted, — namely, that if the consciences of men be not regulated, in the choice and practice of religion, by the authority of the magistrate over them, they will undoubtedly run into principles and practices inconsistent with the safety of human society, and such as will lead them to seditions and tumults; and hence (if I understand him, a matter I am continually jealous about, from the looseness of his expressions, though I am satisfied I constantly take his words in the sense which is received of them by the most intelligent persons) he educeth all his reasonings, and not from a mere dissent from the magistrate's injunctions, without the entertainment of such principles or an engagement into such practices. I cannot, I say, find the arguments that arise from a mere supposition that men, in some things relating to the worship of God, will or do practice otherwise than the magistrate commands, which are used to prove the inconsistency of such a posture of things with public tranquillity; which yet alone was the province our author ought to have managed. But there is another supposition added, — that where conscience is in any thing left unto its own liberty to choose or refuse in the worship of God, there it will embrace, sure enough, such wicked, debauched, and seditious principles as shall dispose men unto commotions, rebellions, and all such evils as will actually evert all rule, order, and policy amongst men. But now this supposition will not be granted him, in reference unto them who profess to take up all their profession of religion from the command of God or the revelation of his will in the Scripture, wherein all such principles and practices as those mentioned are utterly condemned; and the whole profession of Christianity being left for three hundred years without the rule, guidance, and conduct of conscience now contended for, did not once give the least disturbance unto the civil governments of the world. Disturbances, indeed, there were, and dreadful revolutions of governments, in those days and places when and where the professors of it lived; but no concerns of religion being then involved in or with the civil rights and interests of men, as the professors of it had no engagements in them, so from those alterations and troubles no reflection could be made on their profession. And the like peace, the like innocency of religion, the like freedom from all possibility of such imputations as are now cast upon it, occasioned merely by its intertexture with the affairs, rights, and laws of the nations, and the interests of its professors as such therein, will ensue when it shall be separated from that relation wherein it stands to this world, and left at the pure, naked tendency of the souls of men to another, and not before.

But what says our author? "If for the present the minds of men happen to be tainted with such furious and boisterous conceptions of religion as incline them to stubbornness and sedition, and make them unmanageable to the laws of government, shall not a prince be allowed to give check to such unruly and dangerous persuasions?" I answer, That such principles which, being professed and avowed, are in their own nature and just consequence destructive to public peace and human society, are all of them directly opposite to the light of human nature, that common reason and consent of mankind wherein and whereon all government is founded, with the prime fundamental laws and dictates of the Scripture, and so may and ought to be restrained in the practices of the persons that profess them; and with reference unto them the magistrate "beareth not the sword in vain:" for human society being inseparably consequent unto, and an effect of, the law of our nature, or concreated principles of it, which hath subdued the whole race of mankind, in all times and places, unto its observance; opinions, persuasions, principles opposite unto it, or destructive of it, manifesting themselves by any sufficient evidence or in overt acts, ought to be no more allowed than such as profess an enmity to the being and providence of God himself. For men's inclinations, indeed, as in themselves considered, there is no competent judge of them amongst the sons of men; but as to all outward actions that are of the tendency described, they are under public inspection, to be dealt withal according to their demerit.

I shall only add, that the mormo here made use of is not now first composed or erected; it hath, for the substance of it, been flourished by the Papists ever since the beginning of the Reformation. Neither did they use to please themselves more in or to dance more merrily about any thing than this calf: "Let private men have their consciences exempted from a necessary obedience to the prescriptions of the church, and they will quickly run into all pernicious fancies and persuasions." It is known how this scare-crow hath been cast to the ground, and this calf stamped to powder, by divines of the church of England. It is no pleasant thing, I confess, to see this plea revived now with respect to the magistrate's authority, and not the pope's; for I fear that when it shall be manifested, and that by the consent of all parties, that there is no pleadable argument to bottom this pretension for the power of the magistrate upon, some, rather than forego it, will not be unwilling to recur to the fountain from whence it first sprang, and admit the pope's plea as meet to be revived in this case. And, indeed, if we must come at length, for the security of public peace, to deprive all private persons of the liberty of judging what is right and wrong in religion in reference to their own practice, or what is their duty towards God about his worship, and what is not, there are innumerable advantages attending the design of devolving the absolute determination of these things upon the pope, above that of committing it to each supreme magistrate in his own dominions; for besides the plea of at least better security in his determinations than in that of any magistrate, if not his infallibility, which he hath so long talked of, and so sturdily defended, as to get it a great reputation in the world, the delivering up of the faith and consciences of all men unto him will produce a seeming agreement, at least of incomparably a larger extent than the remitting of all things of this nature to the pleasure of every supreme magistrate, which may probably establish as many different religions in the world as there are different nations, kingdoms, or commonwealths.

That which alone remains seeming to give countenance to the assertions before laid down, is our author's assignation of the priesthood by natural right unto the supreme magistrate, which in no alteration of religion he can be divested of, but by virtue of some positive law of God, as it was for a season in the Mosaical institution and government. But these things seem to be of no force; for it never belonged to the priesthood to govern or to rule the consciences of men with an absolute, uncontrollable power, but only in their name, and for them, to administer the holy things which by common consent were admitted and received amongst them. Besides, our author, by his discourse, seems not to be much acquainted with the rise of the office of the priesthood amongst men; as shall be demonstrated if farther occasion be given thereunto. However, by the way, we may observe what is his judgment in this matter. The magistrate, we are told, hath not his ecclesiastical authority from Christ, and yet this is such that the power of the priesthood is included therein, the exercise whereof, "as he is pleased to transfer to others, so he may, if he please, reserve it to himself," p. 32; whence it follows, not only that it cannot be given by Christ unto any other, for it is part of the magistrate's power, which he hath not limited or confined by any subsequent law, nor can there be a coordinate subject of the same power of several kinds; so that all the interest or right any man or men have in or unto the exercise of it is but transferred to them by the magistrate; and therefore they act therein in his name and by his authority only; and hence the bishops, as such, are said to be "ministers of state," p. 49. Neither can it be pretended that this was indeed in the power of the magistrate before the coming of Christ, but not since; for he hath, as we are told, all that he ever had, unless there be a restraint put upon him by some express prohibition of our Saviour, p. 41, — which will hardly be found in this matter. I cannot, therefore, see how, in the exercise of the Christian priesthood, there is (on these principles) any the least respect unto Jesus Christ or his authority: for men have only the exercise of it transferred to them by the magistrate, by virtue of a power inherent in him antecedent unto any concessions of Christ; and, therefore, in his name and authority they must act in all the sacred offices of their functions. It is well if men be so far awake as to consider the tendency of these things.

At length Scripture proofs for the confirmation of these opinions are produced, pp. 35, 36; and the first pleaded is that promise, that "kings shall be nursing fathers unto the church." It is true this is promised, and God accomplish it more and more! but yet we do not desire such nurses as beget the children they nurse. The proposing, prescribing, commanding, binding religion on the consciences of men, is rather the *begetting* of it than its *nursing*. To take care of the church and religion, that it receive no detriment, by all the ways and means appointed by God and useful thereunto, is the duty of the magistrates: but it is so also, antecedently to their actings unto this purpose, to discern aright which is the church whereunto this promise is made; without which they cannot duly discharge their trust nor fulfil the promise itself. The very words, by the rules of the metaphor, do imply that the church and its religion, and the worship of God observed therein, are constituted, fixed, and regulated by God himself, antecedently unto the magistrate's duty and power about it. They are to nurse that which is committed to them, and not what themselves have framed or begotten. And we contend for no more but a rule concerning religion and the worship of God antecedent unto the magistrate's interposing about it, whereby both his actings in his place, and those of subjects in theirs, are to be regulated. Mistakes herein have engaged many sovereign princes, in pursuit of their trust as nursing fathers to the church, to lay out their strength and power for the utter ruin of it; as may be evidenced in instances too many of those who, in a subserviency to and by the direction of the papal interest, have endeavoured to extirpate true religion out of the world. Such a nursing mother we had some time in England, who, in pursuit of her care, burned so many bishops and other holy men to ashes.

He asks farther, "What doth the Scripture mean when it styles our Saviour the King of kings, and maketh princes his vicegerents here on earth?" I confess, according to this gentleman's principles, I know not what it means in so doing. Kings, he tells us, have not their authority in and over religion and the consciences of men from him, and therefore in the exercise of it cannot be his vicegerents; for none is the vicegerent of another in the exercise of any power and authority, if he have not received that power and authority from him. Otherwise the words have a proper sense, but nothing to our author's purpose. It is his power over them, and not theirs over the consciences of their subjects, that is intended in the words. Of no more use, in this controversy is the direction of the apostle, that we "should pray for kings, that under them we may lead a quiet and peaceable life;" for no more is intended therein but that, under their peaceable and righteous administration of human affairs, we may live in that godliness and honesty which is required of us. Wherefore, then, are these weak attempts made to confirm and prove what is not? Those, or the most of them, whom our author in this discourse treats with so much severity, do plead that it is the duty of all supreme magistrates to find out, receive, embrace, and promote, the truths of the gospel, with the worship of God appointed therein; confirming, protecting, and defending them, and those that embrace them, by their power and authority: and in the discharge of this duty they are to use the liberty of their own judgments, informed by the ways that God hath appointed, independently of the dictates and determinations of any other persons whatever. They affirm, also, that to this end they are intrusted with supreme power over all persons in their respective dominions; who on no pretence can be exempted from the exercise of that power, as occasion, in their judgments, shall require it to be exercised: as also, that all causes wherein the profession of religion in their dominions is concerned, which are determinable in "foro civili," by coercive umpirage or authority, are subject unto their cognizance and power. The sovereign power over the consciences of men, to institute, appoint, and prescribe religion and the worship of God, they affirm to belong unto Him alone who is the "author and finisher of our faith, who is the head over all things to the church." The administration of things merely spiritual in the worship of God is, they judge, derived immediately from him to the ministers and administrators of the gospel, possessed of their offices by his command and according to his institution. As to the external practice of religion, and religious worship as such, it is, they say, in the power of the magistrate to regulate all the outward civil concernments of it, with reference unto the preservation of public peace and tranquillity, and the prosperity of his subjects; and herein also they judge that such respect is to be had to the consciences of men as the Scripture, the nature of the thing itself, and the right of the Lord Christ to introduce his spiritual kingdom into all nations, do require.

That which seems to have imposed on the mind of this author is, that if the magistrate may make laws for the regulating of the outward profession of religion, so as public peace and tranquillity may be kept, added to what is his duty to do in the behalf of the truth, then he must have the power over religion and the consciences of men by him ascribed unto him; but there is no privity of interest between these things. The laws which he makes to this purpose are to be regulated by the word of God and the good of the community over which, in the name of God, he doth preside; and whence he will take his warranty to forbid men the exercise of their consciences in the duties of spiritual worship, whilst the principles they profess are suited to the light of nature and the fundamental doctrines of the gospel, with the peace of mankind, and their practices absolutely consistent with the public welfare, I am yet to seek; and so, as far as I can yet perceive, is the author of the discourse under consideration. It will not arise, from a parity of reason, from the power that he hath to restrain cursed swearing and blasphemies by penal coercions; for these things are no less against the light of nature, and no less condemned by the common suffrage of mankind (and the persons that contract the guilt of them may be no less effectually brought to judge and condemn themselves), than are the greatest outrages that may be committed in and against human society. That the gospel will give no countenance hereunto he seems to acknowledge, in his assignation of several reasons why the use of the power, and exercise of it in the way of compulsion by penalties, pleaded for by him, is not mentioned therein. That "Christ and his apostles behaved themselves as subjects; that he neither took nor exercised any sovereign power; that he gave his laws to private men as such, and not to the magistrate; that the power that then was was in bad hands," are pleaded as excuses for the silence of the gospel in this matter. But, lest this should prove farther prejudicial to his present occasion, he adds, p. 42, "The only reason why the Lord Christ bound not the precepts of the gospel upon men's consciences by any secular compulsories was, not because compulsion was an improper way to put his laws in execution, for then he had never established them with more enforcing sanctions, but only because himself was not vested with any secular power, and so could not use those methods of government which are proper to its jurisdiction." This in plain English is, that if Christ had had power, he would have ordered the gospel to have been propagated as Mohammed hath done his Alcoran; an assertion untrue and impious, contrary to the whole spirit and genius of the gospel and of the author of it, and the commands and precepts of it. And it is fondly supposed that the Lord Christ suited all the management of the affairs of the gospel unto that state and condition in this world wherein he emptied himself, and took upon him the form of a servant, making himself of no reputation, that he might be obedient unto death, the death of the cross. He lays the foundation of the promulgation and propagation of it in the world in the grant of all power unto him in heaven and earth. "All power," saith he to his apostles, "is given unto me in heaven and in earth. Go ye therefore, and teach all nations, baptizing them in the name of the Father, and of the Son, and of the Holy Ghost: teaching them to observe all things whatsoever I have commanded you," Matt. xxviii. 18–20. He is considered, in the dispensation of the gospel, as he who is "head over all things to the church," the "Lord of lords, and King of kings," whom our author acknowledgeth to be his vice-gerents. On this account the gospel, with all the worship instituted therein and required thereby, is accompanied with a right to enter into any of the kingdoms of the earth, and spiritually to make the inhabitants of them subject to Jesus Christ, and so to translate them out of the power of darkness into the kingdom of the Son of God; and this right is antecedent and paramount to the right of all earthly kings and princes whatever, who have no power or authority to exclude the gospel out of their dominions, and what they exercise of that kind is done at their peril.

The "penalties that he hath annexed to the final rejection of the gospel and disobedience thereunto" are pleaded by our author to justify the magistrate's power of binding men to "the observation of his commands in religion on temporal penalties, to be by him inflicted on them." Unto that is the discourse of this chapter arrived, which was designed unto another end. I see neither the order, method, nor projection of this procedure, nor know

"Amphora cum cœpit institui, cur urceus exit."
[Altered from Hor. ad Pison. 21.]

However, the pretence itself is weak and impertinent. Man was originally made under a law and constitution of eternal bliss or woe. This state, with regard to his necessary dependence on God and respect to his utmost end, was absolutely unavoidable unto him. All possibility of attaining eternal happiness by himself he lost by sin, and became inevitably obnoxious to eternal misery and the wrath to come. In this condition the Lord Jesus Christ, the supreme Lord of the souls and consciences of men, interposeth his law of relief, redemption and salvation, the great means of man's recovery, together with the profession of the way and law hereof. He lets them know that those by whom it is refused shall perish under that wrath of

God which before they were obnoxious unto, with a new aggravation of their sin and condemnation, from the contempt of the relief provided for them and tendered to them. This he applies to the souls and consciences of men, and to all the inward secret actings of them in the first place, — such as are exempted not only from the judicature of men, but from the cognizance of angels. This he doth by spiritual means, in a spiritual manner, — with regard to the subjection of the souls of men unto God, and with reference unto their bringing to him and enjoyment of him, or their being eternally rejected by him. Hence to collect and conclude that earthly princes, — who (whatever is pretended) are not the sovereign lords of the souls and consciences of men, nor do any of them, that I know of, plead themselves so to be; who cannot interpose any thing by their absolute authority that should have a necessary respect unto men's eternal condition; who have no knowledge of, no acquaintance with, nor can judge of, the principal things whereon it doth depend; from whose temporal jurisdiction and punishment the things of the gospel and the worship of God, as purely such, are by the nature of them (being spiritual and not of this world, though exercised in it, having their respect only unto eternity), and by their being taken into the sole disposal of the sovereign Lord of consciences, who hath accompanied his commands concerning them with his own promises and threatenings, plainly exempted, — should have power over the consciences of men, so to lay their commands upon them in these spiritual things as to back them with temporal, corporeal restraints and punishments, is a way of arguing that will not be confined unto any of those rules of reasoning which hitherto we have been instructed in. When the magistrate hath "an arm like God," and can "thunder with a voice like him;" when he "judgeth not after the sight of his eyes, nor reproveth after the hearing of his ears;" when he can "smite the earth with the rod of his mouth," and "slay the wicked with the breath of his lips;" when he is constituted a judge of the faith, repentance, and obedience of men, and of their efficacy in their tendency unto the pleasing of God here and the enjoyment of him hereafter; when spiritual things, in order to their eternal issues and effects, are made subject unto him; — in brief, when he is Christ let him act as Christ, or rather most unlike him, and guide the consciences of men by rods, axes, and halters (whereunto alone his power can reach), who in the meantime have an express command from the Lord Christ himself not to have their consciences influenced in the least by the consideration of these things.

Of the like complexion is the ensuing discourse, wherein our author, p. 43, having spoken contemptuously of the spiritual institutions of the gospel, as altogether "insufficient for the accomplishment of the ends whereunto they are designed," — forgetting that they respect only the consciences of men, and are His institutions who is the Lord of their consciences, and who will give them power and efficacy to attain their ends, when administered in his name and according to his mind, and that because they are his, — would prove the necessity of temporal coercions and penalties in things spiritual, from the extraordinary effects of excommunication in the primitive times, in the "vexation and punishment of persons excommunicate, by the devil." This work the devil now ceasing to attend unto, he would have the magistrate to take upon him to supply his place and office, by punishments of his own appointment and infliction, and so at last, to be sure of giving him full measure, he hath ascribed two extremes unto him about religion, — namely, to act the part of God and the devil! But as this inference is built upon a very uncertain conjecture, — namely, that upon the giving up of persons to Satan in excommunication, there did any visible or corporeal vexation of them by his power ensue, or any other effects but what may yet be justly expected from an influence of his terror on the minds of men who are duly and regularly cast out of the visible kingdom of Christ by that censure, — and whereas, if there be any truth in it, it was confined unto the days of the apostles, and is to be reckoned amongst the miraculous operations granted to them for the first confirmation of the gospel, and the continuance of it all the time the church wanted the assistance of the civil magistrate is most unduly pretended, without any colour of proof or instance beyond such as may be evidenced to continue at this day; — supposing it to be true, the inference made from it, as to its consequence, on this concession, is exceeding weak and feeble; for the argument here amounteth to no more but this: God was pleased, in the days of the apostles, to confirm their spiritual censures against stubborn sinners, apostates, blasphemers, and such like heinous offenders, with extraordinary spiritual punishments (so in their own nature, or in the manner or way of their infliction); therefore, the civil magistrate hath power to appoint things to be observed in the worship of God, and forbid other things which the light and consciences of men, directed by the word of God, require the observation of, upon ordinary, standing, corporeal penalties, to be inflicted on the outward man, "quod erat demonstrandum."

To wind up this debate, I shall commit the umpirage of it to the church, of England, and receive her determination in the words of one who may be supposed to know her sense and judgment as well as any one who lived in his days or since; and this is Dr Bilson, bishop of Winchester, a learned man, skilled in the laws of the land, and a great adversary unto all that dissented from church constitutions. This man, therefore, treating by way of dialogue, in answer to the Jesuits' Apology and Defence, in the third part, p. 293, thus introduceth Theophilus, a protestant divine, arguing with Philander, a Jesuit, about these matters:—
"*Theoph.* As for the ' supreme head of the church,' it is certain that title was first transferred from the pope to King Henry the Eighth by the bishops of your side, not of ours. And though the pastors in King Edward's time might not well dislike, much less dissuade, the style of the crown, by reason the king was under years, and so remained until he died; yet as soon as it pleased God to place her majesty in her father's throne, the nobles and preachers, perceiving the words 'head of the church' (which is Christ's proper and peculiar honour) to be offensive unto many that had vehemently repelled the same in the pope, besought her highness the meaning of that word which her father had used might be expressed in some plainer, apter terms, and so was the prince called supreme governor of the realm, — that is, ruler and bearer of the sword, with lawful authority to command and punish, answerable to the word of God, in all spiritual or ecclesiastical things or causes, as well as in temporal, and no foreign prince or prelate to have any jurisdiction, superiority, pre-eminence, or authority to establish, prohibit, correct and chastise, with public laws or temporal pains, any crimes or causes ecclesiastical or spiritual within her realm. *Philand.* Calvin saith this is sacrilege and blasphemy. Look you, therefore, with what consciences you take that oath which your own master so mightily detesteth. *Theoph.* Nay, look you with what faces you allege Calvin, who maketh that style to be sacrilegious and blasphemous as well in the pope as in the prince; reason, therefore, you receive or refuse his judgment in both. If it derogate

from Christ in the prince, so it doth in the pope. Yet we grant the sense of the word 'supreme,' as Calvin perceived it by Stephen Gardiner's answer and behaviour, is very blasphemous and injurious to Christ and his word, whether it be prince or pope that so shall use it." What this sense is he declares in the words of Calvin, which are as followeth, in his translation of them: "That juggler, which after was chancellor, I mean the bishop of Winchester, when he was at Rentzburge, neither would stand to reason the matter nor greatly cared for any testimonies of the Scripture, but said it was at the king's discretion to abrogate that which was in use and appoint new. He said the king might forbid priests' marriage; the king might bar the people from the cup in the Lord's supper; the king might determine this or that in his kingdom: and why? forsooth, the king had *supreme* power. This sacrilege hath taken hold on us, whilst princes think they cannot reign except they abolish all the authority of the church, and be themselves supreme judges, as well in doctrine as in all spiritual regimen." To which he subjoins: "This was the sense which Calvin affirmed to be sacrilegious and blasphemous, for princes to profess themselves to be supreme judges of doctrine and discipline; and, indeed, it is the blasphemy which all godly hearts reject and abomine in the bishop of Rome. Neither did King Henry take any such thing on him, for aught that we can learn. But this was Gardiner's stratagem to convey the reproach and shame of the Six Articles[6] from himself and his fellows, that were the authors of them, and to cast it on the king's supreme power. Had Calvin been told that 'supreme' was first received to declare the prince to be superior to the prelates (which exempted themselves from the king's authority by their church liberties and immunities) as well as to the laymen of this realm, and not to be subject to the pope the word would never have offended him." Thus far he; and if these controversies be any farther disputed, it is probable the next defence of what is here pleaded will be in the express words of the principal prelates

---

6   These Articles are well known by the name of the "Bloody Statute," 31 Henry VIII., cap. 14, entitled, "An Act for the Abolishing Diversity of Opinions in certain Articles concerning Christian Religion." They affirmed transubstantiation, communion in one kind, clerical celibacy, vows of chastity, private masses, and auricular confession — ED.

of this realm since the Reformation, until their authority be peremptorily rejected.

Upon my first design to take a brief survey of this discourse, I had not the least intention to undertake the examination of any particular assertions or reasonings that might fall under controversy, but merely to examine the general principles whereon it doth proceed. But passing through these things "currente calamo," I find myself engaged beyond my thoughts and resolutions; I shall therefore here put an end to the consideration of this chapter, although I see sundry things as yet remaining in it that might immediately be discussed with ease and advantage, as shall be manifest if we are called again to a review of them. I have neither desire nor design "serram reciprocare," or to engage in any controversial discourses with this author; and I presume himself will not take it amiss that I do at present examine those principles whose novelty justifies a disquisition into them, and whose tendency, as applied by him, is pernicious and destructive to so many quiet and peaceable persons who dissent from him. And yet I will not deny but that I have that valuation and esteem for that sparkling of wit, eloquence, and sundry other abilities of mind which appear in his writing, that if he would lay aside the manner of his treating those from whom he dissents, with revilings, contemptuous reproaches, personal reflections, sarcasms, and satirical expressions, and would candidly and perspicuously state any matter in difference, I should think that what he hath to offer may deserve the consideration of them who have leisure for such a purpose. If he be otherwise minded, and resolved to proceed in the way and after the manner here engaged in, as I shall in the close of this discourse absolutely give him my "salve æternumque vale," so I hope he will never meet with any one who shall be willing to deal with him at his own weapons.

A SURVEY OF THE SECOND CHAPTER

Alleged power of the magistrate over the conscience in matters of morality refuted — Distinction between moral virtue and grace — Meaning of the terms — Four propositions of Parker on grace and virtue considered — Agreement between the views of Parker and those of the Socinian Seidelius — Exceptions taken to these views — Power of the magistrate in reference to moral duties — The true ground of obligation to these duties.

THE "summary" of this chapter must needs give the reader a great expectation, and the chapter itself no less of satisfaction, if what is in the one briefly proposed be in the other as firmly established: for, amongst other things, a scheme of religion is promised, reducing all its branches either to "moral virtues" or "instruments of morality;" — which being spoken of Christian religion, is, as far as I know, an undertaking new and peculiar unto this author, in whose management all that read him must needs weigh and consider how dexterously he hath acquitted himself; for as all men grant that morality hath a great place in religion, so, that all religion is nothing but morality many are now to learn. "The villany of those men's religion that are wont to distinguish between grace and virtue" (that is, moral virtue) is nextly traduced and inveighed against. I had rather, I confess, that he had affixed the term of "villany" to the men themselves whom he intended to reflect on than to their religion, because, as yet, it seems to me that it will fall on Christianity, and no other real or pretended religion that is or ever was in the world; for if the professors of it have, in all ages, according to its avowed principles, never before contradicted, made a distinction between *moral virtues* (since these terms were known in the church) and *evangelical graces*, if they do so at this day, what religion else can be here branded with this infamous and horrible reproach I know not. A farther inquiry into the chapter itself may possibly give us farther satisfaction; wherein, we shall deal as impartially as we are able, with a diligent watchfulness against all prejudicate affections, that we may discover what there is of sense and truth in the discourse, being ready to receive whatever shall be manifested to have an interest in them. The civil magistrate, we are also here informed, amongst many other things that he may do, "may command any thing in the worship of God that doth not tend to debauch men's practices or to disgrace the Deity;" and that "all subordinate duties, both of morality and religious worship" (such as elsewhere we are told the sacraments are), "are equally subject to the determination of human authority." These things, and sundry others represented in this summary, being new, yea some of them, as far as I know, unheard of amongst Christians until within a few years last past, any reader may justify himself in the expectation of full and demonstrative arguments to be produced in their proof and confirmation. What the issue will be, some discovery may be made by the ensuing inquiry, as was said, into the body of the chapter itself.

The design of this chapter, in general, is to confirm the power of the magistrate over religion and the consciences of men, ascribed unto him in the former, and to add unto it some enlargements not therein insisted on. The argument used to this purpose is taken from "the power of the magistrate over the consciences of men in matters of morality," or with respect unto moral virtue; whence it is supposed the conclusion is so evident unto his "power over their consciences in matters of religious worship," that it strikes our author with wonder and amazement that it should not be received and acknowledged. Wherefore, to further the conviction of all men in this matter, he proceeds to discourse of moral virtue, of grace, and of religious worship, with his wonted reflections upon and reproaches of the Nonconformists for their ignorance about and villanous misrepresentation of these things; which seem more to be aimed at than the argument itself.

I must here wish again that our author had more perspicuously stated the things which he proposeth to debate for the subject of his disputation; but I find an excess of art is as troublesome sometimes as the greatest defect therein. From thence I presume it is that things are so handled in this discourse that an ordinary man can seldom discern satisfactorily what it is that directly and determinately he doth intend beyond reviling of Nonconformists; for in this proposition, — which is the best and most intelligible that I can reduce the present discourse unto, — "The supreme civil magistrate hath power over the consciences of men in morality, or with respect unto moral virtue," excepting only the subject of it, there is not one term in it that may not have various significations, and those such as have countenance given unto them in the ensuing disputation itself. But "contenti sumus hoc Catone," and make the best we can of what lies before us.

I do suppose that in the *medium* made use of in this argument, there is, or I am sure there may be, a controversy of much more importance than that principally under consideration. It, therefore, shall be stated and cleared in the first place; and then the concernment of the argument itself, in what is discoursed thereupon, shall be manifested. It is about *moral virtue* and *grace*, their coincidence or distinction, that we are in the first place to inquire; for without a due stating of the conception of these things, nothing of this argument nor what belongs unto it can be rightly understood. We shall, therefore, be necessitated to premise a brief explanation of these terms themselves, to remove as far as may be all ambiguity from our discourse.

First, then, the very name of *virtue*, in the sense wherein it is commonly used and received, comes from the schools of philosophy, and not from the Scripture. In the Old Testament we have "uprightness, integrity, righteousness, doing good and eschewing evil, fearing, trusting, obeying, believing in God, holiness," and the like; but the name of "virtue" doth not occur therein. It is true, we have translated אֵשֶׁת חַיִל, "a virtuous woman," and once or twice the same word "virtuously," Ruth iii. 11, Prov. xii. 4, xxxi. 10, 29; but that word signifies, as so used, "strenuous, industrious, diligent," and hath no such signification as that we now express by "virtue." Nor is it anywhere rendered ἀρετή by the LXX., although it may have some respect unto it, as ἀρετή may be derived from ἄρης, and peculiarly denote the exercise of industrious strength, such as men use in battle; for חַיִל is "vis, robur, potentia," or "exercitus" also. But in the common acceptation of it, and as it is used by philosophers, there is no word in the Hebrew or Syriac properly to express it. The rabbins do it by מִדָּה, which signifies properly "a measure;" for, studying the philosophy of Aristotle, and translating his Ethics into Hebrew, which was done by Rabbi Meir, and finding his "virtue" placed in mediocrity, they applied מִדָּה to express it: so they call Aristotle's Ethics סֵפֶר הַמִּדּוֹת, "The Book of Measures," — that is, of virtues; and מִדּוֹת טוֹבוֹת are "boni mores." Such a stranger is this very word unto the Old Testament. In the New Testament ἀρετή occurs four times; but it should not seem anywhere to be taken in the sense now generally admitted. In some of the places it rather denotes the excellency and praises that do attend virtue, than virtue itself. So we render ἀρετάς "praises," 1 Pet. ii. 9, as the Syriac doth also תֶּשְׁבּוּחְתָּא, "praises;" and the same translation, Phil. iv. 8, renders εἴ τις ἀρετή, "if there be any virtue," by עֲבָדָא דְשׁוּבְחָא, "works glorious" or "praiseworthy," 1 Pet. ii. 19. It is a peculiar gracious disposition and operation of mind, distinguished from "faith, temperance, patience, brotherly-kindness, godliness, charity," etc., and so cannot have the common sense of the word there put upon it.

The word "moral" is yet far more exotic to the church and Scripture. We are beholden for it, if there be any advantage in its use, merely to the schools of the philosophers, especially of Aristotle. His doctrine περὶ ἠθῶν, commonly called his Ἠθικά or "Moralia," his Morals, hath begotten this name for our use. The whole is expressed, in Isocrates to Demonicus, by ἡ τῶν τρόπων ἀρετή, "the virtue of manners." If, then, the signification of the words be respected as usually taken, it is virtue in men's manners that is intended. The schoolmen brought this expression with all its concerns, as they did the rest of Aristotle's philosophy, into the church and divinity; and I cannot but think it had been well if they had never done it, as all will grant they might have omitted some other things without the least disadvantage to learning or religion. However, this expression of "moral virtue" having absolutely possessed itself of the fancies and discourses of all, and, it may be, of the understanding of some, though with very little satisfaction when all things are considered, I shall not endeavour to dispossess it or eliminate it from the confines of Christian theology. Only, I am sure had we been left unto the Scripture expressions of "repentance toward God, and faith toward our Lord Jesus Christ, of the fear of God, of holiness, righteousness, living unto God, walking with God, and before him," we might have been free from many vain, wordy perplexities, and the whole wrangle of this chapter in particular had been utterly prevented; for let but the Scripture express what it is to be religious, and there will be no contesting about the difference or no difference between grace and moral virtue. It is said that "some judge those who have moral virtue to want grace, not to be gracious;" but say that men are "born of God, and do not commit sin," that they "walk before God and are upright," that they " cleave unto God with full purpose of heart," that they are "sanctified in Christ Jesus," and the like, and no man will say that they have not grace, or are not gracious, if they receive your testimony. But having, as was said, made its entrance amongst us, we must deal with it as well as we can, and satisfy ourselves about its common acceptation and use.

Generally, moral virtues are esteemed to be the duties of the *second table*: for although those who handle these matters more accurately do not so straiten or confine them, yet it is certain that in vulgar and common acceptation (which strikes no small stroke in the regulating of the conceptions of the wisest men about the signification of words) nothing else is intended by "moral virtues," or "duties of morality," but the observation of the precepts of the second table; nor is any thing else designed by those divines who, in their writings, so frequently declare that it is not *morality alone* that will render men acceptable to God. Others do extend these things farther, and fix the denomination of moral firstly upon the law or rule of all those habits of the mind and its operations which afterward thence they call moral. Now, this moral law is nothing but the law of nature, or the law of our creation, which the apostle affirms to lie equally obligatory on all men, even all the Gentiles themselves, Rom. ii. 14, 15, and whereof the decalogue is summarily expressive. This moral law is, therefore, the law written in the hearts of all men by nature; which is resolved partly into the nature of God himself, which cannot but require most of the things of it from rational creatures, partly into that state and condition of the nature of thing and their mutual relations wherein God was pleased to create and set them. These things might be easily instanced and exemplified, but that we must not too much divert from our present occasion. And herein lies the largest sense and acceptation of the law moral, and consequently of moral virtues, which have their form and being from their relation and conformity thereunto. Let it be, then, that moral virtues consist in the universal observance of the requisites and precepts of the law of our creation, and dependence on God thereby. And this description, as we shall see, for the substance of it, is allowed by our author.

Now, these virtues, or this conformity of our minds and actions unto the law of our creation, may be, in the light and reason of Christian religion, considered two ways:— First, as with respect unto the substance or essence of the duties themselves, they may be performed by men in their own strength, under the conduct of their own reason, without any special assistance from the Spirit or sanctifying grace of Christ. In this sense they still bear the name of "virtues," and, for the substance of them, deserve so to do. Good they are in themselves, useful to mankind, and seldom, in the providence of God, go without their reward in this world. I grant, I say, that they may be obtained and acted without special assistance of grace evangelical, though the wiser heathens acknowledged something divine in the communication of them to men. Papinius speaks to that purpose:—

"Diva Jovis solio juxta comes; unde per orbem
Rara dari, terrisque solet contingere virtus.
Seu Pater Omnipotens tribuit, sive ipsa capaces
Elegit penetrare viros." —

But old Homer put it absolutely in the will of his god:—

Ζεὺς δ' ἀρετὴν ἄνδρεσσιν ὀφέλλει τε μινύθει τε
Ὅππως κεν ἐθέλῃσι —

[Il. Υ., 242.]

Thus we grant moral virtue to have been in the heathen of old, for this is that alone whereby they were distinguished amongst themselves: and he that would exclude them all from any interest in moral virtue takes away all difference between Cato and Nero, Aristides and Tiberius, Titus and Domitian, and overthrows all natural difference between good and evil; which, besides other abominations that it would plentifully spawn in the world, would inevitably destroy all human society. But now, these moral virtues, thus performed, whatever our author thinks, are distinct from grace, may be without it, and in their present description, which is not imaginary, but real, are supposed so to be; and, if he please, he may exercise himself in the longsome disputes of Bellarmine, Gregory de Valentia, and others to this purpose innumerable, — not to mention reformed divines, lest they should be scornfully rejected as systematical. And this is enough, I am sure, to free their religion from villany who make a distinction between moral virtue and grace; and if our author is otherwise minded, and doth believe that there is grace evangelical wherever there is moral virtue, or that moral virtues may be so obtained and exercised without the special assistance of grace as to become a part of our religion and accepted with God, and will maintain his opinion in writing, I will promise him, if I live, to return him an answer, on one only condition, which is, that he will first answer what Augustine hath written against the Pelagians on this subject.

Again; these moral virtues, this observance of the precepts of the law of our creation, in a consonancy whereunto originally the image of God in us did consist, may now under the gospel be considered, as men are principled, assisted, and enabled to and in their performance by the grace of God, and as they are directed unto the especial end of living unto him in and by Jesus Christ. What is particularly required hereunto shall be afterward declared. Now, in this sense no man living ever distinguished between grace and virtue any otherwise than the cause and the effect are to be, or may be, distinguished; much less was any person ever so brutish as to fancy an inconsistency between them: for, take grace in one sense, and it is the efficient cause of this virtue, or of these virtues, which are the effects of it; and in another, they are all graces themselves, for that which is wrought in us by grace is grace, as that which is born of the Spirit is spirit. To this purpose something may be spoken concerning *grace* also, the other term, whose ambiguity renders the discourse under consideration somewhat intricate and perplexed. Now, as the former term of "moral virtue" owes its original to the schools of philosophy, and its use was borrowed from them, so this of "grace" is purely scriptural and *evangelical*. The world knows nothing of it but what is declared in the word of God, especially in the gospel; for "the law was given by Moses, but grace and truth came by Jesus Christ." All the books of the ancient philosophers will not give us the least light into that notion of grace which the Scripture declares unto us. As, then, we allowed the sense of the former term, given unto it by its first coiners and users, so we cannot but think it equal that men be precisely tied up in their conceptions about grace unto what is delivered in the Scripture concerning it, as having no other rule either to frame them or judge of them; and this we shall attend unto. Not that I here design to treat of the nature of gospel grace in general; but whereas all the divines that ever I have read on these things, whether ancient or modern (and I have not troubled myself to consider whether they were systematical ones only, or otherwise qualified), allow some distinctions of this term to be necessary for the right understanding of those passages of Scripture wherein it is made use of, I shall mention that or those only which are so unto the right apprehension of what at present under debate.

First, therefore, Grace in the Scripture is taken for the *free grace or favour of God towards sinners by Jesus Christ*. By this he freely pardoneth them their sins, justifieth and accepteth them, or makes them "accepted in the Beloved." This, certainly, is distinct from moral virtue. Secondly, It is taken for *the effectual working of the Spirit of God* in and upon the minds and souls of believers, thereby quickening them when they were "dead in trespasses and sins," regenerating of them, creating a new heart in them, implanting his image upon them. Neither, I presume, will this be called moral virtue. Thirdly, For the *actual supplies of assistance and ability given to believers*, so to enable them unto every duty in particular which in the gospel is required of them; for he "worketh in them both to will and to do of his own good pleasure." As yet the former distinction will appear necessary. Fourthly, For *the effects wrought and produced by this operation of God* and his grace in the hearts and minds of them that believe; which are either habitual, in the spiritual disposition of their minds, or actual, in their operation: all which are called "grace." It may be our author will be apt to think that I "cant," "use phrases," or "fulsome metaphors." But besides that I can confirm these distinctions, and the necessity of them, and the words wherein they are expressed, from the Scriptures and ancient fathers, I can give them him, for the substance of them, out of very learned divines, — whether systematical or no I know not; but this I know, they were not long since *bishops of the church of England*.

We are now, in the next place, to inquire into the mind of our author in these things; for, from his apprehensions about them, he frames a mighty difference between himself, and those whom he opposeth, and from thence takes occasion and advantage afresh to revile and reproach them.

First, therefore, He declares his judgment, that the moral virtues which he treats of do "consist of men's observance of the law of nature, of the dictates of reason, and precepts thereof." Secondly, That "the substance, yea, the whole of religion, consists in these virtues or duties, so that by the observation of them men may attain everlasting happiness" Thirdly, That "there is no actual concurrence of present grace enabling men to perform these duties, or to exercise these virtues, but they are called grace on another account." Fourthly, That "his adversaries are so far from making virtue and grace to be the same, that they make them inconsistent."

And these things shall we take into a brief examination, according as indeed they do deserve.

The first of them he plainly and more than once affirms, nor shall I contend with him about it. So he speaks, p. 68: "The practice of virtue consists in living suitably to the dictates of reason and nature; and this is the substance and main design of all the laws of religion, to oblige mankind to behave themselves in all their actions as becomes creatures endowed with reason and understanding, and, in ways suitable to rational beings, to prepare and qualify themselves for the state of glory and immortality." This is a plain description both of the rule of moral virtues and of the nature of them. The law of reason and nature is the rule; and their own nature, as acting or acted, consists in a suitableness unto rational beings acting to prepare themselves for the state of immortality and glory, — the first end of all virtue, no doubt. We need not, therefore, make any farther inquiry into this matter, wherein we are agreed.

Secondly, That the *substance,* yea, the *whole* of religion, consists in these moral virtues he fully also declares, p. 69: "Moral virtue having the strongest and most necessary influence upon the end of all religion, namely, man's happiness, it is not only its most material and useful part, but the ultimate end of all its other duties" (though I know not how the practice of virtue in this life can be the ultimate end of other duties); "and all true religion can consist in nothing else but either the practice of virtue itself or the use of those means and instruments that contribute unto it." So also, p. 70: "All duties of devotion, excepting only our returns of gratitude, are not essential parts of religion, but are only in order to it, as they tend to the practice of virtue and moral goodness, and their goodness is derived upon them from the moral virtues to which they contribute; and in the same proportion they are conducive to the ends of virtue, they are to be valued among the ministers of religion." So, then, the whole duty of man consists in being virtuous, and all that is enjoined beside is in order thereunto. Hence we are told elsewhere that "outward worship is no part of religion." Again, p. 76: "All religion must of necessity be resolved into enthusiasm or morality; the former is mere imposture, and therefore all that is true must be reduced to the latter." But we need not insist on particulars, seeing he promoteth this to confirmation by the best of demonstrations, — that is, an induction of all particulars, which he calls "a scheme of religion;" wherein, yet, if any thing necessary be left out or omitted, this best of demonstrations is quickly turned into one of the worst of sophisms. Therefore we have here, no doubt, a just and full representation of all that belongs to Christian religion; and it is as follows, p. 69: "The whole duty of man refers either to his Creator, or his neighbour, or himself. All that concerns the two last is confessedly of a moral nature, and all that concerns the first consists either in praising of God or praying to him. The former is a branch of the virtue of gratitude, and is nothing but a thankful and humble temper of mind, arising from a sense of God's greatness in himself and his goodness to us: so that this part of devotion issues from the same virtuous quality, — that is, the principle of all other resentments and expressions of gratitude; only, those acts of it that are terminated on God as their object are styled "religious;" — and therefore gratitude and devotion are not diverse things, but only differing names of the same thing, devotion being nothing else but the virtue of gratitude towards God. The latter, namely, prayer, is either put up in our own or other men's behalf. If for others, it is an act of that virtue we call kindness or charity; if for ourselves, the things we pray for, unless they be the comforts and enjoyments of this life, are some or other virtuous qualities; — and therefore the proper and direct use of prayer is, to be instrumental to the virtues of morality." It is of Christian religion that this author treats, as is manifest from his ensuing discourse, and the reason he gives why moral virtues are styled "graces." Now, I must needs say, that I look on this of our author as the rudest, most imperfect, and weakest scheme of Christian religion that ever yet I saw; so far from comprising an induction of all particulars belonging to it, that there is nothing in it that is constitutive of Christian religion, as such, at all. I wish he had given us a summary of the "credenda" of it, as he hath done of its "agenda," that we might have had a prospect of the body of his divinity. The ten commandments would, in my mind, have done twice as well on this present occasion, with the addition of the explication of them given us in the church catechism; but I am afraid that very catechism may, ere long, be esteemed fanatical also. One, I confess, I have read of before who was of this opinion, that all religion consisted in morality alone; but withal he was so ingenuous as to follow the conduct of his judgment in this matter unto a full renunciation of the gospel, which is certainly inconsistent with it. This was one Martin Seidelius, a Silesian, who gave the ensuing account of his faith unto Faustus Socinus and his society at Cracovia:—

"Cæterum ut sciatis cujus sim religionis, quamvis id scripto meo quod habetis, ostenderim, tamen hic breviter repetam. Et primum quidem doctrina de Messia, seu Rege illo promisso, ad meam religionem nihil pertinet; nam Rex ille tantum Judæis promissus erat, sicut et bona illa Canaan. Sic etiam circumcisio, sacrificia, et reliquæ ceremoniæ Mosis ad me non pertinent, sed tantum populo Judaico promissa, data, et mandata sunt. Neque ista fuerunt cultus Dei apud Judæos, sed inserviebant cultui divino, et ad cultum deducebant Judæos. Verus autem cultus Dei quem meam religionem appello est decalogus, qui est æterna Dei voluntas; qui decalogus ideo ad me pertinet, quia etiam mihi a Deo datus est, non quidem per vocem sonantem de cœlo sicut populo Judaico, at per creationem insita est menti meæ. Quia autem insitus decalogus, per corruptionem naturæ humanæ et pravis consuetudinibus, aliquâ ex parte obscuratus est, ideo ad illustrandum eum adhibeo vocalem decalogum, qui vocalis decalogus ideo etiam ad me, ad omnes populos pertinet, quia cum insito nobis decalogo consentit, imo idem ille decalogus est. Hæc est mea sententia de Messiâ seu Rege illo promisso, et hæc est mea religio, quam coram vobis ingenuè profiteor. Martin Seidelius Olavensis Silesius."

That is, "But that you may know of what religion I am, although it is expressed in that writing which you have already, yet I will here briefly repeat it. And, first of all, the doctrine of the Messiah or King that was promised doth not belong to my religion; for that King was promised to the Jews only, as was the good land of Canaan. So in like manner circumcision, sacrifices, and the rest of the ceremonies of Moses, belong not to me, but were promised, given, and granted unto the people of the Jews alone. Neither were they the worship of God among the Jews, but were only subservient unto divine worship, and led the Jews unto it" (the same opinion is maintained by our author concerning all exterior worship). "But the true worship, which I call my religion, is the decalogue; which is the eternal and immutable will of God" (and here also he hath the consent and concurrence of our author): "which decalogue doth therefore belong unto me, because it is given by God to me also; not, indeed, by a voice sounding from heaven, as he gave it to the people of the Jews, but it is implanted in my mind by nature. But because this implanted decalogue, by reason of the corruption of human nature and through depraved customs, is in some measure obscured, for the illustration of it I make use of the vocal decalogue; which therefore also belongs unto me and all people, because it consenteth with the decalogue written in our hearts, yea, is the same law with it. This is my opinion concerning the Messiah or the promised King, and this is my religion, which I freely acknowledge before you." So he. This is plain dealing. He saw clearly that if all religion and the worship of God consisted in *morality only*, there was neither need nor use of Christ nor the gospel; and accordingly, having no outward advantage by them, he discarded them. But setting aside his bold renunciation of Christ as promised, I see not any material difference between the religion of this man and that now contended for. The poor deluded souls among ourselves, who, leaving the Scripture, pretend that they are guided by the light within them, are, upon the matter, of the same religion: for that light being nothing but the dictates of reason and a natural conscience, it extends not itself beyond morality; which some of them understanding, we know what thoughts and apprehensions they have had of Christ and his gospel, and the worship of God instituted therein; for hence it is (and not as our author pretends, with a strange incogitancy concerning them and the Gnostics, that they assert the Scripture to be the only rule of religious worship) that they are fallen into these fond imaginations. And these are the effects which this principle doth naturally lead unto. I confess, then, that I do not agree with our author in and about this scheme of Christian religion; which I shall, therefore, first briefly put in my exceptions unto, and then offer him another in lieu of it.

First, then, This scheme seems to represent religion unto us as suited to the state of innocency, and that very imperfectly also; for it is composed to answer the former assertion of confining religion to moral virtues, which are granted to consist in our conformity unto and expression of the dictates of reason and the law of nature. Again, the "whole duty of man" is said to refer "either to his Creator, or his neighbour, or himself." Had it been said to God absolutely, another interpretation might have been put upon the words; but being restrained unto him as our Creator, all duties referring to our Redeemer are excluded, or not included, which certainly have some place in Christian religion. Our obedience therein is the "obedience of faith," and must answer the special objects of it, And we are taught in the church catechism to believe in God the Father, who made us and all the world; and in God the Son, who redeemed us and all mankind; and in God the Holy Ghost, who sanctifies us and all the elect people of God. Now, these distinct acts of faith have distinct acts of obedience attending them; whereas none here are admitted, or at least required, but those which fall under the first head. It is also very imperfect as a description of natural religion, or the duties of the law of nature: for the principal duties of it, such as fear, love, trust, affiance of and in God, are wholly omitted, nor will they be reduced unto either of the heads which all religion is here distributed into; for gratitude unto God hath respect formally and directly to the benefits we ourselves are made partakers of; but these duties are eternally necessary on the consideration of the nature of God himself, antecedent unto the consideration, of his communicating of himself unto us by his benefits. Prayer proceeds from them, and it is an odd method, to reduce the cause under the head of its effect; and prayer itself is made at length not to be so much a moral virtue as somewhat instrumental to the virtues of morality.

Secondly, I cannot think we have here a complete representation of Christian religion, nor an induction of all its particulars, because we have neither supposition nor assertion of sin, or a Redeemer, or any duty with respect unto them. Gratitude and prayer, I confess, are two heads whereunto sundry duties of natural religion, without respect unto these things, may be reduced; but since the fall of Adam, there was never any religion in the world accepted with God that was not built and founded on the supposition of them, and whose principal duties towards God did not respect them. To prescribe now unto us a religion, as it respects God, without those duties which arise from the consideration of sin and a Redeemer, is to persuade us to throw away our Bibles. Sin, and the condition of all men on the account thereof; what God requires of them with reference thereunto; the way that God hath found out, proposed, and requires of us to make use of, that we may be delivered from that condition; with the duties necessary to that end, — do even constitute and make up that religion which the Scripture teacheth us, and which, as it summarily expresseth itself, consists in "repentance toward God and faith toward our Lord Jesus Christ, neither of which, nor scarce any thing that belongs unto them, appears in this scheme: so that, —

Thirdly, The most important duties of Christian religion are here not only omitted but excluded. Where shall we find any place here to introduce repentance, and, as belonging thereunto, conviction of sin, humiliation, godly sorrow, conversion itself to God? For my part, I will never be of that religion where these duties towards God have no place. Faith in our Lord Jesus Christ, with all that is necessary to it, preparatory for it, included in it, and consequential on it, are in like manner cast out of the verge of religious duties here schematized. An endeavour to flee from the wrath to come, to receive Jesus Christ, to accept of the atonement, to seek after the forgiveness of sins by him (that we may cant a little), and to give up our souls in universal obedience to all his commands, belong also to the duties of that religion towards God which the Scripture prescribeth unto us; but here they appear not in the least intimation of them. No more do the duties which, though generally included in the law of loving God above all, yet are prescribed and determined in the gospel alone; such are self- denial, readiness to take up the cross, and the like. Besides, all the duties wherein our Christian conflict against our spiritual adversaries doth consist, and, in especial, the whole of our duty towards God in the mortification of sin, can be of no consideration, there where no supposition of sin is made or allowed.

But there would be no end, if all exceptions of this nature, that readily offer themselves, might here have admittance. If this be the religion of our adversaries in these things, if this be a perfect scheme of its duties towards God and induction of all its particulars, let our author insult over and reproach them whilst he pleaseth who blame it as insufficient without grace and godliness, I would not be in the condition of them who trust their eternal concernment to mere observance of it, as knowing that there is no name under heaven given unto men whereby they may be saved, but only the name of Jesus Christ. It will be in vain pretended that it is not a description of Christian religion, but of religion as religion in general, that is here attempted; for besides that it is Christian religion, and that as used and practised by Christians, which is alone under consideration, and an introduction of religion here under any other notion would be grievously inconsistent and incoherent with the whole discourse, it is acknowledged by our author in the progress of his disputation, as was before observed, when he gives a reason why moral virtue is styled "grace," which is peculiar and appropriate to Christian religion alone. Besides, to talk now of a religion in the world, which either hath been or may be since the fall of Adam, without respect unto sin, is to build castles in the air. All the religion that God now requires, prescribes, accepts, that is or can be, is the religion of sinners, or of those who are such, and of them as such, though also under other qualifications. On many accounts, therefore, this scheme of religion, or religious duties towards God, is exceedingly insufficient and imperfect. To lay it, therefore, as a foundation whereon to stand and revile them who plead for a super-addition unto it of grace and godliness, is an undertaking from whence no great success is to be expected.

I can easily supply another *scheme of religion* in the room of this, which though it have not any such contexture of method, nor is set out with such gaudy words as those which our author hath at his disposal, yet I am confident, in the confession of all Christians, shall give a better account than what is here offered unto us both of the religion we profess and of the duties that God requires therein, — and this taken out of one epistle of St Paul, namely, that to the Romans; and I shall do it as things come to mind in the haste wherein I am writing. He, then, gives us his scheme to this purpose: as, first, That all men sinned in Adam, came short of the glory of God, and rendered themselves liable to death and the whole curse of the law; then, that they do all, as left to themselves, accumulate their original sin and transgression with a world of actual sins and provocations of God; that against men in this condition God testifies his wrath and displeasure, both in his works and by his word. Hence it necessarily follows that the first duty of man towards God is to be sensible of this condition, of the guilt of sin, with a fear of the wrath and judgment due to them. Then he informs us that neither the Jews by the law, nor the Gentiles by the light of nature, could disentangle themselves from this state, or do that which is pleasing unto God, so as they might obtain forgiveness of sin and acceptance with him. This bespeaks unto all the great duty towards God of their acknowledgment unto him of their miserable and helpless condition, with all those affections and subordinate duties wherewith it is attended. In this state he declares that God himself, in his infinite wisdom, goodness, and grace, provided a remedy, a way of relief, on which he hath put such an impression of his glorious excellencies as may stir up the hearts of his creatures to endeavour a return unto him from their apostasy; and that this remedy consists in his setting forth Jesus Christ to be a propitiation through faith in his blood, to declare his righteousness for the forgiveness of sin; which he proposeth unto men for their receiving and acceptance. This renders it the greatest duty of mankind towards God to believe in the Son of God so set forth, to seek after an interest in him, or being made partakers of him; for this is the great work that God requires, namely, that we believe on him whom he hath sent. Again; he declares that God justifieth them who so believe, pardoning their sins, and imputing righteousness unto them; whereon innumerable duties do depend, even all the obedience that Christ requires of us, seeing in our believing in him we accept him to be our king, to rule, govern, and conduct our souls to God. And all these are religious duties towards God. He declares, moreover, that whereas men are by nature dead in trespasses and sins, and stand in need of a new spiritual life, to be born again, that they may live unto God, that God in Jesus Christ doth, by his Spirit, quicken them and regenerate them, and work in them a new principle of spiritual life; whence it is their great duty towards God (in this religion of St Paul) to comply with, and to yield obedience unto, all the ways and methods that God is pleased to use in the accomplishment of this, work upon them, the especial duties whereof are too many to be instanced in. But he farther manifests, that notwithstanding the regeneration of men by the Spirit and their conversion to God, there yet continues in them a remainder of the principle of corrupted nature, which he calls "the flesh," and "indwelling sin," that is of itself wholly "enmity against God," and, as far [as] it abides in any, inclines the heart and mind unto sin; which is to be watched against and opposed. And on this head he introduceth the great religious duty towards God of our spiritual conflict against sin, and of the mortification of it; wherein those that believe are to be exercised all the days of their lives, and wherein their principal duty towards God doth consist, and without which they can perform no other in a due manner. Moreover, he farther adds the great gospel privilege of the communication of the Spirit of Christ unto believers, for their sanctification, consolation, and edification, with the duties of thankfulness towards God, joy and rejoicing in him, cheerfulness under trials, afflictions, and persecutions, and sundry others that on that account are required of us; — all religious duties towards God, in the religion by him proposed unto us. Having laid these foundations, and manifested how they all proceed from the eternal counsel and free grace of God, in which it is our duty to admire, adore, and praise him, he declareth how hereby, and on the account of these things, we are bound unto all holiness, righteousness, godliness, honesty, and usefulness in this world, in all relations and conditions whatsoever; — declaring our duties in churches, according to our especial interest in them, towards believers, and towards all men in the world in our several relations; in obedience to magistrates and all superiors; in a word, in universal observance of the whole will and all the commands of God. Now, whether any one will call this a "scheme" or no, or allow it to have any thing of method in it or no, I neither know nor care, but am persuaded that it makes a better, more plain and intelligible, representation of the religious duties towards God which Christian religion requires of us, unto all that suppose this whole religion to depend on divine revelation, than that of our author. But I find myself in a digression. The end of this discourse was only to manifest the sentiments of our author on the second head before laid down; which, I think, are sufficiently evinced.

The third is, That there is no actual work of present grace, either to fit the persons of whom these duties of moral virtues are required unto the performance of them or to work and effect them in them; for although they are called "graces," and the "graces of the Spirit," in the Scripture, yet that is upon another account, as he declares himself, p. 72: "All that the Scripture intends by the 'graces of the Spirit' are only virtuous qualities of the soul; that are therefore styled 'graces,' because they are derived purely from God's free grace and goodness, in that, in the first ages of Christianity, he was pleased, out of his infinite concern for its propagation, in a miraculous manner to inspire its converts with all sorts of virtue."

"Virtuous qualities of the soul" is a very ambiguous expression. Take these virtuous qualities for a new principle of spiritual life, consisting in the habitual disposition, inclination, and ability of mind unto the things required of us in the will of God, or unto the acts of religious obedience, and it may express the graces of the Spirit; which are yet far enough from being so called upon the account here mentioned. But these virtuous qualities are to be interpreted according to the tenor of the preceding discourses that have already passed under examination. Let now our author produce any one writer of the church of God, from first to last, of any repute or acceptation, from the day that the name of Christian was known in the world unto this wherein we live, giving us this account why the fruits of the Spirit, the virtuous or gracious qualities of the minds of believers, are called "graces" that here he gives, and I will give him my thanks publicly for his discovery; for if this be the only reason why any thing in believers is called "grace," why virtues are graces, — namely, because God was pleased in the first ages of Christianity miraculously to inspire its converts with all sorts of virtue, — then there is no communication of grace unto any, no work of grace in and upon any, in an ordinary way, through the ministry of the gospel in these latter ages! The whole being and efficacy of grace, according to this notion, is to be confined unto the miraculous operations of God in gospel concernments in the first ages, whence a denomination in the Scripture is cast upon our virtues, when obtained and exercised by and in our own strength! Now, this plainly overthrows the whole gospel, and contains a Pelagianism that Pelagius himself never did nor durst avow.

Are these things, then, so indeed, that God did, from his free grace and goodness, miraculously inspire the first converts of Christianity with all sorts of virtues, but that he doth not still continue to put forth in any actually the efficacy of his grace, or make them gracious, holy, believing, obedient to himself, and to work in them all suitable actings towards himself and others? Then farewell Scripture, the covenant of grace, the intercession of Christ, yea, all the ancient fathers, councils, schoolmen, and most of the Jesuits themselves! Many have been the disputes amongst Christians about the nature of grace, the rule of its dispensation, the manner and way of its operation, its efficacy, concurrence, and cooperation in the wills of men; but that there is no dispensation of it, no operation but what was miraculous in the first converts of the gospel, was, I think, until now undiscovered. Nor can it be here pretended that the virtuous qualities of our minds and their exercise, — by which is intended all the obedience that God requireth of us, in principle and practice, that we may please him and come to the enjoyment of him, — are not said to be called graces only on the account mentioned; for as in respect of us they are not so termed at all, so if the term "only" be not understood, the whole discourse is impertinent and ridiculous: for those other reasons and accounts that may be taken in will render that given utterly useless unto our author's intention, and, indeed, are altogether inconsistent with it, and he hath given us no reason to suppose that he talks after such a weak and preposterous rate. This, then, is that which is here asserted: The qualities of our minds and their exercise, wherein the virtues pleaded about and affirmed to contain the whole substance of religion do consist, are not wrought in us by the grace or Spirit of God through the preaching of the gospel, but are only called "graces,"as before. Now, though here be a plain contradiction to what is delivered but two pages before, namely, "that we pray for some or other virtuous qualities," — that is, doubtless, to be wrought in us by the grace of God, — yet this present discourse is capable of no other interpretation but that given unto it. And, indeed, it seems to be the design of some men to confine all real gifts and graces of the Spirit of God to the first ages of the gospel, and the miraculous operations in it; which is to overthrow the whole gospel, the church, and the ministry of it, as to their use and efficacy, leaving men only the book of the Bible to philosophize upon, as shall be elsewhere demonstrated. Our author, indeed, tells us, that on the occasion of some men's writings in theology, "there hath been a buzz and a noise of the Spirit of God in the world." His expressions are exceedingly suited to pour contempt on what he doth not approve, not so to express what he doth himself intend. But I desire that he and others would speak plain and openly in this matter, that neither others may be deceived nor themselves have occasion to complain that they are misrepresented; a pretence whereof would probably give them a dispensation to deal very roughly, if not despitefully, with them with whom they shall have to do. Doth he, therefore, think or believe that there are not now any real gracious operations of the Spirit of God upon the hearts and minds of men in the world? that the dispensation of the Spirit is ceased, as well unto ordinary ministerial gifts, with its sanctifying, renewing, assisting grace, as unto gifts miraculous and extraordinary? that there is no work at all of God upon the hearts of sinners but that which is purely moral and persuasive by the word? that what is asserted by some concerning the efficacy of the grace of the Spirit, and concerning his gifts, is no more but "a buzz and a noise?" I wish he would explain himself directly and positively in these things, for they are of great importance; and the loose expressions which we meet with do give great offence unto some, who are apt to think that as pernicious a heresy as ever infested the church of God may be covered and cloaked by them.

But to return: in the sense that mortal virtue is here taken, I dare boldly pronounce that there is *no villany in the religion of those men who distinguish between virtue and grace*, — that is, there is not in their so doing, — this being the known and avowed religion of Christianity. It is granted that wherever grace is, there is virtue; for grace will produce and effect all virtues in the soul whatever. But virtue, on the other side, may be where there is no grace; which is sufficient to confirm a distinction between them. It was so in sundry of the heathen of old; though now it be pretended that grace is nothing but an occasional denomination of virtue, not that it is the cause or principle of it. But the proofs produced by our author are exceedingly incompetent unto the end whereunto they are applied. For that place of the apostle, Gal. v. 22, 23, "The fruit of the Spirit is love, joy, peace, long-suffering, gentleness, goodness, faith, meekness, temperance," though our author should be allowed to turn "joy" into "cheerfulness," "peace" into "peaceableness," "faith" into "faithfulness," as he hath done, corruptly enough, to accommodate it to his purpose, yet it will no way reach his end, nor satisfy his intention; for doth it follow, that because the Spirit effects all these moral virtues in a new and gracious manner, and with a direction to a new and special end in believers, either that these things are nothing but mere moral, virtues, not wrought in us by the grace of God (the contrary whereof is plainly asserted in calling them "fruits of the Spirit"), or that wherever there is moral virtue, though not so wrought by the Spirit, that there is grace also, because virtue and grace are the same? If these are the expositions of Scripture which we may expect from them who make such outcries against other men's perverting and corrupting of it, the matter is not like to be much mended with us, for aught I can see, upon their taking of that work into their own hands.

And indeed his quotation of this place is pretty odd. He doth not in the print express the words as he useth, and as he doth those of another scripture immediately, in a different character, as the direct words of the apostle, that no man may charge him with a false allegation of the text; yet he repeats all the words of it which he intends to use to his purpose, somewhat altering the expressions. But he hath had, I fear, some unhappiness in his explanations. By "joy" he would have "cheerfulness" intended; but what is meant by cheerfulness is much more uncertain than what is intended by joy. Mirth, it may be, in conversation is aimed at, or somewhat of that nature; but how remote this is from that spiritual joy which is recommended unto us in the Scripture, and is affirmed to be "unspeakable and full of glory," he that knows not is scarce meet to paraphrase upon St Paul's epistles. Neither is that "peace with God through our Lord Jesus Christ," which is wrought in the hearts of believers by the Holy Ghost, who "creates the fruit of the lips, peace, peace, unto them," a matter of any more affinity with a moral peaceableness of mind and affections. Our faith also in God, and our faithfulness in our duties, trusts, offices, and employments, are sufficiently distinct. So palpably must the Scripture be corrupted and wrested to be made serviceable to this presumption! He yet adds another proof to the same purpose, — if any man know distinctly what that purpose is, — namely, Tit. ii. 11; where he tells us that the same apostle makes the "grace of God" to consist in gratitude towards God, temperance towards ourselves, and justice towards our neighbours. But these things are not so; for the apostle doth not say that the grace of God doth consist in these things, but that the "grace of God teacheth" us these things. Neither is the grace here intended any subjective or inherent grace, nor, to speak with our author, any "virtuous quality, or virtue;" but the love and grace of God himself in sending Jesus Christ, as declared in the gospel, as is manifest in the words and context beyond contradiction. And I cannot but wonder how our author, desirous to prove that the whole of our religion consists in moral virtues, and these only called "graces" because of the miraculous operations of God from his own grace in the first, gospel converts, should endeavour to do it by these two testimonies; the first whereof expressly assigns the duties of morality, as in believers, to the operations of the Spirit; and the latter, in his judgment, makes them to proceed from grace.

Our last inquiry is into what he ascribes unto his adversaries in this matter, and how he deals with them thereupon. This, therefore, he informs us, p. 71: "'It is not enough,' say they, 'to be completely virtuous, unless ye have grace too.'" I can scarce believe that ever he heard any one of them say so, or ever read it in any of their writings: for there is nothing that they are more positive in than that men cannot, in any sense, be *completely* virtuous unless they have grace; and so they cannot suppose them to be so who have it not. They say, indeed, that moral virtues, as before described, so far as they are attainable by, or may be exercised in the strength of, men's own wills and natural faculties, are not enough to please God and to make men accepted with him; so that virtue as it may be without grace, and some virtues may be so for the substance of them, is not available unto salvation. And I had almost said, that he is no Christian that is of another mind. In a word, virtue is or may be without grace, in all or any of the acceptations of it before laid down. Where it is without the favour of God and the pardon of sin, where it is without the renewing of our natures and the endowment of our persons with a principle of spiritual life, where it is not wrought in us by present efficacious grace, it is not enough, nor will serve any man's turn with respect unto the everlasting concernments of his soul.

But he gives in his exceptions, p. 71: "But when," saith he, "we have set aside all manner of virtue, let them tell me what remains to be called grace, and give me any notion of it distinct from all morality, that consists in the right order and government of our actions in all our relations, and so comprehends all our duty; and therefore if grace be not included in it, it is but a phantasm and an imaginary thing." I say, first, Where grace is, we cannot set aside virtue, because it will and doth produce and effect it in the minds of men; but virtue may be where grace is not, in the sense so often declared. Secondly, Take moral virtue in the notion of it here received and explained by our author, and I have given sundry instances before of gracious duties that come not within the verge or compass of the scheme given us of it. Thirdly, The whole aimed at lies in this: That virtue that governs our actions in all our duties may be considered either as the duty we owe to the law of nature for the ends of it, to be performed in the strength of nature, and by the direction of it; or it may be considered as it is an especial effect of the grace of God in us, which gives it a new principle and a new end, and a new respect unto the covenant of grace wherein we walk with God; — the consideration whereof frustrates the intention of our author in this discourse.

But he renews his charge, p. 73: "So destructive of all true and real goodness is the very religion of those men that are wont to set grace at odds with virtue, and are so far from making them the same that they make them inconsistent; and though a man be exact in all the duties of moral goodness, yet if he be a graceless person (that is, void of I know not what imaginary godliness) he is but in a cleaner way to hell, and his conversion is more hopeless than the vilest and most notorious sinner's; and the morally righteous man is at a greater distance from grace than the profane; and better be lewd and debauched than live an honest and virtuous life, if you are not of the godly party," — with much more to this purpose. For the "men that are wont to set grace at odds with virtue, and are so far from making them the same that they make them inconsistent," I wish our author would discover them, that he might take us along with him in his detestation of them. It is not unlikely, if all be true that is told of them, but that the Gnostics might have some principles not unlike this; but beside them, I never heard of any that were of this mind in the world. And, in truth, the liberty that is taken in these discourses is a great instance of the morality under consideration. But the following words will direct us where these things are charged; for some say that if "a man be exact in all the duties of moral goodness, yet if he be a graceless person, void of I know not what imaginary godliness, he is but in a cleaner way to hell." I think I know both what and who are intended, and that both are dealt withal with that candour we have been now accustomed unto. But, first, you will scarce find those you intend over-forward in granting that men may be "exact in all the duties of moral goodness," and yet be "graceless persons:" for taking moral virtues to comprehend, as you do, their duties towards God, they will tell you such persons cannot perform one of them aright, much less all of them exactly; for they can neither believe in God, nor trust him, nor fear him, nor glorify him, in a due manner. [Secondly,] Take the duties of moral goodness for the duties of the law between man and man, and the observation of the outward duties of God's worship, and they say, indeed, that they may be so performed as that in respect of them men may be blameless, and yet be graceless; for that account, if they mistake not, the apostle Paul gives of himself, Phil. iii. 6–9. They do say, therefore, that many of these duties, so as to be useful in the world and blameless before men, they may perform who are yet graceless. Thirdly, This gracelessness is said to consist in being "void of I know not what imaginary godliness." No, no; — it is to be void of the Spirit of God, of the grace of Christ; not to be born again, not to have a new spiritual life in Christ; not to be united to him or ingrafted in him; not to be accepted and made an heir of God, and enabled to a due, spiritual, evangelical performance of all duties of obedience, according to the tenor of the covenant. These are the things intended. And as many with their "moral duties" may come short of them and be "graceless," so those to whom they are "imaginary" must reject the whole gospel of Christ as an imagination. And I must say (to give matter of a new charge), that, to the best observation that I have been able to make in the world, none have been, nor are, more negligent in the principal duties of morality than those who are aptest to exalt them above the gospel and the whole mystery of it; unless morality do consist in such a course of life and conversation as I will not at present characterize.

It is farther added, that the "conversion of such a one is more hopeless than the vilest and most notorious sinner's; and the morally righteous man," etc. Setting aside the invidious expression of what is here reflected upon, there is nothing more openly taught in the gospel. The Pharisees were a people *morally righteous*, whereon they "trusted in themselves that they were righteous;" and, yet our Lord Jesus Christ told them that "publicans and harlots," the vilest and most notorious of sinners, entered before them into the kingdom of God. And where men trust to their own righteousness, their own duties, be they moral or what they will, there are no men farther from the way of the gospel than they; nay, our Saviour lets us know that, as such, the gospel is not concerned in them, nor they in it. "I came not," he says, "to call the righteous, but sinners to repentance," — not men justifying or lifting up themselves in a conceit of their moral duties, but those who are burdened and laden with a sense of their sins; and so, in like manner, that "the whole have no need of a physician, but the sick." And St Paul declares what enemies they were to the righteousness of God who went about to set up their own righteousness, Rom. x. 3. Now, because moral duties are incumbent on all persons at all times, they are continually pressed upon all, from a sense of the authority and command of God, indispensably requiting all men's attendance unto them. Yet such is the deceitfulness of the heart of man and the power of unbelief, that oftentimes persons who, through their education or following convictions, have been brought to some observance of them, being not enlightened in their minds to discern their insufficiency unto the great end of salvation in and of themselves, are apt to take up with them and to rest in them, without ever coming to sincere repentance towards God, or faith in our Lord Jesus Christ; whereas others, the guilt of whose sins doth unavoidably press upon them, as it did on the publicans and sinners of old, are ofttimes more ready to look out after relief. And those who question these things do nothing but manifest their ignorance in the Scripture, and want of experience in the work of the ministry. But yet, upon the account of the charge mentioned, so unduly framed and impotently managed, our author makes an excursion into such an extravagancy of reproaches as is scarce exceeded in his whole book; part of it I have considered before in our view of his preface, and I am now so used to the noise and bluster wherewith he pours out the storm of his indignation, that I am altogether unconcerned in it, and cannot prevail with myself to give it any farther consideration.

These things, though not direct to the argument in hand, and which on that account might have been neglected, yet supposing that the author placed as much of his design in them as in any part of his discourse, I could not wholly omit the consideration of; not so much out of a desire for their vindication who are unduly traduced in them, as to plead for the gospel itself, and to lay a foundation of a farther defence of the truths of it, if occasion shall so require. And we have also here an insight into the judgment of our author, or his mistake in this matter. He tells us that it is better to tolerate debaucheries and immoralities than liberty of conscience for men to worship God according to their light and persuasion! Now, all religion, according to him, consisting in morality, to tolerate immoralities and debaucheries in conversation is plainly to tolerate atheism; which, it seems, is more eligible than to grant liberty of conscience unto them who differ from the present establishment only as to some things belonging to the outward worship of God!

These things being premised, the argument itself pleaded in this chapter is capable of a speedy despatch. It is to this purpose: "The magistrate hath power over the consciences of men in reference to morals or moral virtues, which are the principal things in religion; and therefore much more hath so in reference to the worship of God, which is of less importance." We have complained before of the ambiguity of these general terms, but it is to no purpose to do so any more, seeing that we are not like to be relieved in this discourse. Let us, then, take things as we find them, and satisfy ourselves on the intention of the author by that declaration which he makes of it up and down the chapter. But yet here we are at a loss also. When he speaks, or seems to speak, to this purpose, whether in the confirmation of the proposition, or the inferences whereof his arguments consist, what he says is cast into such an intertexture with invectives and reproaches, and expressed in such a loose, declamatory manner, as it is hard to discover or find out what it is that he intends. Suppose, therefore, in the first place, that a man should call his consequent into question, — namely, that because the magistrate hath power over the consciences of his subjects in morals, that therefore he hath so also in matters of instituted worship, — how would he confirm and vindicate it? Two things are all I can observe that are offered in the confirmation of it:— First, That "these things of morality, moral virtues, are of more importance in religion than the outward worship of God," which the amplitude of power before asserted is now reducing to a respect unto. Secondly, That "there is much more danger of his erring and mistaking in things of morality than in things of outward worship, because of their great weight and importance." These things are pleaded, p. 28, and elsewhere up and down. That any thing else is offered in the confirmation of this consequent I find not. And it may be some will think these proofs to be very weak and feeble, unable to sustain the weight that is laid upon them; for it is certain that the first rule, — that he that hath power over the greater hath so over the lesser, — doth not hold unless it be in things of the same nature and kind. And it is no less certain and evident that there is an especial and formal difference between these things, — namely, moral virtues and instituted worship; the one depending, as to their being and discovery, on the light of nature, and the dictates of that reason which is common to all, and speaks the same language in the consciences of all mankind; the other, on pure revelation, which may be and is variously apprehended. Hence it is, that whereas there is no difference in the world about what is virtue and what is not, there is no agreement about what belongs to divine worship and what doth not.

Again; *lesser* things may be exempted from that power and authority, by especial privilege or law, which hath the disposal of *greater* committed unto it, and intrusted with it; as the magistrate amongst us may take away the life of a man, which is the greatest of his concernments, the name of his all, for felony, but cannot take his estate or inheritance of land, which is a far less concernment unto him, if it be antecedently settled by law to other uses than his own. And if it cannot be proved that the disposal of the worship of God, as to what doth really and truly belong unto it, and all the parts of it, is exempted from all human power by special law and privilege, let it be disposed of as whoso will shall judge meet.

Nor is the latter consideration suggested to enforce this consequent of any more validity, — namely, "that there is more danger of the magistrate's erring or mistaking about moral virtue than about rites of worship," because that is of most concernment in religion; for it is true, that suppose a man to walk on the top of a high house or tower, on a plain floor, with battlements or walls round about him, there will be more danger of breaking his neck if he should fall from thence than if he should fall from the top of a narrow wall that had not the fourth part of the height of the house. But there would not be so much danger of falling: for from the top of the house, as circumstantiated, he cannot fall, unless he will willfully and violently cast himself down headlong; and on the top of the wall, it may be, he cannot stand, with the utmost of his heed and endeavours. The magistrate cannot mistake about moral virtues, unless he will do it willfully. They have their station fixed in the world on the same ground and evidence with the magistracy itself. The same evidence, the same common consent and suffrage of mankind, is given unto moral virtues, as is to any government in the world; and to suppose a supreme magistrate, a lawgiver, to mistake in these things, in judging whether justice, and temperance, or fortitude, be virtues or no, and that in his legislative capacity, is ridiculous. Neither Nero nor Caligula was ever in danger of any such misadventure. All the magistrates in the world at this day are agreed about these things. But as to what concerns the worship of God, they are all at variance. There is no such evidence in these things, no such common suffrage about them, as to free any absolutely from failings and mistakes; so that in respect of them, and not of the other, lies the principal danger of miscarrying as to their determination and administration. Supposing, therefore, the premises our author lays down to be true, his inference from them is feeble and obnoxious to various impeachments, whereof I have given some few instances only, which shall be increased if occasion require.

But the assertion itself which is the foundation of these consequences is utterly remote from accuracy and truth. It is said that "the magistrate hath power over the consciences of men in reference unto moral duties, which are the principal parts of religion." Our first and most difficult inquiry is after the meaning of this proposition; the latter, after its truth. I ask, then, first, Whether he hath power over the consciences of men with respect unto moral virtue, and over moral virtue itself as virtue and as a part of religion, or on some other account? If his power respect virtue as a part of religion, then it equally extends itself to all that is so, by virtue of a rule which will not be easily everted. But it doth not appear that it so extends itself as to plead an obliging authority in reference unto all duties; for let but the scheme of moral duties, especially those whose object is God, given us by our author, be considered, and it will quickly be discerned how many of them are exempted from all human cognizance and authority, and that from and by their nature, as well as their use in the world. And it is in vain to ascribe an authority to magistrates which they have no power to exert, or take cognizance whether it be obeyed or no. And what can they do therein with respect unto "gratitude to God," which holds the first place in the scheme of moral virtues here given in unto us? We are told, also, p. 83, "That in matters both of moral virtue and divine worship, there are some rules of good and evil that are of an eternal and changeable obligation, and these can never be prejudiced or altered by any human power, because the reason of their obligation arises from a necessity and constitution of nature, and therefore must be as perpetual as that; but then there are other rules of duty that are alterable according to the various accidents, changes, and conditions of human life, and depend chiefly upon contracts and positive laws of kingdoms." It would not be unworthy our inquiry to consider what rules of moral duty they are which are alterable and depend "on accidents and contracts;" but we might easily find work enough should we call all such fond assertions to a just examination. Neither doth the distinction here given us between various rules of moral virtue very well answer what we are told, p. 69, — namely, "that every particular virtue is therefore such, because it is a resemblance and imitation of some of the divine attributes;" which I suppose they are not whose rules and forms are alterable upon accidents and occasions. And we are taught also, p. 68, that the "practice of virtue consists in living suitably to the dictates of reason and nature;" which are rules not variable and changeable. There must be some new distinction to reconcile these things, which I cannot at present think of. That which I would enquire from hence is, Whether the magistrate have power over the consciences of men in reference unto those things in morality whose rules of good and evil are of an eternal obligation? That he hath not is evidently implied in this place. And I shall not enter into the confusion of the ensuing discourse, where the latter sort of rules for virtue, the other member of the distinction, are turned into various methods of executing laws about outward acts of virtue or vice, and the virtues themselves into outward expressions and significations of duty; for I have at present no contest with this author about his manner of writing, nor do intend to have. It is enough that here at once all the principal and most important virtues are vindicated to their own unalterable rules as such, and the consciences of men in reference unto them put under another jurisdiction. And what, then, becomes of this argument, "That the magistrate must have power over the consciences of men in matters of divine worship, because he hath so in things moral, which are of greater importance," when what is so of importance is exempted from his power?

Hence it sufficiently appears that the authority of the magistrate over men, with reference unto moral virtue and duty, doth not respect virtue as virtue, but hath some other consideration. Now what this is, is evident unto all. How moral virtues do belong unto religion, and are parts of it, hath been before declared. But God, who hath ordered all things in weight and measure, hath fore-designed them also to another end and purpose. For preparing mankind for political society in the world among themselves for a time, as well as for religious obedience unto himself, he inlaid his nature and composition with principles suited to both those ends, and appointed them to be acted with different respects unto them. Hence moral virtues, notwithstanding their peculiar tendency unto him, are appointed to be the instrument and ligament of human society also; — as the law of Moses had in it a typical end, use, and signification, with respect to Christ and the gospel; and a political use, as the instrument of the government of the nation of the Jews. Now, the power of the magistrate in respect to moral virtues is in their latter use, — namely, as they relate to human policy, which is concerned in the outward actings of them. This, therefore, is granted; and we shall inquire farther, whether any more be proved, namely, that the magistrate hath power over the outward actings of virtue and vice, so far as human society or public tranquillity is concerned in them, and on that account?

Secondly, It may be inquired, What is the power and authority over moral virtues which is here ascribed unto the civil magistrate, and over the consciences of men with respect unto them? Is it such as to make that to be virtue which was not virtue before, or which was vice, and oblige men in conscience to practice it as virtue? This would go a great way indeed, and answer somewhat of what is, or, as it is said, may be, done in the worship of God, when that is made a part of it which was not so before. But what name shall these new virtues be called by? A new virtue, both as to its acts and objects, will as much fly the imaginations of men as a sixth sense doth. It may be our author will satisfy us as to this inquiry; for he tells us, p. 80, that "he hath power to make that a particular of the divine law that God hath not made so." I wish he had declared himself how and wherein; for I am afraid this expression, as here it lies, is offensive. The divine law is divine, and so is every particular of it; and how a man can make a thing divine that is not so of itself, nor by divine institution, is hard to find out. It may be that only the subject-matter of the law, and not the law itself formally, is intended; and to make a thing a particular of the divine law is no more but to make the divine law require that in particular of a man which it did not require of him before. But this particular refers to the nature, essence, and being of the thing, or to the acting and occasion of it in particular. And if it be taken in the latter sense, there is no more ascribed unto the magistrate than is common with him to every man in the world: for every one that puts himself into new circumstances or new relations, doth so make that unto him to be a particular of the divine law which was not so before; for he is bound and obliged unto the actual performance of many duties which, as so circumstantiated, he was not bound unto before.

But somewhat else seems to be intended from the ensuing discourse: "They are fully empowered to declare new instances of virtue and vice, and to introduce new duties in the most important parts of religion." And yet I am still at the same loss; for by his "declaring new instances of virtue and vice," I suppose he intends an authoritative declaration, such as that they have no other foundation, nor need none to make them what they are. They are new instances of virtue and vice, because so declared. And this suits unto the "introducing of new duties in the most important parts of religion," — made duties by that introduction. I wish I could yet learn what these "new instances of virtue and vice" are or mean; whether they are new as virtues and vices, or as instances. For the first, would I could see a new practice of old virtues! but, to tell you the truth, I care not for any of the new virtues that I have lately observed in the world, nor do I hope ever to see any better new ones.

If it be the *instances that are new*, I wish again I knew what were more in them than the actual and occasional exercise of old duties. Pages 79, 80, conduce most to extricate us out of these ambiguities. There we are informed that "the laws of every nation do distinguish and settle men's rights and properties, and that distinctly; with respect whereunto justice, that prime natural virtue, is in particular instances to be exercised. And, p. 84, it is farther declared, that "in the administration of justice there may be great difference in the constitution of penalties and execution of them." This, it seems, is that which is aimed at: The magistrate, by his laws, determines whether Titius have set his hedge upon Caius' ground, and whether Sempronius have rightly conveyed his land or house to his son or neighbour; whereby what is just and lawful in itself is accommodated to the use of political society. He determines, also, how persons guilty of death shall be executed, and by whom, and in what manner. Whence it must needs follow, that he hath power to assign new particulars of the divine law, to declare new bounds or hedges of right and wrong, which the law of God neither doth nor can limit, or hath power over the consciences of men with respect to moral virtues; which was to be demonstrated. Let us lay aside these swelling expressions, and we shall find that all that can be ascribed unto the civil magistrate in this matter is no more than to preserve property and peace by that rule and power over the outward actions of men which is necessary thereunto.

Having made some inquiry into the terms of "moral virtue" and the "magistrate's power," it remains only that we consider what respect this case hath unto the consciences of men, with reference unto them; and I desire to know whether all mankind be not obliged in conscience to the observation of all moral virtues antecedently to the command or authority of the magistrate, who doth only inspect their observation of them as to the concerns of public peace and tranquillity? Certainly, if all moral virtues consist in "living suitably to the dictates of reason," as we are told, — and in a sense rightly, if the rule of them all and every one, which gives them their formal nature, be the law of our creation, which all mankind enter the world under an indispensable obligation unto, — it cannot be denied but that there is such an antecedent obligation on the consciences of men as that inquired after. But the things mentioned are granted by our author; nor can by any be denied without offering the highest outrage to Scripture, reason, and the common consent of mankind. Now, if this obligation be thus on all men, unto all virtue as virtue, and this absolutely, from the authority of God over them and their consciences, how comes an inferior authority to interpose itself between that of God and their consciences, so as immediately to oblige them? It is granted that when the magistrate commandeth and requireth the exercise of any moral duty, in a way suited unto public good and tranquillity, he is to be obeyed for conscience' sake, because he who is the Lord of conscience doth require men to be obedient unto him, whereon they are obliged in conscience so to be: but if the things required of them be in themselves moral duties, as they are such, their consciences are obliged to observe and exercise them from the command of God; and other obligation unto them, as such, they neither have nor can have. But the direction and command for the exercise of them in these and those circumstances, for the ends of public good whereunto they are directed, belongs unto the magistrate, who is to be obeyed: for as in things merely civil, and which have nothing originally of morality in them, but secondarily only, as they tend to the preservation and welfare of human society, which is a thing morally good, the magistrate is to be obeyed for conscience' sake, and the things themselves, as far as they partake of morality, come directly under the command of God, which affects the conscience; — so in things that have an inherent and inseparable morality, and so respect God in the first place, when they come to have a civil sanction in reference to their exercise unto public political good, that sanction is to be obeyed out of conscience; but the antecedent obligation that was upon the conscience unto a due exercise of those duties, when made necessary by circumstances, is not superseded, nor any new one added thereunto.

I know what is said, but I find not as yet what is proved, from these things, concerning the uncontrollable and absolute power of the supreme magistrate over religion and the consciences of men. Some things are added indeed here, up and down, about circumstances of divine worship, and the power of ordering them by the magistrate; which though there may be some different conceptions about, yet they no way reach the cause under debate. But as they are expressed by our author, I know not of any one writer in and of the church of England that hitherto has so stated them as they are by him; for he tells us, p. 85, that "all rituals, ceremonies, postures, and manners of performing the outward expressions of devotion, that are not chargeable with countenancing vice or disgracing the Deity, are capable of being adopted into the ministries of divine service, and are not exempted from being subject to the determinations of human power." Whether they are so or no, the magistrate, I presume, is to judge, or all this flourish of words and concessions of power vanish into smoke. His command of them binds the consciences of men to observe them, according to the principle under consideration. Hence it must be absolutely in the power of every supreme magistrate to impose on the Christian subjects a greater number of ceremonious observances in the worship of God, and those of greater weight, than ever were laid upon the Jews; for who knows not that under the names of "rituals, ceremonies, postures, manners of performing all divine service," what a burdensome heap of things are imposed in the Roman church? whereunto, as far as I know, a thousand more may be added, not chargeable in themselves with either of the crimes which alone are allowed to be put in, in bar or plea against them. And whether this be the liberty whereunto Jesus Christ hath vindicated his disciples and church, is left unto the judgment of sober men. Outward religious worship, we know, is to be performed by natural actions. These have their circumstances; and those ofttimes, because of the public concernment of the exercise of religion, of great importance. These may be ordered by the power and according to the wisdom of those in authority; but that they should make so many things as this assertion allows them to make to belong unto and to be parts of the worship of God, whereof not one is enjoined or required by him, and the consciences of men be thereby obliged unto their observance, I do not believe, nor is it here at all proved.

    To close this discourse about the power of obliging the consciences of men; I think our author grants that conscience is immediately obliged to the observation of all things that are good in themselves, from the law of our creation. Such things as either the nature of God or our own requires from us, our consciences surely are obliged immediately by the authority of God to observe: nor can we have any dispensation for the non-performance of our duty from the interposition of the commands and authority of any of the sons of men; for this would be openly and directly to set up men against God, and to advance them or their authority above him or his. Things evidently deduced and necessarily following the first principles and dictates of nature are of the same kind with themselves, and have the authority of God no less enstamped on them than the other; and in respect unto them, conscience cannot by virtue of inferior commands plead an exemption. Things of mere revelation do remain; and concerning them I desire to know, whether we are not bound to observe and do whatever God in his revealed will commands us to observe and do, and to abstain from whatever he forbids, and this indispensably? If this be denied, I will prove it with the same arguments whereby I can prove that there is a God and that we are his creatures, made to serve him; for the reason of these things is inseparable from the very being of God. Let this be granted, and ascribe what ye will, or please, or can, to the supreme magistrate, and you shall not from me have the least contradiction.

A SURVEY OF THE THIRD CHAPTER

Liberty of conscience — The obligation to comply with its dictates not superseded by the authority of the magistrate — External worship an essential part of religion — External worship not left to be regulated by man — The rite of sacrifice shown to be of divine original — Alleged right of the magistrate to appoint ceremonies — Distinction between words and ceremonies as signs.

THE third chapter entertains us with a magnificent grant of *liberty of conscience*. The very first paragraph asserts a "liberty of conscience in mankind over all their actions, whether moral or strictly religious." But lest this should prove a bedlam concession, that might mischief the whole design in hand, it is delivered to the power of a keeper; who yet, upon examination, is no less wild and extravagant than itself is esteemed absolutely to be. This is, "That they have it as far as concerns their judgments, but not their practice;" — that is, they have liberty of conscience over their *actions* but not their *practices*, or *over their practices* but *not over their practices*! for, upon trial, their actions and practices will prove to be the same. And I do not as yet well understand what is this liberty of conscience over men's actions. Is it to do or not to do, as their consciences dictate to them? This is absolutely denied and opposed in the chapter itself. Is it to judge of their actions, as done, whether they be good or evil? This, conscience is at no liberty in; for it is determined to a judgment in that kind naturally and necessarily, and must be so whilst it hath the light of nature and word of God to regard, so far as a rule is capable of giving a measure and determination to things to be regulated by it, — that is, its moral actings are morally determined. What, then, this liberty of conscience over men's actions should be, when they can neither act freely according to their consciences what they are to do, nor abstain from what they are not to do, nor are at liberty to judge what they have done to be good or bad, I cannot divine.

Let us search after an explication of these things in the paragraph itself, whose contents are represented in the words mentioned. Here we are told that this liberty consists in "men's thinking of things according to their own persuasion, and therein asserting the freedom of their judgments." I would be loath to think that this liberty of men's consciences over all their moral actions should, at first dash, dwindle into a liberty in speculations, — that men may think what they will, opine as they please, in or about things that are not to be brought into practice; but yet, as far as I can perceive, I must think so, or matters will come to a worse issue.

But these things must be a little farther examined, and that very briefly. Here is mention of "liberty of conscience;" but what conscience is, or what that liberty is, is not declared. For conscience, it is called sometimes "the mind," sometimes "the understanding," sometimes "opinion," sometimes described by the "liberty of thinking,"sometimes termed an *"imperious faculty;"* which things, without much discourse and more words than I can now afford to use, are not reconcilable among themselves. Besides, liberty is no proper affection of the mind or understanding. Though I acknowledge the mind and its actings to be naturally free from outward compulsion or coaction, yet it is capable of such a determination from the things proposed unto it, and the manner of their proposal, as to make necessary the elicitation of its acts. It cannot but judge that two and three make five. It is the will that is the proper seat of *liberty*; and what some suppose to be the ultimate determination of the practical understanding is indeed *an act of the will*. It is so if you speak of liberty naturally and morally, and not of state and condition, which are here confounded. But suppose what you will to be conscience, it is moral actions or duties that are here supposed to be the objects of its actings. Now, what are or can be the thoughts or actings of the mind of man about moral actions, but about their virtue or their vice, their moral good or evil? Nor is a conclusion of what is a man's own duty in reference to the practice of them possibly to be separated from them. That, then, which is here asserted is, That a man may think, judge, or conceive such or such a thing to be his duty, and yet have thereby no obligation put upon him to perform it; for conscience, we are informed, hath nothing to do beyond the inward thoughts of men's minds!

To state this matter a little more clearly, let us take conscience in the most usual acceptation of it, and that which answers the experience of every man that ever looks into the affairs and concerns within; and so it is the practical judgment that men make of themselves and of their actions, or what they are to do and what they are not to do, what they have done or what they have omitted, with reference unto the judgment of God, at present declared in their own hearts and in his word, and to be fully executed at the last day: for we speak of conscience as it is amongst Christians, who acknowledge the word of God, and that for a double end; first, as the rule of conscience itself; secondly, as the declaration of the will of God, as to his approbation or rejecting of what we do or omit. Suppose, then, that a man make a judgment in his conscience, regulated by the word of God, and with respect unto the judgment of God concerning him, that such and such a thing is a duty, and whose performance is required of him, I desire to know whether any obligation be upon him from thence to act according? It is answered, that "the territory of conscience is confined unto men's thoughts, judgments, and persuasions, and these are free" (Yea, no doubt); "but for outward actions there is no remedy, but they must be subject to the cognizance of human laws," p. 9. Who ever doubted of it? He that would have men so have liberty from outward actions as not to have those actions cognoscible by the civil power as to the end of public tranquillity, but to have their whole station firmed absolutely in the world upon the plea of conscience, would, no doubt, lay a foundation for confusion in all government. But what is this to the present inquiry, Whether conscience lay an obligation on men, as regulated by the word of God, and respecting him, to practice according to its dictates? It is true enough, that if any of its practices do not please or satisfy the magistrate, their authors must, for aught I know, stand to what will follow or ensue on them to their prejudice; but this frees them not from the obligation that is upon them in conscience unto what is their duty. This is that which must be here proved, if any thing be intended unto the purpose of this author, — namely, that notwithstanding the judgment of conscience concerning any duty, by the interposition of the authority of the magistrate to the contrary, there is no obligation ensues for the performance of that duty. This is the answer that ought plainly to be returned, and not a suggestion that outward actions must fall under the cognizance of the magistrate, which none ever doubted of, and which is nothing to the present purpose, unless he would have them so to fall under the magistrates cognizance as that his will should be the supreme rule of them; which, I think, he cannot prove. But what sense the magistrate will have of the outward actions, wherein the discharge of man's duty doth consist, is of another consideration.

This, therefore, is the state of the present case applied unto religious worship: Suppose the magistrate command such things in religion as a man in his conscience, guided by the word and respecting God, doth look upon as unlawful and such as are evil, and sin unto him if he should perform them, and forbid such things in the worship of God as he esteems himself obliged in conscience to observe as commands of Christ; if he practice the things so commanded, and omit the things so forbidden, I fear he will find himself within doors continually at confession, saying, with trouble enough, "I have done those things which I ought not to have done, and I have left undone those things which I ought to have done, and there is no health in me;" unless this author can prove that the commands of God respect only the minds of men, but not their outward actions, which are left unto the authority of the magistrate alone. If no more be here intended, but that whatever conscience may require of any, it will not secure them but that, when they come to act outwardly according to it, the civil magistrate may and will consider their actions, and allow them or forbid them, according to his own judgment, it were surely a madness to deny it, as great as to say the sun shineth not at noonday. If conscience to God be confined to thoughts, and opinions, and speculations about the general notions and notices of things, about true and false, and unto a liberty of judging and determining upon them what they are, whether they are so or no, the whole nature and being of conscience, and that to the reason, sense, and experience of every man, is utterly overthrown. If conscience be allowed to make its judgment of what is good or evil, what is duty or sin, and no obligation be allowed to ensue from thence unto a suitable practice, a wide door is opened unto atheism, and thereby the subversion of all religion and government in the world.

This, therefore, is the sum of what is asserted in this matter: Conscience, according to that apprehension which it hath of the will of God about his worship (whereunto we confine our discourse), obligeth men to act or forbear accordingly. If their apprehensions are right and true, just and equal, what the Scripture, the great rule of conscience, doth declare and require, I hope none, upon second thoughts, will deny but that such things are attended with a right unto a liberty to be practised, while the Lord Jesus Christ is esteemed the Lord of lords and King of kings, and is thought to have power to command the observance of his own institutions. Suppose their apprehensions to be such as may in those things, be they more or less, be judged not to correspond exactly with the great rule of conscience, yet supposing them also to contain nothing inconsistent with, or of a disturbing nature to, civil society and public tranquillity, nothing that gives countenance to any vice or evil, or is opposite to the principal truths and main duties of religion, wherein the minds of men in a nation do coalesce, nor to carry any politic entanglements along with them; and add thereunto the peaceableness of the persons possessed with those apprehensions, and the impossibility they are under to divest themselves of them; — and I say natural right, justice, equity, religion, conscience, God himself in all, and his voice in the hearts of all unprejudiced persons, do require that neither the persons themselves, on the account of their consciences, have violence offered unto them, nor their practices in pursuit of their apprehensions be restrained by severe prohibitions and penalties But whereas the magistrate is allowed to judge and dispose of all outward actions in reference to public tranquillity, if any shall assert principles, as of conscience, tending or obliging unto the practice of vice, immorality, or sin, or to the disturbance of public society, such principles being all notoriously judged by Scripture, nature, the common consent of mankind, and inconsistent with the fundamental principles of human polity, may be, in all instances of their discovery and practice, coerced and restrained. But, plainly, as to the commands of conscience, they are of the same extent with the commands of God; — if these respect only the inward man, or the mind, conscience doth no more; if they respect outward actions, conscience doth so also.

From the liberty of conscience a proceed is made to Christian liberty, which is said to be "a duty or privilege founded upon the" (chimerical) "liberty of conscience" before granted. But these things stand not in the relation imagined. Liberty of conscience is of natural right, Christian liberty is a gospel privilege, though both may be pleaded in unwarrantable impositions on conscience. But these things are so described by our author as to be confounded: for the Christian liberty described in this paragraph is either restrained to matters of pure speculation, wherein the mind of man is left entirely free to judge of the truth and falsehood of things; or as it regards things that fall under laws and impositions, wherein men are left entirely free to judge of them, as they are objects of mere opinion. Now, how this differs from the liberty of conscience granted before I know not. And that there is some mistake in this description of Christian liberty needs no other consideration to evince but this, namely, that Christian liberty, as our author tells us, is a privilege; but this is not so, being that which is equally common unto all mankind. This liberty is necessary unto human nature, nor can it be divested of it; and so it is not a privilege that includes a speciality in it. Every man cannot but think what he thinks, and judge what he judgeth, and that when he doth so, whether he will or no; for every thing when it is, and as it is, is necessary. In the use of what means they please, to guide, direct, and determine their thoughts, their liberty doth consist. This is equal in all, and natural unto all. Now, this inward freedom of our judgment is, it seems, our Christian liberty, consistent with any impositions upon men in the exercise of the worship of God, with an obligation on conscience unto their use and practice! a liberty, indeed, of no value, but a mere aggravation of bondage. And these things are farther discoursed, sect. iii., p. 95; wherein we are told, that "this prerogative of our Christian liberty is not so much any new favour granted in the gospel, as the restoration of the mind of man to its natural privilege, by exempting us from the yoke of the ceremonial law, whereby things in themselves indifferent were tied upon the conscience with as indispensable an obligation as the rule of essential goodness, and equity, during the whole period of the Mosaic dispensation; which being corrected by the gospel, those indifferent things, that have been made necessary by a divine, positive command, returned to their own nature, to be used or omitted only as occasion shall direct."

It is true that a good part of our Christian liberty consists in our deliverance from the yoke of Mosaical institutions; but that this "is not so much a new favour granted in the gospel as the restoration of the mind of man to its natural privilege," is an assertion that runs parallel with many others in this discourse. This privilege, as all others of the gospel are, is spiritual, and its outward concerns and exercise are of no value where the mind is not spiritually made free by Christ. And it is uncertain what is meant by the "restoration of the mind to its natural privilege." If the privilege of the mind in its natural purity is intended, as it was before the entrance of sin, it is false; if any privilege [which] the mind of man, in its corrupt, depraved condition, is capable of, be designed, it is no less untrue. In things of this nature the mind in that condition is in bondage, and not capable of any liberty; for it is a thing ridiculous to confound the mere natural liberty of our wills, which is an affection inseparable from that faculty, with a moral or spiritual liberty of mind relating unto God and his worship. But this whole paragraph runs upon no small mistake, — namely, that the yoke of Mosaical institutions consisted in their impositions on the minds and judgments of men, with an opinion of the antecedent necessity of them; for although the words recited, "Things in themselves indifferent were tied upon the conscience with as indispensable an obligation as the rules of essential goodness and equity," may be restrained to their use, exercise, and observation, yet the conclusion of it, that "whatever our superiors impose upon us, whether in matters of religious worship or any other duties of morality, there neither is nor can be any intrenchment upon our Christian liberty, provided it be not imposed with an opinion of the antecedent necessity of the thing itself," with: the whole scope of the argument insisted on, makes it evident to be the sense intended. But this is wide enough from the mark. The Jews were never obliged to judge the whole system of their legal institutions to be any way necessary antecedent unto their institution and appointment; nor were they obliged to judge their intrinsic nature changed by their institution: only, they knew they were obliged to their constant and indispensable practice, as parts of the worship of God, instituted and commanded by him who hath the supreme authority over their souls and consciences. There was, indeed, a bondage frame of spirit upon them in all things, especially in their whole worship of God, as the apostle Paul several times declares. But this is a thing of another nature, though our delivery from it be also a part of Christian liberty. This was no part of their inward no more than their outward bondage, that they should think, believe, judge, or esteem the things themselves enjoined them to be absolutely of any other nature than they were. Had they been obliged unto any such judgment of things, they had been obliged to deceive themselves, or to be deceived. But, by the absolute authority of God, they were indispensably bound in conscience to the actual observance and continual use of such a number of ceremonies, carnal ordinances, and outward observances, as, being things in themselves low and mean, called by the apostle "beggarly elements," and enjoined with so great strictness, and under so severe penalties, — many of them, of excision, or extermination from among the people, — so became an intolerable and insupportable yoke unto them. Neither doth the apostle Peter dispute about a judgment of their nature, but the necessity of their observation, when he calls them "a yoke which neither they nor their fathers were able to bear," Acts xv. 10. And when St Paul gives a charge to believers to "stand fast in the liberty wherewith Christ hath made them free," it is with respect to the outward observation of Mosaical rites, as by him instituted, and not as to any inward judgment of their minds concerning their nature antecedent unto that institution. His whole disputation on that subject respects only men's practice with regard unto an authoritative obligation thereunto, which he pleaded to be now expired and removed. And if this Christian liberty, which he built and proceeded upon, be of force to free, not our minds from the judgments that they had before of things in themselves, but our persons from the necessary practice and observance of things instituted of God, however antecedently indifferent in themselves, I think it is, at least, of equal efficacy to exempt us from the necessary practice of things imposed on us in the worship of God by men. For, setting aside the inequality of the imposing authority, which casts the advantage on the other side (for these legal impositions were imposed on the church by God himself; those now intended are such masters as our superiors of themselves impose on us in religious worship), the case is absolutely the same: for as God did not give the "law of commandments contained in ordinances" unto the Jews from the goodness of the things required therein antecedent to his command, which should make them necessary to be practised by them for their good, but did it of his own sovereign, arbitrary will and pleasure; so he obliged not the people themselves unto any other judgment of them, but that they were necessarily to be observed. And, setting aside the consideration of his command, they were things in their own nature altogether indifferent. So is it in the present case. It is pleaded that there is no imposition on the minds, consciences, or judgments of men, to think or judge otherwise of what is imposed on them than as their nature is and doth require; only they are obliged unto their usage, observance, and practice: which is to put us into a thousand times worse condition than the Jews, if instances of them should be multiplied, as they may lawfully be every year, seeing it much more quiets the mind, to be able to resolve its thoughts immediately into the authority of God under its yoke than into that of man. If, therefore, we are freed from the one by our Christian liberty, we are so much more from the other; so as that, "being made free by Christ," we should not be the "servants of men" in things belonging to his service and worship.

From this discovery here made of the nature of Christian liberty, our author makes some deductions, pp. 98, 99, concerning the nature of religious worship; wherein he tells us that "the whole substance of religious worship is transacted within the mind of man, and dwells in the heart and thoughts, the soul being its proper seat and temple, where men may worship their God as they please without offending their prince; and that external worship is no part of religion itself." I wish he had more clearly and distinctly expressed his mind in this matter, for his assertions, in the sense the words seem to bear, are prodigiously false, and such as will open a door to atheism, with all the villany and confusion in the world; for who would not think this to be his intention: Let men keep their minds and inward thoughts and apprehensions right for God, and then they may practice outwardly in religion what they please; one thing one day, another another; be Papists and Protestants, Arians and Homo-ousians, yea, Mohammedans and Christians, any thing, every thing, after the manner of the country and laws of the prince where they are and live; — the rule that Ecebolius[7] walked by

---

7   Ecebolius was a sophist of Constantinople, a zealous Christian under Constantine the Great, and equally zealous as a Pagan under Julian. — ED.

of old? I think there is no man that owns the Scripture but will confess that this is, at least, if not a direct, yet an interpretative rejection of the whole authority of God. And may not this rule be quickly extended unto oaths themselves, the bonds and ligaments of human society? for whereas, in their own formal nature, they belong to the worship of God, why may not men pretend to keep up their reverence unto God in the internal part of them, or their esteem of him in their invocation of his name, but as to the outward part accommodate it unto what by their interest is required of them; so swearing with their tongues, but keeping their mind at liberty? If the principles laid down be capable of any other more tolerable sense, and such as may be exclusive of these inferences, I shall gladly admit it; at present, what is here deduced from them seems to be evidently included in them.

It is true, indeed, that natural, moral, or internal worship, consisting in faith, love, fear, thankfulness, submission, dependence, and the like, hath its constant seat and residence in the souls and minds of men; but that the ways whereby these principles of it are to be outwardly exercised and expressed, by God's command and appointment, are not also indispensably necessary unto us, and parts of his worship, is utterly false. That which principally in the Scripture comes under the notion of the worship of God, is the due observance of his outward institutions; which divines have, upon unquestionable grounds, contended to be commanded and appointed in general in the second commandment of the decalogue, whence all particular institutions in the several seasons of the church are educed, and resolved into the authority of God therein expressed. And that account which we have here given us of outward worship, — namely, that it is "no part of religion itself, but only an instrument to express the inward generation of the mind by some outward action or posture of the body," — as it is very difficultly to be accommodated unto the sacrifices of old or the present sacraments of the church, which were and are parts of outward worship, and, as I take it, of religion; so the being an instrument, unto the purpose mentioned, doth not exclude any thing from being also a part of religion and worship itself, if it be commanded by God to be performed in his service unto his glory. It is pretended that all outward worship is only "an exterior signification of honour;" but yet all the parts of it in their performance are acts of obedience unto God, and are the proper actings of faith, love, and submission of soul unto God; which if they are not his worship, and parts of religion, I know not what may be so esteemed. Let, then, outward worship stand in what relation it will to inward spiritual honour, where God requires it and commands it, it is no less necessary and indispensably to be performed than any part of inward worship itself, and is a no less important duty of religion; for any thing comes to be a part of religious worship outwardly to be performed, not from its own nature, but from its respect unto the commands of God, and the end whereunto it is by him designed. So the apostle tells us, that "with the heart man believeth unto righteousness, and with the mouth confession is made unto salvation," Rom. x. 10. Confession is but the "exterior signification" of the faith that is in our hearts; but yet it is no less necessary to salvation than faith itself is to righteousness. And those who regulate their obedience and religious worship by the commands of God, knowing that which way soever they are signified, by inbred light or superadded revelation, it is they which give their obedience its formal nature, making it religious, will not allow that place and use of the outward worship required by God himself which should exclude it from being religious, or a part of their religion.

But upon the whole matter our author affirms, "That in all ages of the world, God hath left the management of his outward worship unto the discretion of men, unless when to determine some particulars hath been useful to some other purpose, p. 100. "The management of outward worship" may signify no more but the due performance of it; and so I acknowledge that though it be not left unto men's discretion to observe or not observe it, yet it is, too, their duty and obedience, which are their discretion and their wisdom. But the management here understood is opposed to God's own determination of particular forms, — that is, his especial institutions; and hereof I shall make bold to say, that it was never in any age so left to the discretion of men. To prove this assertion, sacrifices are singled out as an instance. It is known and granted that these were the most solemn part of the outward worship of God for many ages, and that there was a general consent of mankind unto the use of them, so that however the greatest part of the world apostatized from the true, only, and proper object of all religious worship, yet they retained this mode and medium of it. These sacrifices, we are told, p. 101, "did not owe their original unto any divine institution, but were made choice of by good men as a fit way of imitating the grateful resentments of their minds." The argument alone, as far as I can find, fixed on to firm this assertion is, that those who teach the contrary, and say that this mode of worship was commanded, do say so without proof or evidence. Our author, for the most part, sets off his assertions at no less rate than as such without whose admittance all order and government, and almost every thing that is good amongst mankind, would be ruined and destroyed. But he hath the unhappiness to found them, ordinarily, not only on principles and opinions dubious and uncertain, but on such paradoxes as have been by sober and learned men generally decried. Such is this of the original of sacrifices, here insisted on. The divines of the church of Rome do generally contend that religion and sacrifices are so related that the one cannot be without the other. Hence, they teach [that] God would have required sacrifices in the state of innocency had mankind continued therein. And though the instance be ill laid and not proved, yet the general rule applied unto the religion of sinners is not easily to be evicted; for as in Christian religion we have a Sacrifice that is πρόσφατος καὶ ζῶσα, as to its efficacy, always "newly offered and living," so before the personal offering of it in the body of Christ, there was no season or age without a due representation of it in sacrifices typical and of mystical signification. And although there be no express mention in the Scripture of their institution (for these are ancient things), yet there is as good warrant for it as for offering and burning incense only with sacred fire taken from the altar, which was of a heavenly traduction, for a neglect whereof the priests were consumed with fire from before the Lord; that is, though an express command be not recorded for their institution and observation, yet enough may be collected from the Scripture that they were of a divine extract and original. And if they were arbitrary inventions of some men, I desire to have a rational account given me of their catholicism in the world, and one instance more of any thing not natural or divine that ever prevailed to such an absolute universal acceptance amongst mankind. It is not so safe, I suppose, to assign an arbitrary original unto any thing that hath obtained a universal consent and suffrage, lest men be thought to set their own houses on fire, on purpose to consume their neighbours'.

Besides, no tolerable colour can be given to the assertion that they were the "invention of good men." The first notice we have of them is in those of Cain and Abel, whereof one was a bad man and of the evil one, and yet must be looked on as the principal inventor of sacrifices, if this fiction be allowed. Some of the ancients, indeed, thought that Adam sacrificed the beasts to God whose skins his first garments were made of; and if so, he was very pregnant and sudden in his invention, if he had no direction from God. But more than all this, bloody sacrifices were types of Christ, from the foundation of the world; and Socinus himself, who and his followers are the principal assessors of this paradox, grants that Christ is called the "Lamb of God," with respect unto the sacrifices of old, even before the law, as he is termed "a Lamb slain from the foundation of the world," not only with respect unto the efficacy of his sacrifice, but to the typical representation of it. And he that shall deny that the patriarchs in their sacrifices had respect unto the promised Seed will endeavour the shaking of a pillar of the church's creed. Now, I desire to know how men, by their own invention or authority, could assign such an end unto their sacrifices, if they were not of divine prescription, if not designed of God thereunto.

Again, the apostle tells us, Abel offered his sacrifice by faith, Heb. xi. 4; and faith hath respect unto the testimony of God, revealing, commanding, and promising to accept our duty. Wherever any thing is done in faith, there an assent is included to this, "that God is true," John iii. 33; and what it doth is thereby distinguished from will-worship, that is resolved into the commandments and doctrines of men, which whoso rest on make void the commandment of God, Matt. xv. 3, 6. And the faith of Abel, as to its general nature, was "the substance of things hoped for, and the evidence of things not seen," Heb. xi. 1; which in this matter it could not be if it had neither divine command nor promise to rest upon. It is evident, therefore, that sacrifices were of a *divine original*; and the instance in them to prove that the "outward worship of God hath, in all ages, been left unto the prudence and management of men," is feeble, and such as will give no countenance unto what it is produced in the justification of. And herewith the whole discourse of our author on this subject falls to the ground; where I shall at present let it lie, though it might, in sundry particulars, be easily crumbled into useless asseverations and some express contradictions.

In the close of this chapter an application is made of what hath been before argued, or rather dictated, upon a particular controversy about "significant ceremonies." I am not willing to engage in any contests of that nature, seeing to the due handling of them a greater length of discourse would be necessary than I think meet at present to draw forth this survey unto. Only, seeing a very few words may serve to manifest the looseness of what is here discoursed, to that purpose I shall venture on the patience of the reader with an addition of them. We have, therefore, in the first place, a reflection on "the prodigious impertinency of the clamour against the institution of significant ceremonies, when it is the only use of ceremonies, as of all other outward expressions of religion, to be significant," I do somewhat admire at the temper of this author, who cannot express his dissent from others in controversial points of the meanest and lowest concernment, but with crying out, "prodigies," "clamours," "impertinencies," and the like expressions of astonishment in himself and contempt of others. He might reserve some of these great words for more important occasions. But yet I join with him thus far in what he pleads, that ceremonies instituted in the worship of God that are *not significant* are very *insignificant*, and such as deserve not the least contention about them. He truly, also, in the next words, tells us that all "outward worship is a sign of inward honour." It is so, both in civil things and sacred. All our question is, How these instituted ceremonies come to be significant, and what it is they signify, and whether it be lawful to assign a significancy to them in the worship of God, when indeed they have none of the kind intended? To free us from any danger herein he informs us, p. 108, "That all the magistrate's power of instituting significant ceremonies amounts to no more than a power of determining what shall or what shall not be visible signs of honour; and this can be no usurpation upon the consciences of men." This is new language, and such as we have not formerly been used unto in the church of England, — namely, that of the '"magistrate's instituting significant ceremonies." It was of old, the "church's appointing ceremonies for decency and order." But all the terms of that assertion are metamorphosed; the "church" into the "magistrates;" "appointing," which respects exercise, into "institution," which respects the nature of the thing, and hath a singular use and sense in this matter (or let them pass for the same); and "order and decency" into "ceremonies significant." These things were indeed implied before, but not so fully and plainly expressed or avowed. But the "honour" here intended in this matter is the honour, which is given to God in his worship. This is the honour of faith, love, fear, obedience, spiritual and holy, in Jesus Christ. To say that the magistrate hath power to institute visible signs of this honour, to be observed in the outward worship of God, is upon the matter to say that he hath power to institute new sacraments, for so such things would be, and to say what neither is nor can be proved, nor is here either logically or any way regularly attempted so to be.

The comparing of the *ceremonies* and their, signification, with *words* and their signification, will not relieve our author in this matter. Some things are naturally significant of one another: so effects are of causes; so is smoke of fire; and such were the signs of the weather mentioned by our Saviour, Matt. xvi. 2, 3. Thus, I suppose, ceremonies are not significant, They do not naturally signify the things whereunto they are applied; for if they did there would be no need of their institution, and they are here said to be *instituted by the magistrate*. Again, there are customary signs, — some, it may be, *catholic*, many *topical*, — that have prevailed by custom and usage to signify such things as they have no absolute natural coherence with or relation unto; such is *putting off the hat* in sign of reverence, with others innumerable. And both these sorts of signs may have some use about the service and worship of God, as might be manifested in instances. But the signs we inquire after are voluntary, arbitrary, and instituted, as our author confesseth; for we do not treat of appointing some ceremonies for order and decency, which our canons take notice of, but of instituting ceremonies for signification, such as neither naturally nor merely by custom and usage come to be significant, but only by virtue of their institution. Now, concerning these, one rule may be observed, — namely, that they cannot be of one kind and signify things of another, by virtue of any command and consent of men, unless they have an absolute authority both over the sign and thing signified, and can change their natures, or create a new relation between them. To take, therefore, things natural, that are outward and visible, and appoint them to be signs, not natural, nor civil, nor customary, but mystical, of things spiritual, supernatural, inward, and invisible, and as such to have them observed in the church or worship of God, is a thing which is not as yet proved to be lawful. Signify thus naturally they never can, seeing there is no natural relation between them; civilly, or by consent, they do not so, for they are things sacred which they am supposed to signify, and are so far from signifying by consent, that those who plead for their signification do not agree wherein it doth consist. They must, therefore, signify so mystically and spiritually, and "signa cum ad res divinas pertinent sunt sacramenta," says Austin; — these things are sacraments. And when men can give mystical and spiritual efficacy to any of their own institutions; when they can make a relation between such signs and the things signified by them; when they can make that teaching and instructing in spiritual things and the worship of God which he hath not made so or appointed, blessed or consecrated to that end; when they can bind God's promises of assistance and acceptance to their own inventions; when they can advance what they will into the same rank and series of things in the worship of God with the sacrifices of old, or other parts of instituted worship in the church, by God's command, and attended with his promise of gracious acceptance; — then, and not before, may they institute the "significant ceremonies" here contended for. Words, it is true, are signs of things, and those of a mixed nature, partly natural, partly by consent: but they are not of one kind and signify things of another; for, say the schoolmen, "Where Words are signs of sacred things, they are signs of them as things, but not as sacred."

A SURVEY OF THE FOURTH CHAPTER

Conscience exempted from human authority, where there is an antecedent obligation from divine authority.

IN the fourth chapter we have no concern. The hypothesis whose confutation he hath undertaken, as it is in itself false, so it is rather suited to promote what he aims at than what he opposeth; and the principles which himself proceedeth on do seem to some to *border on*, if not to be *borrowed from* his, and those which are here confuted. And thence it is that the foundations which he lays down in the entrance of this discourse are as destructive of his own pretensions as of those against which they are by himself improved: for it is granted and asserted by him that there are actions and duties in and about which the consciences of men are not to be obliged by human authority, but have an antecedent obligation on them from the authority of God himself; "so that disobedience unto the contrary commands of human authority is no sin, but an indispensable duty." And although he seems at first to restrain things of this nature unto things natural, and of an essential rectitude, — that is, to the prime dictates of the law of nature, — yet he expressly extends it in instances unto the belief of the truth of the gospel, which is a matter of mere and pure revelation. And hereon he adds the formal and adequate reason of this exemption of conscience from human authority, and its obligation unto duty, before its consideration without it and against it; "which is, not because subjects are in any thing free from the authority of the supreme power on earth, but because they are subject to a superior in heaven; and they are then only excused from the duty of obedience to their sovereign, when they cannot give it without rebellion against God: so that it is not originally any right of their own that exempts them from a subjection to the sovereign power in all things, but it is purely God's right of governing his own creatures that magistrates then invade when they make edicts to violate or control his laws."

It is about religion and the worship of God that we are discoursing. Now, in these things no man ever thought that it was originally a right of subjects, as subjects, abstracting from the consideration of the authority of God, that should exempt them from a subjection to the sovereign power; for though some of the ancients discourse at large that it is of natural right and equity that every one should worship God as he would himself, yet they founded this equity in the nature of God and the authority of his commands. This exemption, then, ariseth merely, as our author observes, because they are subject to a superior power in heaven, which excuseth them from the duty of obedience to their superiors on earth, when they cannot give it without rebellion against God: whence it undeniably follows, that that supreme power in heaven exempted these things from all inferior powers on earth. Extend this, now, unto all things wherein men have, and ought to have, a regard unto that superior power in heaven, as it must be extended, or the whole is ridiculous (for that heavenly supremacy is made the formal reason of the exemption here granted), and all that our author hath been so earnestly contending for in the preceding chapters falls to the ground: for no man pleads exemption from subjection unto, yea, from giving active obedience unto, the authority and commands of the magistrate, even in things religious, but merely on the account of his subjection to the authority of God in heaven; and, where this is so, he is set at liberty by our author from all contrary commands of men. This is Bellarmine's "Tutissimum est," which, as King James observed, overthrows all that he had contended for in his five books De Justificatione.[8]

---

8   See vol. xiv., p. 204 of Owen's works. — Ed.

A SURVEY OF THE FIFTH CHAPTER

Alleged evils from the free exercise of conscience — Charges of Parker against Nonconformists — Mischief of different sects in a commonwealth — Duties of a prince in regard to divided interests in religion — Principle of toleration asserted.

THE fifth chapter is at such variance with itself and what is elsewhere dictated in the treatise, that it would require no small labour to make any tolerable composition of things between them. This I shall not engage in, as not being of my present concernment. What seems to tend unto the carrying on of the design of the whole may be called unto some account. In the beginning of it he tells us that "a belief of the indifferency, or rather imposture, of all religions is made the most effectual, not to say the most fashionable, argument for liberty of conscience," For my part, I never read, I never heard of this pretence or argument, to be used to that purpose. It wants no such defence. Nay, the principle itself seems to me to be suited directly to oppose and overthrow it: for if there be no such thing in reality as religion in the world, it is certainly a very foolish thing to have differences perpetuated amongst men upon the account of conscience; which, without a supposition of religion, is nothing but a vain and empty name. But hence our author takes occasion to discourse of the use of religion and conscience in the government of affairs in the world; and proves in many words that "conscience unto God, with a regard to future eternal rewards or punishments, is the great ligament of human society, the security of government, the strongest bond of laws, and only support of rule; without which every man would first and last be guided by mere self-interest, which would reduce all power and authority to mere force and violence." To this purpose doth he discourse at large in one section of this chapter; and in another, with no less earnestness and elegancy of words, and repetition of various expressions of the same signification, that "the use and exercise of conscience will certainly overthrow all government, and fill the world with confusion"! In like manner, whereas we have been hitherto throughly instructed, as I thought, that men may think what they will in the matters of religion, and be of what persuasion they please, [and] no man can or ought to control them therein, here we are told that "no power nor policy can keep men peaceable until some persuasions are rooted out of their minds by severity of laws and penalties"! p. 145. And whereas heretofore we were informed that "men might believe what they would," princes were concerned only in their outward practice, now are we assured that "above all things it concerns princes to look to the doctrines and articles of men's belief"! p. 147. But these things, as was before intimated, are not of our concern.

Nor can I find much of that importance in the third and fourth paragraphs of this declamatory invective. It is evident whom he regards and reflects upon, and with what false, unmanly, unchristian revilings he endeavours to traduce them. He would have the world believe that there is a generation of men whose principles of religion teach them to be proud, peevish, malicious, spiteful, envious, turbulent, boisterous, seditious, and whatever is evil in the world; when others are all for candour, moderation, and ingenuity, — amongst whom, no doubt, he reckons himself for one, and gives in this discourse in evidence thereof. But what are those doctrines and articles of men's belief, which dispose them inevitably to all the villanies that our author could find names for? A catalogue of them he gives us, pp. 147, 148. Saith he, "What if they believe that princes are but the executioners of the decrees of the presbytery; and that in case of disobedience to their spiritual governors they may be excommunicated, and by consequence deposed? What if they believe that dominion is founded in grace, and therefore all wicked kings forfeit their crowns, and that it is in the power of the people of God to bestow them where they please? And what if others believe that to pursue their successes in villany and rebellion is to follow providence?" All the world knows what it is that hath given him the advantage of providing a covering for these monstrous fictions, and an account thereof hath been given elsewhere. And what, now, if those intended do not believe these things, nor any one of them? What if they do openly disavow every one of them, as, for aught I ever heard or know, they do, and as I do myself? What if some of them are ridiculously framed into articles of faith, from the supposed practices of some individual persons? And what if men be of never so vile opinions about the pursuit of their successes, so they have none to countenance them in any unlawful enterprises; which, I think, must go before successes? What if only the Papists be concerned in these articles of faith, and they only in one of them, about the excommunication and deposition of princes, and that only some of them; and not one of those has any concern in them whom he intends to reproach? I say, if these things are so, we need look no farther for the principles of that religion which hath furnished him with all this candour, moderation, and ingenuity, and hath wrought him to such a quiet and peaceable temper, by teaching him that humility, charity, and meekness, which here bewray themselves.

Let it be granted, as it must and ought to be, that all principles of the minds of men, pretended to be from apprehensions of religion, that are in themselves inconsistent with any lawful government, in any place whatever, ought to be coerced and restrained; for our Lord Jesus Christ, sending his gospel to be preached and published in all nations and kingdoms of the world, then and at all times under various sorts of governments, all for the same end of public tranquillity and prosperity, did propose nothing in it but what a submission and obedience unto might be consistent with the government itself, of what sort soever it were. He came, as they used to sing of old, "to give men a heavenly kingdom, and not to deprive them or take from them their earthly temporal dominions." There is, therefore, nothing more certain than that there is no principle of the religion taught by Jesus Christ which either in itself, or in the practice of it, is inconsistent with any righteous government on the earth. And if any opinions can truly and really be manifested so to be, I will be no advocate for them nor their abettors. But such as these our author shall never be able justly to affix on them whom he opposeth, nor the least umbrage of them, if he do but allow the gospel and the power of Christ to institute those spiritual ordinances, and require their administration, which do not, which cannot, extend unto any thing wherein a magistrate, as such, hath the least concernment in point of prejudice; for if, on a false or undue practice of them, any thing should be done that is not purely spiritual, or that, being done, should be esteemed to operate upon may of the outward concerns, relations, interests, or occasions of men, they may be restrained by the power of him who presides over public good.

But besides these pretences, our author, I know not how, chargeth also the humours, inclinations, and passions of some men as inconsistent with government, and always disposing men to fanaticism and sedition; and on occasion thereof falls out into an excess of intemperance in reproaching them whom he opposeth, such as we have not above once or twice before met with the like; and in particular, he raves about that "zeal," as he calls it, for the glory of God, which hath "turned whole nations into shambles, filled the world with butcheries and massacres, and fleshed itself with slaughters of myriads of mankind." Now, omitting all other controversies, I shall undertake to maintain this against any man in the world, that the effects here so tragically expressed have been produced by the *zeal* our author pleads for, in compelling all unto the same sentiments and practices in religion, incomparably above what hath ensued upon any other pretence in or about religion whatever. This, if need require, I shall evince with such instances, from the entering of Christianity into the world to this very day, as will admit of no competition with all those together which, on any account or pretence, have produced the like effects. This it was and is that hath soaked the earth with blood, depopulated nations, ruined families, countries, kingdoms, and at length made innumerable Christians rejoice in the yoke of Turkish tyranny, to free themselves from their perpetual persecutions on the account of their dissent from the worship publicly established in the places of their nativity. And as for the humours, inclinations, and passions of men, when our author will give such rules and directions as whereby the magistrate may know how to make a true and legal judgment of who are fit on their account to live in his territories, and who are not, I suppose there will not be any contest about them. Until then, we may leave them, as here displayed and set up by our author, for every one to cast a cudgel at them that hath a mind thereunto.

For to what purpose is it to consider the frequent occasions he takes to discourse about the ill tempers and humours of men, or of inveighing against them for being "morose and ungentle, unsociable, peevish, censorious," with many other terms of reproach that do not at present occur to my memory, nor are, doubtless, worth the searching after? Suppose he hath the advantage of a better natural temper, have more sedate affections, a more compliant humour, be more remote from giving or receiving provocations, and have learned the ways of courtly deportment, only was pleased to veil them all and every one in the writing of this discourse, is it meet that they should be persecuted and destroyed, be esteemed seditious, and I know not what, because they are of a natural temper not so disposed to affability and sweetness of conversation as some others are? For my part, I dislike the humour and temper of mind characterized by our author, it may be as much as he, — I am sure, I think, as much as I ought; but to make it a matter of such huge importance as solemnly to introduce it into a discourse about religion and public tranquillity will not, it may be, on second thoughts, be esteemed over-considerately done. And it is not unlikely but that our author seems of as untoward a composition and peevish a humour to them whom he reflects upon as they do to him, and that they satisfy themselves as much in their disposition and deportment as he doth himself in his.

"Nimirum idem onmes fallimur; neque est quisqam,
Quem non in aliqua re, videre Suffenum Possis."
[Catull., xxii. 18]

Sect. v. pp. 155, 156, he inveighs against the events that attend the permission of *different sects of religion* in a commonwealth; and it is not denied but that some inconveniences may ensue thereon. But, as himself hath well observed in another place, we do not in these things inquire what is absolutely best, and what hath no inconvenience attending it; but what is the best which, in our present condition, we can attain unto, and what in that state answers the duty that God requireth of us. Questionless, it were best that we should be all of one mind in these things of God, and it is no doubt also our duty on all hands to endeavour so to be; but seeing, "de facto," this is not so, nor is it in the power of men, when and how they will, to depose those persuasions of their minds and dictates of their consciences from whence it is not so, on the one part or the other (although in some parts of our differences some may do so and will not, namely, in things acknowledged to be of no necessity antecedent to their imposition, and some would do so and cannot), it is now inquired, What is the best way to be steered in for the accomplishment of the desired end of peace and tranquillity for the future, and maintaining love, quietness, and mutual usefulness at present amongst men? Two ways are proposed to this purpose. The one is, to exercise mutual forbearance to each other whilst we are inevitably under the power of different persuasions in these things, producing no practices that are either injurious unto private men in their rights, or hurtful unto the state as to public peace; endeavouring, in the meantime, by the evidence of truth, and a conversation suited unto it, to win upon each other to a consent and agreement in the things wherein we differ. The other is, by severe laws, penalties, outward force, as imprisonments, mulcts, fines, banishments, or capital punishments, to compel all men out of hand to a uniformity of practice, whatever their judgments be to the contrary. Now, as the state of things is amongst us, which of these ways is most suitable to the law of our being and creation, the best principles of the nature of man, and those which have the most evident resemblance of divine perfections, the gospel, the spirit and letter of it, with the mind of its author, our Lord Jesus Christ, — which is most conducing to attain the end aimed at, in ways of a natural and genuine compliance with the things themselves of religion, conscience, and divine worship, — is left unto the judgment of God and all good men.

In the meantime, if men will make declamations upon their own surmises, jealousies, and suspicions of things which are either so indeed, that is, really surmised, or pretended to be so, for some private interests or advantages of their own, which no man can answer or remove; if they may fancy at their pleasure ghosts, goblins, fiends, walking sprights, seditions, drums, trumpets, armies, bears and tigers; every difference in religion, be it never so small, be the agreement amongst them that differ never so great; be it the visible, known, open interest of them that dissent from what is established to live quietly and peaceably, and to promote the good of the commonwealth wherein they live; do they profess that it is their duty, their principle, their faith and doctrine, to obey constantly their rulers and governors in all things not contrary to the mind of God, and pretend no such commands of his as should interfere in the least with their power in order to public tranquillity; do they offer all the security of their adherence to such declared principles as mankind is necessitated to be contented and satisfied with in things of their highest concernment; do they avow an especial sense of the obligation that is put upon them by their rulers when they are protected in peace; have they no concernment in any such political societies, combinations, interests as might alone give countenance unto any such disturbance; — all is one, every different *opinion is press-money,* and *every sect is an army,* although they be all and every one of them Protestants, of whom alone we do discourse, Other answer, therefore, I shall not return unto this part of our author's arguing than what he gave of old, —

> "Ne admittam culpam, ego meo sum promus pectori,
> Suspicio est in pectore alieno sita.
> Nam nunc ego te si surripuisse suspicer,
> Jovi coronam de capite e Capitolio,
> Quod in culmine astat summo, si non id feceris,
> Atque id tamen mihi lubeat suspicarier;
> Quî tu id prohibere me potes, ne suspicer." —
>   [Plaut., Trin. i. 2, 44.]

Only, I may add, that sundry of the instances our author makes use of are false and unduly alleged; for what is here charged on differences in and about religion, in reference unto public tranquillity, might have been, yea, and was, charged on *Christian religion* for three hundred years, and is so by many still on *Protestancy,* as such; and that it were a very easy and facile task to set out the pernicious evils of a compelled agreement in the practice of religion, and those not fancied only or feigned, but such as do follow it, have followed it, and will follow it in the world.

An inquiry in this invective, tending to evince its reasonableness, is offered in p. 158, — namely, "Where there are divided interests in religion in the same kingdom, it is asked, how shall the prince behave himself towards them?" The answer thereunto is not, I confess, easy, because it is not easy to be understood what is intended by "divided interests in religion." We will, therefore, lay that aside, and consider what really is amongst us, or may be, according to what we understand by these expressions. Suppose, then, that in the same profession of protestant religion, some different ways and observances in the outward worship of God should be allowed, and the persons concerned herein have no other, cannot be proved to have any other interest, with respect unto religion, but to "fear God and honour the king," it is a very easy thing to return an answer to this inquiry: for, not entering into the profound political speculation of our author about "balancing of parties, or siding with this or that party," where the differences themselves constitute no distinct parties, in reference to civil government and public tranquillity, let the prince openly avow, by the declaration of his judgment, his constant practice, his establishing of legal rights, disposing of public favours in places and preferments, that way of religion which himself owns and approves; and let him indulge and protect others of the same religion, for the substance of it, with what himself professeth, in the quiet and peaceable exercise of their consciences in the worship of God, keeping all dissenters within the bounds allotted to them, that none transgress them to the invasion of the rights of others; — and he may have both the reality and glory of religion, righteousness, justice, and all other royal virtues; which will render him like to Him whose vicegerent he is; and he will undoubtedly reap the blessed fruits of them in the industry, peaceableness, and loyalty of all his subjects whatever.

There are sundry things, in the close of this chapter, objected against such a course of procedure, but those such as are all of them resolved into a supposition that they who in any place or part of the world desire liberty of conscience for the worship of God have indeed no conscience at all; for it is thereon supposed, without farther evidence, that they will thence fall into all wicked and unconscientious practices. I shall make, as I said, no reply to such surmises. Christianity suffered under them for many ages; Protestancy hath done so in sundry places for many years; and those who now may do so must, as they did, bear the effects of them as well as they are able. Only I shall say, first, Whatever is of real inconvenience in this pretension, on the supposition of liberty of conscience, is no way removed by taking away all different practices, unless ye could also obliterate all different persuasions out of the minds of men; which, although in one place he tells us ought to be done by severe penalties, yet in another he acknowledgeth that the magistrate hath no cognizance of any such things, who yet alone is the inflicter of all penalties. Nay, where different apprehensions are, the absolute prohibition of different answerable practices doth a thousand times more dispose the minds of men to unquietness than where they are allowed both together, as hath been before declared. And he that can obliterate out of and take away all different apprehensions and persuasions about the worship of God from the minds and consciences of men, bringing them to centre in the same thoughts and judgments absolutely, in all particulars about them,

> "Dicendum est, Deus ille fuit, Deus, inclute Memmi!Qui
> princeps vitæ rationem invenit eam;" —
> [Lucret., v. 8,]

he is God, and not man.

Secondly, It is granted that the magistrate may and ought to restrain all principles and outward practices that have any natural tendency unto the disturbance of the peace; which being granted, and all obligations upon dissenting parties being alone put upon them by the supreme legislative and executive power of the kingdoms and nations of the world, public tranquillity is, and will be, as well secured on that respect as such things are capable of security in this world. All the longsome discourse, therefore, which here ensues, — wherein all the evils that have been in this nation are charged on liberty of conscience, from whence not one of them did proceed, seeing there was no such thing granted until, upon other civil and political accounts, the flood-gates were set open unto the following calamities and confusions, — is of no use, nor unto any purpose at all: for until it can be demonstratively proved that those who do actually suffer, and are freely willing so to do (as far as the foregoing otherwise lawful advantages, open unto them as well as others, may be so called), and resolved to undergo what may farther, to their detriment, yea, to their ruin, be inflicted on them, to preserve their consciences entire unto some commands of God, have no respect unto others of as great evidence and light to be his (as are those which concern their obedience unto magistrates, compared with those which they avow about the worship of God); and that private men, uninterested in, and incapable of, any pretence unto public authority of any sort, do always think themselves warranted to do such things as others have done, pleading right and authority for their warranty; and until it be made manifest, also, that they have any other or greater interest than to enjoy their particular conditions and estates in peace, and to exercise themselves in the worship of God according as they apprehend his mind to be, — these declamations are altogether vain, and, as to any solid worth, lighter than a feather.

And I could desire if these controversies must be farther debated, that our author would omit the pursuit of those things which are really ἔξω τοῦ πράγματος, and, according to the ancient custom, attend ἄνευ προοιμίων καὶ παθῶν, without rhetorical prefaces or unreasonable passions, unto the merit of the cause. To this purpose I suppose it might not be amiss for him to consider a few sheets of paper lately published under the title of "A Case Stated," etc, wherein he will find the main controversy reduced to its proper heads, and a modest provocation unto an answer to what is proposed about it.

— "Illum aspice contra
Qui vocat."

A SURVEY OF THE SIXTH CHAPTER

The word of God the sole rule of worship — The light of reason — Vocal revelation — Magistrate's power in regard to things without the church but about it — Testimonies from the ancient fathers as to the supreme authority of Scripture — Alleged instances from the Old Testament of the magistrate appointing religious rites — Parker's answers to certain objections considered — Doctrine of passive obedience refuted — Alleged right of the magistrate to punish his subjects if they will not comply with idolatry or superstition established by law — The true dignity and functions of the magistrate declared — Exhortation to toleration and charity.

THE sixth chapter in this discourse, — which is the last that at the present I shall call to any account, as being now utterly wearied with the frequent occurrence of the same things in various dresses, — is designed to the confutation of a principle which is termed the "foundation of all Puritanism," and that wherein "the mystery of it" consisteth. Now this is, "That nothing ought to be established in the worship of God but what is authorized by some precept or example in the word of God, which is the complete and adequate rule of worship." Be it so that this principle is by some allowed, yea, contended for, it will not be easy to affix a guilt upon them on the account of its being so; for lay aside prejudices, corrupt interests, and passions, and I am persuaded that at the first view, it will not seem to be foreign unto what is in a hundred places declared and taught in the Scripture. And certainly a man must be master of extraordinary projections who can foresee all the evil, confusion, and desolation in the world, which our author hath found out as inevitable consequences of its admittance. It hath, I confess, been formerly disputed with colourable arguments, pretences, and instances, on the one side and the other, and variously stated amongst learned men, by and on various distinctions, and with divers limitations. But the manner of our author is, that whatever is contrary to his apprehensions must presently overthrow all government and bring in all confusion into the world. Such huge weight hath he wonted himself to lay on the smallest different conceptions of the minds of men, where his own are not enthroned! Particularly, it is contended that there can be no peace in any churches or states whilst this principle is admitted; when it is easily demonstrable that without the admittance of it, as to its substance and principal end, all peace and agreement among churches are utterly impossible. The like also may be said of states; which, indeed, are not at all concerned in it, any farther than as it is a principal means of their peace and security where it is embraced, and that which would reduce rulers to a stability of mind in these things, after they have been tossed up and down with the various suggestions of men, striving every one to exalt their own imaginations. But seeing it is pretended and granted to be of so much importance, I shall, without much regard to the exclamations of this author, and the reproachful, contemptuous expressions, which, without stint or measure, he pours out upon the assertors of it, consider both what is the concern of his present adversaries in it and what is to be thought of the principle itself; so submitting the whole to the judgment of the candid reader. Only, I must add one thing to the position, without which it is not maintained by any of those with whom he hath to do, which may deliver him from combating the air in his next assault of it; and this is, That nothing ought to be established in the worship of God, as a part of that worship, or made constantly necessary in its observance, without the warranty before mentioned: for this is expressly contended for by them who maintain it, and who reject nothing upon the authority of it but what they can prove to be a pretended part of religious worship as such. And, as thus laid down, I shall give some farther account both of the principle itself and of the interest of the Nonconformists in it, because both it and they are together here reproached.

    What then, I say, is the true sense and importance of that which our author designs to oppose, according to the mind of them who assert it? How impotent his attempts against it are for its removal shall briefly be declared. In the meantime, I cannot but in the first place tell him, that if by any means this principle, truly stated, as to the expressions wherein it is before laid down, and the formal terms whereof it consisteth, should be shaken or rendered dubious, yet that the way will not be much the plainer or clearer for the introduction of his pretensions. There are yet other general maxims which Nonconformists adhere unto, and suppose not justly questionable, which they can firmly stand and build upon in the management of their plea, as to all differences between him and them; and because, it may be, he is unacquainted with them, I shall reckon over some of them, for his information. And they are these that follow:—

1. That whatever the Scripture hath indeed prescribed and appointed to be done and observed in the worship of God and the government of the church, that is indeed to be done and observed. This, they suppose, will not be opposed; at least, they do not yet know, notwithstanding any thing spoken or disputed in this discourse, any pretences on which it may honestly so be. It is also, as I think, secured, Matt. xxviii. 20.

2. That nothing in conjunction with, nothing as an addition or supplement unto, what is so appointed ought to be admitted, if it be contrary either to the general rules or particular preceptive instructions of the Scripture. And this also, I suppose, will be granted; and if it be not freely, some are ready by arguments to extort the confession of it from them that shall deny it.

3. That nothing ought to be joined with or added unto what in the Scripture is prescribed and appointed in these things without some cogent reason, making such conjunction or addition necessary. Of what necessity may accrue unto the observation of such things by their prescription, we do not now dispute, but at present only desire to see the necessity of their prescription; and this can be nothing but some defect, in substance or circumstance, matter or manner, kind or form, in the institutions mentioned in the Scripture, as to their proper ends. Now, when this is discovered, I will not, for my part, much dispute by whom the supplement is to be made. In the meantime, I do judge it reasonable that there be some previous reasons assigned unto any additional prescriptions in the worship of God unto what is revealed in the Scripture, rendering the matter of those prescriptions antecedently necessary and reasonable.

4. That if any thing or things in this kind shall be found necessary to be added and prescribed, then that and those alone be so which are most consonant unto the general rules of the Scripture given us for our guidance in the worship of God, and

the nature of those institutions themselves wherewith they are conjoined or whereunto they are added. And this also I suppose to be a reasonable request, and such as will be granted by all men who dare not advance their own wills and wisdom above or against the Will and wisdom of God.

Now, if, as was said, the general principle before mentioned should by any means be duly removed, or could be so, or if entangled or rendered dubious, yet, as far as I can learn, the Nonconformists will be very far from supposing the matters in contest between them and their adversaries to be concluded. But as they look upon their concernments to be absolutely secured in the principles now mentioned, all which they know to be true and hope to be unquestionable, so the truth is, there is by this author very small occasion administered unto any thoughts of quitting the former more general thesis as rightly stated; but rather, if his ability be a competent measure of the merit of his cause, there is a strong confirmation given unto it in the minds of considering men, from the impotency and successlessness of the attempt made upon it. And that this may appear to the indifferent reader's satisfaction, I shall so far divert in this place from the pursuit of my first design as to state the principle aright, and briefly to call the present opposition of it unto a new account.

The sum, in general, of what this author opposeth with so much clamour is, That *divine revelation is the sole rule of divine religious worship*; an assertion that, in its latitude of expression, hath been acknowledged in and by all nations and people. The very heathen admitted it of old, as shall be manifested, if need require, by instances sufficient; for though they framed many gods, in their foolish, darkened imaginations, yet they thought that every one of them would be worshipped according to his own mind, direction, and prescription. So did, and I think do, Christians generally believe. Only, some have a mind to pare this generally-avowed principle, to curb it, and order it so, by distinctions and restrictions, that it may serve their turn and consist with their interest; for an opposition unto it nakedly, directly, and expressly, few have had the confidence yet to make. And the Nonconformists need not go one step farther in the expression of their judgments and principles in this matter; for who shall compel them to take their adversaries' distinctions (which have been invented and used by the most learned of them) of "substantial and accidental, proper and reductive, primitive and accessary, direct and consequential, intrinsic and circumstantial worship," and the like, for the most part, unintelligible terms, in their application unto the state of the question? If men have a mind, let them oppose this thesis as laid down; if not, let them let it alone: and they who shall undertake the confirmation of it will no doubt carry it through the briers of those unscriptural distinctions. And that this author may be the better instructed in his future work, I shall give him a farther account of the terms of the assertion laid down.

Revelation is either ἐνδιάθετος or προφορικός, and containeth every discovery or declaration that God hath made of himself or of his mind and will unto men. Thus it is comprehensive of that concreated light which is in all men concerning him and his will; for although we say that this is natural, and is commonly contradistinguished from revelation properly so called, which, for perspicuity's sake, we call revelation supernatural, yet whereas it doth not so necessarily accompany human nature but that it may be separated from it, nor is it educed out of our natural faculties by their own native or primogenial virtue, but is or was distinctly implanted in them by God himself, I place it under the general head of revelation.

Hence, whatever is certainly from God, by the light of nature and instinct thereof declared so to be, is no less a certain rule of worship and obedience, so far forth as it is from him and concerneth those things, than any thing that comes from him by express vocal revelation. And this casts out of consideration a vain exception wherewith some men please themselves, as though the men of this opinion denied the admittance of what is from God, and by the light of nature discovered to be his mind and will. Let them once prove any thing in contest between them and their adversaries to be required, prescribed, exacted, or made necessary, by the light of nature, as the will of God revealed therein, and I will assure them that, as to my concern, there shall be an end to all difference about it. But yet, that I may add a little farther light into the sense of the Nonconformists in this matter, I say, —

1. That this inbred light of reason guides unto nothing at all in or about the worship of God, but what is more fully, clearly, and directly taught and declared in the Scripture. And this may easily be evinced, as from the untoward mixture of darkness and corruption that is befallen our primogenial, inbred princi-

ples of light and wisdom by the entrance of sin, so also from the end of the Scripture itself, which was to restore that knowledge of God and his mind which was lost by sin, and which might be as useful to man in his lapsed condition as the other was in his pure and uncorrupted estate. At present, therefore, I shall leave this assertion, in expectation of some instance, in matters great or small, to the contrary, before I suppose it be obnoxious to question or dispute.

2. As there can be no opposition nor contradiction between the light of nature and inspired vocal or scriptural revelation, because they are both from God, so if in any instance there should appear any such thing unto us, neither faith nor reason can rest in that which is pretended to be natural light, but must betake themselves for their resolution unto express revelation. And the reason hereof is evident, — because nothing is *natural light* but what is common to all men, and where it is denied, it is frustrated as to its ruling efficacy. Again; it is mixed, as we said before, and it is not every man's work to separate the chaff from the wheat, or what God hath implanted in the mind of man when he made him upright, and what is since soaked into the principles of his nature from his own inventions. But this case may possibly very rarely fall out, and so shall not much be insisted on.

3. Our inquiry in our present contest is solely about *instituted worship*, which we believe to depend on supernatural revelation. The light of nature can no way relieve or guide us in it or about it, because it refers universally to things above and beyond that light; but only with reference unto those moral, natural circumstances, which appertain unto those actings or actions of men whereby it is performed, which we willingly submit unto its guidance and direction.

Again, *vocal revelation* hath come under two considerations:— First, As it was occasional. Secondly, As it became stated.

First, As it was occasional. For a long time God was pleased to guide his church in many concerns of his worship by fresh occasional revelations, even from the giving of the first promise unto Adam unto the solemn giving of the law by Moses; for although men had, in process of time, many *stated revelations*, that were preserved by tradition among them, as the first promise, the institution of sacrifices, and the like, yet as to sundry emergencies of his worship, and parts of it, God guided them by new occasional revelations. Now, those revelations being not recorded in the Scripture, as being only for present or emergent use, we have no way to know them but by what those to whom God was pleased so to reveal himself did practice, and which, on good testimony, found acceptance with him. Whatever they so did, they had especial warranty from God for; which is the case of the great institution of sacrifices itself, It is a sufficient argument that they were divinely instituted, because they were graciously accepted.

Secondly, Vocal revelation, as the rule of worship, became stated and invariable in and by the giving and writing of the law. From thence, with the allowances before mentioned, we confine it to the Scripture, and so unto all succeeding generations. I confess, many of our company, who have kept to us hitherto in granting divine revelation to be the sole principle and rule of religious worship, now leave us, and betake themselves to paths of their own. The postmisnical[9] Jews, after many attempts made that way by their predecessors, both before and after the conversation of our Lord Christ in the flesh, at length took up a resolution that all obligatory divine revelation was not contained in the Scripture, but was partly preserved by *oral tradition*; for although they added a multitude of observances unto what were prescribed unto their fathers by Moses, yet they would never plainly forego that principle, nor do to this day, that *divine revelation is the rule of divine worship*. Wherefore, to secure their principle and practice, and to reconcile them together (which are indeed at an unspeakable variance), they have fancied their oral law, which they assert to be of no less certain and divine original than the law that is written. On this pretence they plead that they keep themselves unto the forementioned principle, under the superstition of a multitude of self-invented observances. The Papists also here leave us, but still with a semblance of adhering to that principle, which carries so great and uncontrollable an evidence with it as that there are a very few, as was said, who have hitherto risen up in a direct and open opposition unto it; for whereas they have advanced a double

---

9   The reference is to the Mishna, or the collection of oral traditions, which profess to be a comment on the laws of Moses. The collection of them is ascribed to Rabbi Jehudah Hakkadosh, A.D. 190, or 220. — ED.

principle for the rule of religious worship besides the Scripture, — namely, tradition, and the present determinations of their church, from thence educed, — they assert the first to be divine or apostolical, which is all one, and the latter to be accompanied with infallibility, which is the formal reason of our adherence and submission unto divine revelation: so that they still adhere in general unto the forementioned principle, however they have debauched it by their advancement of those other guides. But herein also we must do them right, that they do not absolutely turn loose those two rude creatures of their own, traditions and present church determinations, upon the whole face of religion, to act therein at their pleasure, but they secure them from whatever is determined in the written word, affirming them to take place only in those things that are not contrary to the word or not condemned in it; for in such, they confess, they ought not nor can take place, — which I doubt whether our author will allow of or no in reference to the power by him asserted.

By "religious worship," in the thesis above, we understand, as was said before, *instituted worship only*, and not that which is purely moral and natural; which, in many instances of it, hath a great coincidence with the light of nature, as was before discoursed.

We understand also *the solemn or stated worship* of the church of God. That worship, I say, which is solemn and stated for the church, the whole church, at all times and seasons, according to the rules of his appointment, is that which we inquire after. Hence, in this matter we have no concernment in the fact of this or that particular person which might be occasionally influenced by necessity, as David's eating of the shew-bread was, and which how far it may excuse or justify the persons that act thereon, or regulate their actions directly, I know not, nor am any way engaged to inquire.

This is the state of our question in hand, the mind of the assertion, which is here so hideously disguised and represented in its pretended consequences. Neither do I think there is any thing needful farther to be added unto it; but yet, for the clearing of it from mistakes, something may be discoursed which relates unto it. We say, then, —

First, That there are sundry things to be used in, about, and with those actions whereby the worship of God is performed, which yet are not sacred, nor do belong unto the worship of

God as such, though that worship cannot be performed without them. The very breath that men breathe and the light whereby they see are necessary to them in the worship of God, and yet are not made sacred or religious thereby. Constantine said of old that he was "a bishop, but without the church;" not a sacred officer, but one that took care and had a supervisorship of things necessarily belonging to the performance of God's worship, yet no parts or adjuncts of it as such, for it was all still *without*. Now, all those things in or about the worship of God that belonged unto Constantine's episcopacy, — that is, the ordering and disposal of things *without* the church but *about* it, *without* worship but *about* it, — we acknowledge to be left unto common prudence, guided by the general rules of Scripture, by which the church is to walk and compose its actings. And this wholly supersedes the discourse of our author concerning the great variety of circumstances wherewith all human actions are attended; for, in one word, all such circumstances as necessarily attend human actions, as such, neither are sacred nor can be made so without an express institution of God, and are disposable by human authority: so that the long contest of our author on that head is altogether vain. So, then, —

Secondly, By "all the concernments of religious worship," which any affirm that they must be directed in by divine revelation or regulated by the Scripture, they intend all that is religious, or whatever belongs to the worship of God, as it is divine worship; and not what belongs unto the actions wherein and whereby it is performed, as they are actions.

Thirdly, That when any part of worship is instituted in special, and general rules are given for the practice of it, "hic et nunc," there the warranty is sufficient for its practice at its due seasons; and for those seasons, the nature of the thing itself, with what it hath respect unto, and the light of the general Scripture rules, will give them an acceptable determination.

And these few observations will abundantly manifest the impertinency of those who think it incumbent on any, by virtue of the principle before laid down, to produce express warranty in words of Scripture for every *circumstance* that doth attend and belong unto the actions whereby the worship of God is performed, which as they require not, so no such thing is included in the principle as duly stated. For particular circumstances that have respect to good order, decency, and external regulation of divine worship, they are all of them either circumstances of the actions themselves whereby divine worship is performed and exercised, and so in general they are natural and necessary, which in particular, or "actu exercito," depend on moral prudence; or religious rites themselves, added in and to the whole, or any parts of divine service, — which alone, in this question, come under inquiry.

I know there are usually sundry exceptions put in to this thesis, as before stated and asserted, and instances to the contrary are pretended, some whereof are touched upon by our author, p. 181, which are not now particularly and at large to be considered. But yet, because I am, beyond expectation, engaged in the explication of this principle, I shall set it so far forth right and straight unto farther examination as to give in such general observations as, being consistent with it and explanatory of it, will serve to obviate the most of the exceptions that are laid against it; as, —

1. Wherever in the Scripture we meet with any religious duty that had a preceding institution, although we find not expressly a consequent approbation, we take it for granted that it was approved; and so, on the contrary, where an approbation appears, an institution is concealed.

2. The question being only about religious duties, or things pertaining to or required in or about the worship of God, no exception against the general thesis can take place but such as consists in things directly of that nature. Instances in and about things civil and belonging merely to human conversation, or things natural, as signs and memorials one of another, are in this matter of no consideration.

3. Things extraordinary in their performance, and which, for aught we know, may have been so in their warranty or rule, have no place in our debate: for we are inquiring only after such things as may warrant a suitable practice in us without any farther authority, which is the end for which instances against this principle are produced; this actions extraordinary will not do.

4. Singular and occasional actions, which may be variously influenced and regulated by present circumstances, are no rule to guide the ordinary stated worship of the church. David's eating of the shew-bread, wherein he was justified because of his hunger and necessity, was not to be drawn into example of giv-

ing the shew-bread promiscuously to the people. And sundry instances to the same purpose are given by our Saviour himself.

5. There is nothing of any dangerous or bad consequence in this whole controversy, but what lies in the imposition on men's practices of the observation of uncommanded rites, making them necessary unto them in their observation. The things themselves are said in their own nature, antecedent to their injunction for practice, to be indifferent, and indifferent as unto practice. What hurt would it be to leave them so? They cannot, say some, be omitted, for such and such reasons. Are there, then, reasons for their observation besides their injunction, and such as on the account whereof they are enjoined? Then are they indeed necessary in some degree before their injunction; for all reason for them must be taken from themselves. And things wholly indifferent have nothing in themselves, one more than another, why one should be taken and another left; for if one have the advantage of another in the reasons for its practice, it is no more indifferent, at least it is not comparatively so. Granting, therefore, things enjoined to be, antecedently to their injunction, equally indifferent in their own nature with all other things of the same or the like kind, which yet are rejected or not enjoined, and then to give reasons taken from themselves, — their decency, their conducingness to edification, their tendency to the increase of devotion, their significancy of this or that, — is to speak daggers and contradictions, and to say, "A thing is indifferent before the injunction of its practice; but yet if we had thought so, we would never have enjoined it, seeing we do so upon reasons." And, without doubt, this making necessary the practice of things in the worship of God, proclaimed to be indifferent in themselves, and no way called for by any antecedent reason, is an act of power.

6. Where things are instituted of God, and he himself makes an alteration in or of his own institutions, those institutions may be lawfully practised and observed until the mind of God for their alteration and abolition be sufficiently revealed, proposed, and confirmed unto them that are concerned in them; for as the making of a law doth not oblige until and without the promulgation of it, so as that any should offend in not yielding obedience unto it, so upon the abrogation of a law, obedience may be conscientiously and without sin yielded unto that law, until the abrogation, by what act soever it was made, be notified and

confirmed. An instance hereof we have in the observation of Mosaical rites, in the forbearance of God, after the law of their institution was enervated and the obligation of it unto obedience really dissolved, at least the foundation of it laid, for the actual dissolution of it depended on the declaration of the fact wherein it was founded.

7. There may be a coincidence of things performed by sundry persons at the same time and in the same place, whereof some may have respect unto religious worship directly, and so belong unto it, and others only occasionally, and so not at all belong thereunto; as if, when the Athenians had been worshipping at their altars, St Paul had come, and reading the inscription of one of them, and thence taking occasion and advantage to preach "the unknown God" unto them, their act was a part of religious veneration, his presence and observation of them, and laying hold of that occasion for his purpose, was not so.

8. Many things which are mere natural circumstances, requisite unto the performance of all actions whatever in communities, and so to be ordered by prudence according unto general rules of the word of God, may seem to be adjuncts of worship, unless they are followed to their original, which will discover them to be of another nature.

9. Civil usages and customs observed in a religious manner, — as they are all to be by them that believe, and directed by them unto moral ends, — may have a show and appearance of religious worship, and so, according to the principle before stated, require express institution; but although they belong unto our living unto God in general, as do all things that we do, seeing "whether we eat or drink, we are to do all to the glory of God," and therefore are to be done in faith, yet they are, or may be, no part of instituted worship, but such actions of life as in our whole course we are to regulate by the rules of the Scripture, so far as they afford us guidance therein.

10. Many observances in and about the worship of God are recorded in the Scripture without especially reflecting any blame or crime on them by whom they were performed (as many great sins are historically only related, and left to be judged by the rule of the word in other places, without the least remark of displeasure on the persons guilty of them), and that by such whose persons were accepted of God; yea, it may be in that very service wherein, less or more, they failed in their ob-

servation, God being merciful to them, though not in all things prepared according to the preparation of the sanctuary; and yet the things themselves not to be approved or justified, but condemned of God. Such was the fact of Judas Maccabæus in his offering sacrifices for the sin of them that were dead; and that of instituting an anniversary feast in commemoration of the dedication of the altar.

This little search have I made into this "great mystery," as it is called, "of Puritanism," after which so mighty an outcry is raised by this author; and if it might be here farther pursued, it would, as stated by us in these general rules and explications, be fully manifested to be a principle in general admitted, until of late, by all sorts of men, some few only having been forced sometimes to corrupt it for the security of some especial interest of their own. And it were an easy thing to confirm this assertion by the testimonies of the most learned protestant writers that have served the church in the last ages. But I know how with many amongst us they are regarded, and that the citation of some of the most reverend names among them is not unlikely to prejudice and disadvantage the cause wherein their witness is produced. I shall not, therefore, expose them to the contempt of those, now they are dead, who would have been unwilling to have entered the lists with them in any kind of learning when they were alive. There is, in my apprehension, the substance of this assertion still retained among the Papists, Bellarmine himself lays it down as the foundation of all his controversies, and endeavours to prove: "Propheticos et apostolicos libros verum esse verbum Dei, et certam et stabilem regulam fidei," De Verbo Dei, lib. i. cap. 1; — "That the prophetical and apostolical books are the true word of God, a certain and stable rule of faith." [This] will go a great way in this matter; for all our obedience in the worship of God is the obedience of faith. And if the Scripture be the rule of faith, our faith is not, in any of its concerns, to be extended beyond it, no more than the thing regulated is to be beyond the rule.

Neither is this opinion of so late a date as our author and others would persuade their credulous followers. The full sense of it was spoken out roundly of old. So speaks the great Constantine (that an emperor may lead the way) in his oration to the renowned fathers assembled at Nice: Εὐαγγελικαὶ βιβλοι καὶ ἀποστολικαὶ, καὶ τῶν παλαιῶν προφητῶν θεσπίσματα σαφῶς ἡμᾶς ἃ χρὴ περὶ τοῦ θείου φρονεῖν ἐκπαιδεύουσι· τὴν πολεμοποιὸν οὖν ἀπελάσαντες ἔριν, ἐκ τῶν θεοπνεύστων λόγων λάβωμεν τῶν ζητουμένων τὴν λύσιν· — that is, "The evangelical and apostolical books and the oracles of the ancient prophets do plainly instruct us what we are to think of divine things. Laying aside, therefore, all hostile discord, let us resolve the things brought into question by the testimonies of the writings given by divine inspiration." We have here the full substance of what is pleaded for; and might the advice of this noble emperor be admitted, we should have a readier way to expedite all our present differences than as yet seems to be provided for us. The great Basil speaks yet more expressly than Constantine the Great, Lib. de Confes. Fid.: Φανερὰ ἔκπτωσις, καὶ ὑπερηφανίας κατηγορία, ἢ ἀθετεῖν τι τῶν γεγραμμένων, ἢ ἐπεισάγειν τῶν μὴ γεγραμμένων· — that is, "It hath the manifest guilt of infidelity and pride, to reject any thing that is written, or to add or introduce any thing that is not written;" which is the sum of all that in this matter is contended for. To the same purpose he discourseth, Epist. lxxx. ad Eustath.; where, moreover, he rejects all pretences of customs and usages of any sorts of men, and will have all differences to be brought for their determination to the Scripture. Chrysostom, in his Homily on Psalm xcv., speaks the same sense. Saith he, Καὶ τίς ὁ ταῦτα ἐγγυώμενος; Παῦλος. Οὐδὲν γὰρ δεῖ λέγειν ἀμάρτυρον, οὐδὲ ἀπὸ λογισμῶν μόνον· ἐάν τι γὰρ ἄγραφον λέγηται, ἡ διάνοια τῶν ἀκροατῶν σκάζει, πῇ μὲν ἐπινεύουσα, πῇ δὲ παραγραφομένη, καὶ ποτὲ μὲν τὸν λόγον ὡς ἕωλον ἀποστρεφομένη, ποτὲ δὲ ὡς πιθανὸν παραδεχομένη. Ὅταν δὲ ἔγγραφος ἡ μαρτυρία τῆς θείας φωνῆς προέλθῃ, καὶ τοῦ λέγοντος τὸν λόγον, καὶ τοῦ ἀκούοντος τὴν διάνοιαν ἐβεβαίωσε· — "Who is it that promiseth these things? Paul. For we are not to say any thing without testimony, nor upon our mere reasoning; for if any thing be spoken without Scripture (testimony), the mind of the hearers fluctuates, now assenting, anon hesitating, sometimes rejecting what is spoken as frivolous, sometimes receiving it as probable. But where the testimony of the divine voice comes forth from the Scripture, it confirmeth the word of the speaker and the mind of the hearer." It is even so. Whilst things relating to religion and the worship of God are debated and disputed by the reasonings of men, or on any other principles besides the express authority of the Scriptures, no certainty or full persuasion of mind can be atoned about them. Men under such actings are as Lucian in his Menippus says he was between the disputations of the philosophers; sometimes he nodded one way, sometimes another, and seemed to give his assent backwards and forwards to express contradictions. It is in the testimony of the Scripture alone about the things of God that the consciences of those that fear him can acquiesce and find satisfaction. The same author, as in many other places, so in his 13th Homily on the Second Epistle to the Corinthians, expressly sends us to the Scripture to inquire after all things, as that which is the exact canon, balance, and rule of religion: Παρὰ τῶν γραφῶν ταῦτα πάντα πυνθάνεσθε. Among the Latins, Tertullian is express to the same purpose. In his book against Hermogenes, "Adoro," said he, "plenitudinem Scripturarum quæ mihi factorem manifestat et facta." Again, "Scriptum esse hoc doceat Hermogenis officina, aut timeat iræ illud adjicientibus aut detrahentibus destinatum;" — "I adore the fulness of the Scripture;" and, "Let Hermogenes prove what he saith to be written, or fear the woe denounced against them who add to or take from the word." And again, in his book, De Carne Christi, "Non recipio quod extra Scripturam de tuo infers;" — "I do not receive what you bring of your own without Scripture." So also in his book, De Præscriptionibus, "Nobis nihil ex nostro arbitrio indulgere licet; sed nec eligere quod aliquis de arbitrio suo induxerit. Apostolos Domini habemus authores, qui nec ipsi quicquam ex suo arbitrio quod inducerent elegerunt; sed acceptam a Christo disciplinam, fideliter nationibus assignaverunt;" — "It is not lawful for us" (in these things) "to indulge unto our own choice, nor to choose what any one brings in of his choosing. We have the apostles of our Lord for our example, who brought in nothing of their own minds or choice; but having received the discipline" (of Christian religion) "from Christ, they faithfully communicated it to the nations." Jerome is plain to the same purpose in sundry places. So Comment. in xxiii. Matthew, "Quod de Scripturis authoritatem non habet, eadem facilitate contemnitur qua probatur;" — "That which hath not authority from the Scripture is as easily despised as asserted." Comm. in Hagg., cap. i., "Sed et alia quæ, absque authoritate et testimoniis Scripturarum, quasi traditione apostolica sponte reperiunt atque confingunt, percutit gladius Dei;" — "But those other things which, without authority or testimony of the Scriptures, they find out or feign of their own accord, as of apostolical tradition, the sword of God smites through." It were easy to produce twenty other testimonies out of the ancient writers of the church, giving sufficient countenance to the assertion contended about. What account our author gives of this principle is now, very briefly, to be considered.

First, therefore, pp. 174, 175, he reviles it as "a pretence wild and humorsome, which men must be absurd if they believe, or impudent if they do not, seeing it hath not the least shadow or foundation either from Scripture or reason;" though it be expressly asserted, either in its own terms, or confirmed by direct deductions, in and from above forty places of Scripture. And so much for that part of the assault.

The next chargeth it with infinite follies and mischiefs in those which allow it, and it is said that "there can never be an end of alterations and disturbances in the church whilst it is maintained;" the contrary whereof is true, confirmed by experience and evidence of the thing itself. The admittance of it would put an end to all disturbances; for let any man judge whether, if there be matters in difference, as in all these things there are and ever were, the bringing them to an issue and settled stability be not likelier to be effected by all men's consenting unto one common rule, whereby they may be tried and examined, than that every party should be left at liberty to indulge to their own affections and imaginations about them. And yet we are told, p. 178, "that all the pious villanies that ever have disturbed the Christian world have sheltered themselves in this grand maxim, that Jesus Christ is the only lawmaker to his church." I confess I could heartily desire that such expressions might be forborne; for let what pretence men please be given to them and colour put upon them, they are full of scandal to Christian religion. The maxim itself here traduced is as true as any part of the gospel; and it cannot be pretended that it is not the maxim itself, but the abuse of it (as all the principles of the gospel, through the blindness and lusts of men, have been abused), that is reflected on, seeing the design of the whole discourse is to evert the maxim itself. Now, whatever apprehensions our author may have of his own abilities, I am satisfied that they are no way competent to disprove this principle of the gospel, as will be evident on the first attempt he shall make to that purpose; let him begin the trial as soon as he pleaseth.

In the third section we have a heap of instances raked together to confront the principle in its proper sense before declared and vindicated, in no one whereof it is at all concerned; for the reasons of things in matters civil and religious are not the same. All political government in the world consists in the exercise of principles of natural right, and their just application to times, ages, people, occasions, and occurrences. Whilst this is done, government is acted regularly to its proper end; where this is missed, it fails. These things God hath left unto the prudence of men and their consent; wherein they cannot for the most part fail, unless they are absolutely given up unto unbridled lusts; and the things whereto they may fail are always convenient or inconvenient, good and useful or hurtful and destructive; not always, yea, very seldom, directly and in themselves morally good or evil. In such things men's ease and profit, not their consciences, are concerned. In the worship of God things are quite otherwise. It is not convenience or inconvenience, advantage or disadvantage, as to the things of this life, but merely good or evil, in reference to the pleasing of God and to eternity, that is in question. Particular applications to the manners, customs, usages of places, times, countries, — which is the proper field of human authority, liberty, and prudence in civil things (because their due, useful, and regular administration depends upon them), — have here no place: for the things of the worship of God, being spiritual, are capable of no variations from temporal, earthly varieties among men; have no respect to climates, customs, forms of civil government, or any thing of that nature; but, considering men quite under other notions, namely, of sinners and believers, with respect utterly unto other ends, namely, their living spiritually unto God here, and the eternal enjoyment of him hereafter, are not subject to such prudential accommodations or applications. The worship of God is, or ought to be, the same at all times, in all places, and amongst all people, in all nations; and the order of it is fixed and determined in all particulars that belong unto it. And let not men pretend the contrary: until they can give an instance of any such defect in the institutions of Christ as that the worship of God cannot be carried on, nor his church ruled and edified, without an addition of something of their own for the supply thereof, which therefore should and would be necessary to that end antecedent unto its addition; and when they have so done, I will subscribe unto whatsoever they shall be pleased to add of that, or indeed any other kind. "Customs of churches," and "rules of decency," which our author here casts under the magistrate's power, are ambiguous terms, and in no sense express the hypothesis he hath undertaken the defence of. In the proper signification of the words, the things intended may fall under those natural circumstances wherein religious actions in the worship of the church may have their concern, as they are actions, and are disposable by human authority; but he will not, I presume, so soon desert his fundamental principle, of the magistrate's appointing things in and parts of religious worship, nowhere described or determined in the word of God, which alone we have undertaken to oppose. The instances he also gives us about actions in their own nature and use indifferent, as going to law or taking physic, are not in the least to his purpose. And yet if I should say that none of these actions are indeed indifferent in "actu exercito," as they speak, and in their individual performance, but have a moral good or evil, as an inseparable adjunct, attending them, arising out of respect to some rule, general or particular, of divine revelation, I know he cannot disprove it; and much more is not pleaded concerning religious worship.

But this principle is farther charged with "mischief equal to its folly;" which is proved by instances in sundry uninstituted observances, both in the Jewish and primitive Christian churches, as also in protestant churches abroad. I answer, that if this author will consent to umpire these differences by either the Old or New Testament, or by any protestant church in the world, we shall be nearer an end of them than, as far as I can see, yet otherwise we are. If he will not be bound neither to the example of the church of the Jews, nor of the churches of the New Testament, nor of the present protestant churches, it must be confessed that their names are here made use of only for a pretence and an advantage. Under the Old Testament we find that all that God required of his church was, that they should "remember the law of Moses his servant, which he commanded unto him in Horeb for all Israel, with the statutes and judgments," Mal. iv. 4. And when God had given out his institutions and the whole order of his worship, it being fixed in the church accordingly, it is added eight or ten times in one chapter that this was done: "As the LORD commanded Moses, so did he,"

Exod. xl.. After this God gives them many strict prohibitions from adding any thing to what he had so commanded: as Deut. iv. 2, xii. 32; Prov. xxx. 6. And as he had in the decalogue rejected any worship not of his own appointment, as such, Exod. xx. 4, 5, so he made it afterward the rule of his acceptation of that people and what they did, or his refusal of them and it, whether it was by him commanded or no. So, in particular, he expressly rejects that which was so added as to days, and times, and places, though of the nearest affinity and cognation to what was appointed by himself, because it was invented by man, yea, by a king, 1 Kings xii. 33. And when, in process of time, many things of an uncertain original were crept into the observance of the church, and had firmed themselves with the notion of "traditions," they were all at once rejected in that word of the blessed Holy One, "In vain do ye worship me, teaching for doctrines" (that is, what is in my worship to be observed) "the traditions of men." For the churches of the New Testament, the foundation of them is laid in that command of our Saviour, Matt. xxviii. 19, 20, "Go ye therefore, and teach all nations, baptizing them in the name of the Father, and of the Son, and of the Holy Ghost: teaching them to observe all things whatsoever I have commanded you: and, lo, I am with you alway, even unto the end of the world." That they should be taught to do or observe any thing but what he commanded, — that his presence should accompany them in the teaching or observation of any superadditions of their own, — we nowhere find written, intimated, or exemplified by any practice of theirs. Nor, however, in that juncture of time, the like whereunto did never occur before, nor ever shall do again, during the expiration and taking down of Mosaical institutions, before they became absolutely unlawful to be observed, the apostles, according to the liberty given them by our Lord Jesus Christ and direction of the Holy Ghost, did practice some things compliant with both church-states, did they, in any one instance, impose any thing on the practice of the churches in the worship of God, to be necessarily and for a continuance observed among them, but what they had express warrant, and authority, and command of our Lord Christ for. Counsel they gave in particular cases, that depended upon present emergencies; directions for the regular and due observation of institutions, and the application of general rules in particular practice; they also taught a due and sanctified use of civil customs, and the proper use of moral or natural symbols: but to impose any *religious* rites on the constant practice of the church in the worship of God, making them necessary to be always observed by that imposition, they did not once attempt to do, or assume power for it to themselves. Yea, when, upon an important difficulty, and to prevent a ruining scandal, they were enforced to declare their judgment to the churches in some points, wherein they were to abridge the practice of their Christian liberty for a season, they would do it only in things made "necessary" by the state of things then among the churches (in reference to the great end of edification, whereby all practices are to be regulated), before the declaration of their judgment for the restriction mentioned, Acts xv. 23–29. So remote were they from assuming unto themselves a dominion over the religion, consciences, or faith of the disciples of Christ, or requiring any thing, in the constant worship of the church, but what was according to the will, appointment, and command of their Lord and Master. Little countenance, therefore, is our author like to obtain unto his sentiments from the Scriptures of the Old and New Testament, or the example either of the Jews or Christians mentioned in them.

The instances he gives from the church of the Jews, or that may be given, are either civil observances, as the feast of purim; or moral conveniencies directed by general rules, as the building of synagogues; or customary signs suited to the nature of things, as wearing of sackcloth; or such as have no proof of their being approved, as the feast of dedication, and some monthly fasts taken up in the captivity; — from none of which any objection can be taken against the position before laid down. Those from the church of the New Testament had either a perpetual binding institution from the authority of Christ, as the Lord's-day Sabbath; or contain only a direction to use civil customs and observances in a holy and sanctified manner, as the love feasts and kiss of charity; or such as were never heard of in the New Testament at all, as the observation of Lent and Easter. He that out of these instances can draw a warranty for the power of the civil magistrate over religion and the consciences of men, to institute new duties in religion when he pleaseth, so these "do not countenance vice nor disgrace the Deity," which all his Christian subjects shall be bound in conscience to observe, or otherwise make good any of those particular conclusions, that therefore Christ is not the only lawgiver to his church, or that divine revelation is not the adequate rule of divine worship, or that men may add any thing to the worship of God, to be observed in it constantly and indispensably by the whole church, will manifest himself, to have an excellency in argumentation beyond what I have ever yet met withal.

A removal of the argument taken from the perfection of the Scripture, and its sufficiency to instruct us in the whole counsel and will of God, concerning his worship and our obedience unto him, is nextly attempted; but with no engines but what have been discovered to be insufficient to that purpose a hundred times. It is alleged, "That what the Scripture commands in the worship of God is to be observed, that what it forbids is to be avoided;" which if really acknowledged, and a concernment of the consciences of men be granted therein, is sufficiently destructive of the principal design of our author. But, moreover, I say that it commands and forbids things by general rules, as well as by particular precepts and inhibitions; and that if what is so commanded be observed, and what is so forbidden be avoided, there is a direct rule remaining in it for the whole worship of God.

But this is said here to be of "substantial duties, but not of external circumstances;" and if it be so even of substantial duties, it perfectly overthrows all that our author hath been pleading in the first three chapters of his discourse. For external circumstances, of what nature those are which are disposable by human authority and prudence hath been now often declared, and needs not here to be repeated.

The sum of his apprehensions in this matter, about the perfection and sufficiency of the Scripture in reference to the worship of God, our author gives us, p. 189: "Any thing," saith he, "is lawful" (that is, in the worship of God) "that is not made unlawful by some prohibition; for things become evil, not upon the score of their being not commanded, but upon that of their being forbidden. And what the Scripture forbids not, it allows; and what it allows is not unlawful; and what is not unlawful may lawfully be done." This tale, I confess, we have been told many and many a time, but it hath been as often answered that the whole of it, as to any thing of reasoning, is captious and sophistical.

Once more, therefore; what is commanded in the worship of God is lawful, yea, is our duty to observe. All particular instances of this sort that are to have actual place in the worship of God were easily enumerated, and so expressly commanded; and why, among sundry things that might equally belong thereunto, one should be commanded, and another left at liberty without any institution, no man can divine. Of particular things not to be observed there is not the same reason. It is morally impossible that all instances of men's inventions, all that they can find out to introduce into the worship of God, at any time, in any age, and please themselves therein, should be beforehand enumerated and prohibited in their particular instances. And if, because they are not so forbidden, they may lawfully be introduced into divine worship, and imposed upon the practice of men, ten thousand things may be made lawful and be so imposed. But the truth is, although a particular prohibition be needful to render a thing evil in itself, a general prohibition is enough to render any thing unlawful in the worship of God. So we grant that what is not forbidden is lawful, but withal say that every thing is forbidden that should be esteemed as any part of divine worship that is not commanded; and if it were not, yet for want of such a command or divine institution, it can have neither use nor efficacy with respect to the end of all religious worship.

Our author speaks with his wonted confidence in this matter; yea, it seems to rise to its highest pitch, as also doth his contempt of his adversaries or whatever is or may be offered by them in the justification of this principle. "Infinite certainty" on his own part, p. 193, "baffled and intolerable impertinencies, weak and puny arguments, cavils of a few hot-headed and brain-sick people," with other opprobrious expressions of the like nature, filling up a great part of his leaves, are what he can afford unto those whom he opposeth. But yet I am not, for all this bluster, well satisfied, much less "infinitely certain," that he doth in any competent measure understand aright the controversy about which he treats with all this wrath and confidence; for the sum of all that here he pleads is no more but this, that "the circumstances of actions in particular are various, and as they are not, so they cannot be, determined by the word of God, and therefore must be ordered by human prudence and authority:" which if he suppose that any man denies, I shall the less wonder at his severe reflections upon them, though I shall never judge them necessary or excusable in any case whatever. Page 198, he imposeth it on others that lie under the power of this persuasion, "that they are obliged in conscience to act contrary to whatever their superiors command them in the worship of God;" which farther sufficiently evidenceth that either he understands not the controversy under debate, or that he believes not himself in what he saith; which, because the harsher imputation, I shall avoid the owning of in the least surmise.

Section 6, from the concession that the "magistrate may take care that the laws of Christ be executed," — that is, command and require his subjects to observe the commands of Christ in that way and by such means as those commands, from the nature of the things themselves, and according to the rule of the gospel, may be commanded and required, — he infers that he hath himself power of making laws in religion! But why so? and how doth this follow? Why, saith he, "It is apparently implied, because whoever hath a power to see that laws be executed cannot be without a power to command their execution." Very good: but the conclusion should have been, "He cannot be without a power to make laws in the matter about which he looks to the execution;" which would be good doctrine for justices of the peace to follow. But what is here laid down is nothing but repeating of the same thing in words a little varied; as if it had been said, "He that hath power to see the laws executed, or a power to command their execution, he hath power to see the laws executed, or a power to command their execution;" which is very true. And this we acknowledge the magistrate hath, in the way before declared. But that, because he may do this, he may also make laws of his own in religion, it doth not at all follow from hence, whether it be true or no. But this is farther confirmed from "the nature of the laws of Christ, which have only declared the substance and morality of religious worship, and therefore must needs have left the ordering of its circumstances to the power and wisdom of lawful authority." "The laws of Christ" which are intended are those which he hath given concerning the worship of God. That these have "determined the morality of religious worship," I know not how he can well allow, who makes the law of nature to be the measure of morality and all moral religious worship. And for "the substance of religious worship," I wish it were well declared what is intended by it. For my part, I think that whatever is commanded by Christ, the observation of it is of the substance of religious worship; else, I am sure the sacraments are not so. Now, do but give men leave, as rational creatures, to observe those commands of Christ in such a way and manner as the nature of them requires them to be observed, as he hath himself in general rules prescribed, as the concurrent actions of many in society make necessary, and all this controversy will be at an end. When a duty, as to the kind of it, is commanded in particular, or instituted by Christ in the worship of God, he hath given general rules to guide us in the individual performance of it, as to the circumstances that the actions whereby it is performed will be attended withal. For the disposal of those circumstances according to those rules, prudence is to take place and to be used; for men, who are obliged to act as men in all other things, are not to be looked on as brutes in what is required of them in the worship of God.

But to institute mystical rites and fixed forms of sacred administrations, whereof nothing in the like kind doth necessarily attend the acting of instituted worship, is not to determine circumstances, but to ordain new parts of divine worship; and such injunctions are here confessed by our author, p. 191, to be "new and distinct commands by themselves," and to enjoin something that the Scripture nowhere commands: which when he produceth a warranty for, he will have made a great progress towards the determining of the present controversy.

Page 192, he answers an objection, consisting of two branches, as by him proposed, whereof the first is, "That it cannot stand with the love and wisdom of God not to take order himself for all things that immediately concern his own worship and kingdom." Now, though I doubt not at all but that God hath so done, yet I do not remember at present that I have read [of] any imposing the necessity hereof upon him in answer to his love and wisdom. I confess Valerianus Magnus, a famous writer of the church of Rome, tells us that never any one did so foolishly institute or order a commonwealth as Jesus Christ must be thought to have done, if he have not left one supreme judge to determine the faith and consciences of men in matters of religion and divine worship; and our author seems not to be remote from that kind of reasoning, who, without an assignment of a power to that purpose, contendeth that all things among men will run into confusion, — of so little concernment do the Scriptures and the authority of God in them to some seem to be. We do indeed thankfully acknowledge that God, out of his love and wisdom, hath ordered all things belonging to his worship and spiritual kingdom in the world; and we do suppose we need no other argument to evince this assertion but to challenge all men who are otherwise minded to give an instance of any defect in his institutions to that purpose. And this we are the more confirmed in, because those things which men think good to add unto them, they dare not contend that they are parts of his worship, or that they are added to supply any defect therein; neither did ever any man yet say that there is a defect in the divine institution of worship, which must be supplied by a minister's wearing a surplice. All, then, that is intended in this consideration, though not urged, as is here pretended, is, that God, in his goodness, love, and care towards his church, hath determined all things that are needful in or to his worship; and about what is not needful, men, if they please, may contend, but it will be to no great purpose.

The other part of the objection which he proposeth to himself is laid down by him in these words: "If Jesus Christ have not determined all particular rites and circumstances of religion, he hath discharged his office with less wisdom and fidelity than Moses, who ordered every thing appertaining to the worship of God, even as far as the pins or nails of the tabernacle." And hereunto in particular he returns in answer not one word, but only ranks it amongst idle and impertinent reasonings. And I dare say he wants not reasons for his silence; whether they be pertinent or no I know not: for setting aside the advantage that, it is possible, he aimed to make in the manner and terms of the proposal of this objection to his sentiments, it will appear that he hath not much to offer for its removal. We dispute not about the "rites and circumstances of religion, which are terms ambiguous, and, as hath been declared, may be variously interpreted, no more than we do about the "nails of the tabernacle," wherein there were none at all; but it is about the worship of God, and what is necessary thereunto. The ordering hereof, — that is, of the house of God and all things belonging thereunto, — was committed to Jesus Christ, "as a Son over his own house," Heb. iii. 1–6. In the discharge of his trust therein he was faithful, as was Moses, who received that testimony from God, that he was "faithful in all his house," upon his ordering all things in the worship of God as he commanded him, without adding any thing of his own thereunto, or leaving any thing uninstituted or undetermined which was to be of use therein. From the faithfulness of Christ, therefore, in and over the house of God, as it is compared with the faithfulness of Moses, it may be concluded, I think, that he ordered all things for the worship of God in the churches of the New Testament, as far as Moses did in and for the church of the Old, and more is not contended for; and it will be made appear that his commission in this matter was as extensive as that of Moses at the least, or he could not, in that trust and the discharge of it, have that preeminence above him which in this place is ascribed unto him.

Section 7, an account is given of the great variety of circumstances which do attend all human actions, whence it is impossible that they should be all determined by divine prescription. The same we say also; but add withal, that if men would leave these circumstances free, under the conduct of common prudence, in the instituted worship of God, as they are compelled so to do in the performance of moral duties, and as he himself hath left them free, it would be as convenient for the reasons and consciences of men as an attempt to the contrary. Thus, we have an instance given us by our author in *the moral duty of charity*, which is commanded us of God himself; but the *times, seasons, manner, objects, measures* of it are left free, to be determined by human prudence upon emergencies and occasions. It may be now inquired whether the magistrate, or any other, can determine those circumstances by a law? or whether they are not, as by God, so by all wise men, left free, under the conduct of their reason and conscience who are obliged to do the duty itself by the command of God? And why may not the same rule and order be observed with respect to the circumstances that attend the performance of the duties of instituted worship? Besides, there are general circumstances that are capable of a determination, — such are time and place as naturally considered, — without such adjuncts as might give them a moral consideration, or render them good or evil; these the magistrate may determine: but for particular circumstances attending individual actions, they will hardly be regulated by a standing law. But none of these things have the least interest in our debate. To add things necessarily to be observed in the worship of God, no way naturally related unto the actions wherewith prescribed worship is to be performed, and then to call them circumstances thereof, erects a notion of things which nothing but interest can digest and concoct.

His eighth section is unanswerable. It contains such a strenuous reviling of the Puritans, and contemptuous reproaches of their writings, with such encomiums of their adversaries, as there is no dealing with it; and so I leave it. And so likewise I do his ninth, wherein, as he saith, he "upbraids the men of his contest with their shameful overthrows, and dares them to look those enemies in the face that have so lamentably cowed them by so many absolute triumphs and victories:" which kind of juvenile exultations on feigned suppositions will, I suppose, in due time receive an alloy from his own more advised thoughts and considerations. The instance wherewith he countenanceth himself in his triumphant acclamations unto the victory of his party is the book of Mr Hooker, and its being unanswered; concerning which I shall only say, that as I wish the same moderation, ingenuity, and learning unto all that engage in the same cause with him in these days, so if this author will mind us of any one argument in his longsome discourse not already frequently answered, and that in print long ago, it shall have its due consideration. But this kind of discourse, it may be, on second thoughts, will be esteemed not so comely. And I can mind him of those who boast as highly of some champions of their own against all Protestants, as he can do of any patron of those opinions which he contendeth for. But it doth not always fall out that those who have the most outward advantages and greatest leisure have the best cause and abilities to manage it.

The next sections treat concerning *superstition, will-worship,* and *Popery*; which, as he saith, having been charged by some on the church unduly, he retorts the crime of them upon the authors of that charge. I love not to strive, nor will I contend about words that may have various significations fixed on them. It is about things that we differ. That which is evil is so, however you call it, and whether you can give it any special name or no. That which is good will still be so, call it what and how men please. The giving of a bad or odious name to any thing doth not make itself to be bad or odious. The managing, therefore, of those appellations, either as to their charge or recharge, I am no way concerned in. When it is proved that men believe, teach, or practice otherwise than in duty to God they ought to do, then they do evil; and when they obey his mind and will in all things, then they do well, and in the end will have the praise thereof. In particular, I confess superstition, as the word is commonly used, denotes a vicious habit of mind with respect unto God and his worship, and so is not a proper denomination for the worship itself, or of any evil or crime in it; but yet, if it were worth contending about, I could easily manifest that, according to the use of the word by good authors, in all ages men have been charged with that crime from the kind and nature of the worship itself observed by them. And when St Paul charged the Athenians with an excess in superstition, it was from the multiplication of their gods, and thronging them together, right or wrong, in the dedication of their altars. But these things belong not at all to our present design. Let them who enjoin things unto an indispensable necessary observation in the worship of God, which are not by him prescribed therein, take care of their own minds that they be free from the vice of superstition, and they shall never be judged or charged by me therewith; though I must say that a multiplication of instances in this kind, as to their own observation, is the principal if not the only way whereby men who own the true and proper object of religious worship do or may manifest themselves to be influenced by that corrupt habit of mind, so that they may relate unto superstition as the effect to its cause. But the recrimination here insisted on, with respect unto them who refuse admittance unto or observance of things so enjoined, is such as ought to be expected from provocations and a desire of retortion. Such things usually taste of the cask, and are sufficiently weak and impertinent; for it is a mistake, that those charged do make, as it is here expressed, "any thing necessary not to be done," or put "any religion in the not doing of any thing," or the non-observance of any rites, orders, or ceremonies, any other than every one puts in his abstinence from what God forbids, which is a part of our moral obedience.

And the whole question in this matter is not, Whether, as it is here phrased, "God hath tied up his creatures to nice and pettish laws, laying a greater stress upon a doubtful or indifferent ceremony than upon the great duty of obedience?" but merely, Whether men are to observe in the worship of God what they apprehend he hath enjoined them, and to abstain from what he doth forbid, according to all the light that they have into his mind and will? which inquiry, as I suppose, may be [thus] satisfied, — that they are so to practice and so to abstain, without being liable to the charge of superstition. No man can answer for the minds of other men, nor know what depraved, vicious habits and inclinations they are subject unto. Outward actions are all that we are, in any case, allowed to pass judgment upon, and of men's minds as those actions are indications of them. Let men, therefore, observe and do in the worship of God whatever the Lord Christ hath commanded them, and abstain from what he hath forbidden, whether in particular instances or by general directive precepts and rules, — by which means alone many things are capable of falling under a prohibition, without the least thought of placing any worship of God in their abstinence from this or that thing in particular, — and I think they need not much concern themselves in the charge of superstition given in or out by any against them.

For what is discoursed, section 11, about will-worship, I cannot so far agree with our author as I could in what passed before about superstition; and that partly because I cannot discern him to be herein at any good agreement with himself: for "superstition," he tells us, "consists in the apprehensions of men, when their minds are possessed with weak and uncomely conceits of God," p. 201; here, that "will-worship consists in nothing else than in men's making their own fancies and inventions necessary parts of religion," which outward actings are not coincident with the inward frame and habit of mind before described. And I do heartily wish that some men could well free themselves from the charge of will-worship, as it is here described by our author, though cautelously expressed, to secure the concernments of his own interest from it; for although I will not call the things they contend to impose on others in the worship of God their "fancies," yet themselves acknowledge them to be their "inventions." And when they make them necessary to be observed in the whole worship of God, as public and stated, and forbid the celebration of that worship without them; when they declare their usefulness and spiritual or mystical significancy in that worship or service, designing to honour God in or by their use, setting up some of them to an exclusion of what Christ hath commanded, — if I cannot understand but that they make them necessary parts of God's worship, as to the actual observance of it, I hope they will not be angry with me, since I know the worst they can possibly with truth charge upon me in this matter is, that I am not so wise nor of so quick an understanding as themselves. Neither doth our author well remove his charge from those whose defence he hath undertaken; for he doth it only by this consideration, "that they do not make the things by them introduced in the worship of God to be parts of religion; they are not so," he saith, "nor are made so by them;" — for this hinders not but that they may be looked on as parts of divine worship, seeing we are taught by the same hand that "external worship is no part of religion at all." And let him abide by what he closeth this section withal, — namely, that they make not any additions to the worship of God, but only provide that what God hath required be performed in an orderly and decent manner, — and, as to my concern, there shall be an end of this part of our controversy.

The ensuing paragraphs about "Christian liberty, adding to the commands of God, and Popery," are of the same nature with those preceding about superstition and will-worship. There is nothing new in them but words, and they may be briefly passed through. For the charge of Popery, on the one side or other, I know nothing in it, but that when any thing is enjoined or imposed on men's practice in the worship of God, which is known to have been invented in and by the papal church during the time of its confessed apostasy, it must needs beget prejudices against it in the minds of them who consider the ways, means, and ends of the fatal defection of that church, and are jealous of a sinful compliance with it in any of those things. The recharge on those who are said "to set up a pope in every man's conscience, whilst they vest it with a power of countermanding the decrees of princes," — if no more be intended by "countermanding" but a refusal to observe their decrees and yield obedience to them in things against their consciences, which is all that can be pretended, — if it fall not on this author himself, as in some cases it doth, and which, by the certain conduct of right reason, must be extended to all wherein the consciences of men are affected with the authority of God, yet it doth on all Christians in the world that I know of, besides himself. [As] for "adding to the law of God," it is not charged on any that they add to his commands, as though they made their own divine, or part of his word and law; but only that they add in his worship to the things commanded by him: which being forbidden in the Scripture, when they can free themselves from it I shall rejoice, but as yet see not how they can so do. Nor are there any, that I know of, who "set up any prohibitions of their own," in or about the worship of God, or any thing thereunto pertaining, as is unduly and unrighteously pretended. There may be, indeed, some things enjoined by men which they do and must abstain from, as they would do from any other sin whatever; but their consciences are regulated by no prohibitions but those of God himself. And things are prohibited and made sinful unto them, not only when in particular, and by a specification of their instances, they are forbidden, but also when there lie general prohibitions against them on any account whatever. Some men, indeed, think that if a *particular prohibition* of any thing might be produced, they would acquiesce in it, whilst they plead an exemption of sundry things from being included in general prohibitions, although they have the direct formal reason attending them on which those prohibitions are founded: but it is to be feared that this also is but a pretence; for let any thing be particularly forbidden, yet if men's interest and superstition induce them to observe or retain it, they will find out distinctions to evade the prohibition and retain the practice. What can be more directly forbidden than the making or using of graven images in or about religious worship? and yet we know how little some men do acquiesce in that prohibition. And it was the observation of a learned prelate[10] of this nation, in his rejection of the distinctions whereby they endeavoured to countenance themselves in their idolatry, that the particular instances of things forbidden in the second commandment are not principally intended, but the general rule of not adding any thing in the worship of God without his institution. "Non imago," saith he, "non simulachrum prohibetur; sed non facies tibi." What way soever, therefore, any thing becomes a sin unto any, be it by a particular or general prohibition, be it from the scandal that may attend its practice, unto him it is a sin. And, it is a wild notion, that when any persons abstain from the practice of that in the worship of God which to them is sinful as so practised, they add prohibitions of their own to the commands of God.

The same is to be said concerning Christian liberty. No man, that I know of, makes "things indifferent to be sinful," as is pretended, nor can any man in his right wits do so; for none can

---

10   Dr Bilson. See page 407.

entertain contradictory notions of the same thing at the same time, as these are, that the same things are indifferent, that is, not sinful, and sinful. But this some say, that things in their own nature indifferent, that is, absolutely so, may be yet relatively unlawful, because, with respect unto that relation, forbidden of God. To set up an altar of old for a civil memorial in any place was a thing indifferent; but to set up an altar to offer sacrifices on, where the tabernacle was not, was a sin. It is indifferent for a man that understands that language to read the Scripture in Latin or in English; but to read it in Latin unto a congregation that understands it not, as a part of God's worship, would be sin. Nor doth our Christian liberty consist alone in our judgment of the indifferency of things in their own nature, made necessary to practice by commands, as hath been showed; and if it doth so, the Jews had that privilege as much as Christians. And they are easily offended who complain that their Christian liberty, in the practice of what they think meet in the worship of God, is intrenched on by such as, leaving them to their pleasure, because of their apprehension of the will of God to the contrary, cannot comply with them in their practice.

The close of this chapter is designed to the removal of an objection, pretended to be weighty and difficult, but indeed made so merely by the novel opinions advanced by this author; for, laying aside all respect unto some uncouth principles broached in this discourse, there is scarce a Christian child of ten years old but can resolve the difficulty pretended, and that according to the mind of God: for it is supposed that the magistrate may "establish a worship that is idolatrous and superstitious," and an inquiry is made thereon what the subject shall do in that case? Why, where lies the difficulty? "Why," saith he, "in this case they must be either rebels or idolaters. If they obey, they sin against God; if they disobey, they sin against their sovereign." According to the principles hitherto received in Christian religion, any one would reply and say, No: for it is certain that men must obey God, and not contract the guilt of such horrible sins as idolatry and superstition; but in so doing they are neither rebels against their ruler nor do sin against him. It is true, they must quietly and patiently submit to what they may suffer from him, but they are in so doing guilty of no rebellion or sin against him. Did ever any Christian yet so much as call it into question whether the primitive Christians were rebels, and sinned against their rulers, because they would not obey those edicts whereby they established idolatrous worship? or did any one ever think that they had a difficult case of conscience to resolve in that matter? They were, indeed, accused by the Pagans as rebels against the emperors; but no Christian ever yet thought their case to have been doubtful. But all this difficulty ariseth from the making of two Gods, where there ought to be but one; and this renders the case so perplexed, that, for my part, I cannot see directly how it is determined by our author. Sometimes he speaks as though it were the duty of subjects to comply with the establishment of idolatry supposed, as pp. 214, 215; for with respect, as I suppose, it is to the case as by him stated that he says, "Men must not withdraw their obedience;" and, "Better submit unto the unreasonable impositions of Nero or Caligula than to hazard the dissolution of the state." Sometimes he seems not to oblige them in conscience to practice according to the public prescription, but only pleads that the magistrate may punish them if they do not, and fain would have it thought that he may do so justly. But these things are certain unto us in this matter, and are so many κύριαι δόξαι in Christian religion:— That if the supreme magistrate command any thing in the worship of God that is idolatrous, we are not to practice it accordingly, because we must obey God rather than men. Nextly, That in our refusal of compliance with the magistrate's commands, we do neither rebel nor sin against him; for God hath not, doth not at any time, shut us up, in any condition, unto a necessity of sinning. Thirdly, That in case the magistrate shall think meet, through his own mistakes and misapprehensions, to punish, destroy, and burn them alive who shall not comply with his edicts, as did Nebuchadnezzar, or as they did in England in times of Popery, after all honest and lawful private ways of self-preservation used, which we are obliged unto, we are quietly and patiently to submit to the will of God in our sufferings, without opposing or resisting by force, or stirring up seditions or tumults, to the disturbance of public peace.

But our author hath elsewhere provided a full solution of this difficulty, chap. viii. p. 308, where he tells us, "That in cases and disputes of a public concern, private men are not properly 'sui juris;' they have no power over their actions; they are not to be directed by their own judgments, or determined by their own wills, but by the commands and determinations of the public conscience; and if there be any sin in the command, he that imposed it shall answer for it, and not I, whose duty it is to obey. The commands of authority will warrant my obedience; my obedience will hallow or at least excuse my action, and so secure me from sin, if not from error, because I follow the best guide and most probable direction I am capable of; and though I may mistake, my integrity shall preserve my innocence; and in all doubtful and disputable cases, it is better to err with authority than to be in the right against it." When he shall produce any one divine writer, any of the ancient fathers, any sober schoolmen or casuists, any learned modern divines, speaking at this rate, or giving countenance unto his direction given to men for the regulating of their moral actions, it shall be farther attended unto. I know some such thing is muttered amongst the pleaders for blind obedience upon vows voluntarily engaged into for that purpose. But as it is acknowledged by themselves that by those vows they deprive themselves of that right and liberty which naturally belong unto them, as unto all other men (wherein they place much of the merit of them); so by others those vows themselves, with all the pretended brutish obedience that proceeds from them, are sufficiently evidenced to be a horrible abomination, and such as make a ready way for the perpetration of all villanies in the world, — to which purpose that kind of obedience hath been principally made use of. But these things are extremely fond, and not only, as applied unto the worship of God, repugnant to the gospel, but also in themselves to the law of our creation, and that moral dependence on God which is indispensable unto all individuals of mankind. We are told in the gospel that "every man is to be fully persuaded in his own mind;" that "whatsoever is not of faith is sin;" that we are not to be (in such things) "the servants of men;" that other men's leading of us amiss, whoever they are, will not excuse us, "for if the blind lead the blind, both shall fall into the ditch," and he that followeth is as sure to perish as he that leadeth. The next guides of the souls and consciences of men are, doubtless, those who speak unto them in the name of God, or preachers of the gospel; yet are all the disciples of Christ frequently warned to "take heed" that they be not deceived by any under that pretence, but diligently examining what is proposed unto them, they discern in themselves what is good and evil. Nor doth the great apostle himself require us to be followers of him any farther than he was a follower of Christ. They will find small relief who, at the last day, shall charge their sins on the commands of others, whatever hope to the contrary they are put into by our author. Neither will it be any excuse that we have done according to the precepts of men, if we have done contrary to those of God. Ephraim of old was "broken in judgment, because he willingly walked after the commandment," Hos. v. 11. But would not his "obedience hallow, or at least excuse, his action?" and would not the "authority of the king warrant his obedience?" or must Ephraim now answer for the sin, and not he only that imposed the command? But it seems that when Jeroboam sinned, who at that time had this goodly creature of the "public conscience" in keeping, he made Israel sin also, who obeyed him. It is, moreover, a brave attempt, to assert that "private men," with respect to any of their moral actions, "are not properly 'sui juris,' have no power over their actions, are not to be directed by their own judgments or determined by their own wills." This is Circe's rod, one stroke whereof turned men into hogs. For to what propose serve their understandings, their judgments, their wills, if not to guide and determine them in their actions? I think he would find hard work that should go about to persuade men to put out their own eyes, or blind themselves, that they might see all by one public eye; and I am sure it is no less unreasonable to desire them to reject their own wills, understandings, and judgments, to be led and determined by a public conscience, considering especially that that public conscience itself is a mere "tragelaphus," which never had existence in "rerum natura."

Besides, suppose men should be willing to accept of this condition of renouncing their own understandings and judgments from being their guides as to their moral actions, I fear it will be found that indeed they are not able so to do. Men's understandings and their consciences are placed in them by him who made them, to rule in them and over their actions in his name, and with respect unto their dependence on him; and let men endeavour it whilst they please, they shall never be able utterly to cast off this yoke of God and destroy this order of things, which is by him inlaid in the principles of all rational beings. Men, whilst they are men, in things that have a moral good or evil in them or adhering to them, must be guided and determined by their own understandings whether they will or no; and if by any means they stifle the actings of them at present, they will not avoid that judgment which, according to them, shall pass upon them at the last day. But these things may elsewhere be farther pursued. In the meantime, the reader may take this case as it is determined by the learned prelate before mentioned, in his dialogue about subjection and obedience, against the Papists, whose words are as follow. Part iii. p. 297:— "*Philand.* If the prince establish any religion, whatever it be, you must by your oath obey it. *Theoph.* We must not rebel and take arms against the prince, but with reverence and humility serve God before the prince; and that is nothing against our oath. *Philand.* Then is not the prince supreme. *Theoph.* Why so? *Philand.* Yourselves are superior, when you serve whom you list. *Theoph.* As though to serve God according to his will were to serve whom we list, and not whom princes and all others ought to serve. *Philand.* But you will be judges when God is well served, and when not. *Theoph.* If you can excuse us before God when you mislead us, we will serve him as you shall appoint us; otherwise, if every man shall answer for himself, good reason he be master of his own conscience in that which toucheth him so near, and no man shall excuse him for. *Philand.* This is to make every man supreme judge of religion. *Theoph.* The poorest wretch that is may be supreme governor of his own heart; princes rule the public and external actions of their countries, but not the consciences of men." This in his days was the doctrine of the church of England; and, as was observed before, no person who then lived in it knew better what was so.

The sole inquiry remaining is, Whether the magistrate, having established such a religion as is idolatrous or superstitious, may justly and lawfully punish and destroy his subjects for their non-compliance therewithal? This is that which, if I understand him, our author would give countenance unto, contrary to the common sense of all Christians, yea, of common sense itself; for whereas he interweaves his discourse with suppositions that men may mistake in religion and abuse it, all such interpositions are purely sophistical, seeing the case proposed to resolution, which ought in the whole to be precisely attended unto, is about the refusal to observe and practise a religion idolatrous or superstitions. Of the like nature is that argument which alone he makes use of here and elsewhere to justify his principles, — namely, the necessity of government, and how much better the worst government is and the most depraved in its administration than anarchy or confusion; for as this by all mankind is unquestioned, so I do not think there is any one among them who can tell how to use this concession to our author's purpose. Doth it follow that because magistrates cannot justly or righteously prescribe an idolatrous religion, and compel their subjects to the profession and obedience of it, and because the subjects cannot nor ought to yield obedience therein, because of the antecedent and superior power of God over them, therefore anarchy or confusion must be preferred before such an administration of government? Let the magistrate command; what he will in religion, yet, whilst he attends unto the ends of all civil government, that government must needs be every way better than none, and is by private Christians to be borne with and submitted unto, until God in his providence shall provide relief. The primitive Christians lived some ages in the condition described, refusing to observe the religion required by law, and exercising themselves in the worship of God, which was strictly forbidden; and yet neither anarchy, nor confusion, nor any disturbance of public tranquillity did ensue thereon. So did the Protestants here in England in the days of Queen Mary, and some time before. The argument which he endeavours in these discourses to give an answer unto is only of this importance: If the supreme magistrate may command what religion he pleaseth, and enact the observation of it under destructive penalties, whereas the greatest part of magistrates in the world will and do prescribe such religions and ways of divine worship as are idolatrous or superstitious, which their subjects are indispensably bound in conscience not to comply withal, then is the magistrate justified in the punishing of men for their serving of God as they ought, and they may suffer as *evil-doers* in what they suffer as *Christians*. This, all the world over, will justify them that are uppermost and have power in their hands (on no other ground but because they are so and have so) in their oppressions and destructions of them that, being under them in civil respects, do dissent from them in things religious. Now, whether this be according to the mind of God or no is left unto the judgment of all indifferent men. We have, I confess, I know not how many expressions interposed in this discourse, as was observed, about "sedition, troubling of public peace, men being turbulent against prescribed rules of worship," whereof if he pretend that every peaceable dissenter and dissent from what is publicly established in religious worship are guilty, he is a pleasant man in a disputation; and if he do any thing, he determines his case proposed on the part of compliance with idolatrous and superstitious worship. If he do not so, the mention of them in this place is very importune and unseasonable. All men acknowledge that such miscarriages and practices may be justly coerced and punished; but what is this to a bare refusal to comply in any idolatrous worship, and a peaceable practice of what God doth require, as that which he will accept and own?

But our author proceeds to find out many pretences on the account whereof persons whom he acknowledgeth to be innocent and guiltless may be punished; and though their "apprehensions in religion be not," as he saith, "so much their crime as their infelicity, yet there is no remedy, but it must expose them to the public rods and axes," p. 219. I have heard of some wise and righteous princes, who have affirmed that they had rather let twenty guilty persons go free than punish or destroy one that was innocent. This seems to render them more like Him whose vicegerents they are than to seek out colourable reasons for the punishment of them whom they know to be innocent; which course is here suggested unto them. Such advice might be welcome to him whom men called $\pi\eta\lambda\grave{o}\nu$ $\alpha\ddot{\iota}\mu\alpha\tau\iota$ $\pi\epsilon\varphi\upsilon\rho\alpha\mu\acute{e}\nu o\nu$, — "clay mingled and leavened with blood;" others, no doubt, will abhor it and detest it. But what spirit of meekness and mercy our author is acted by he discovereth in the close of this chapter, p. 223; for, saith he, "it is easily imaginable how an honest and well-meaning man may, through mere ignorance, fall into such errors, which, though God will pardon, yet governors must punish. His integrity may expiate the crime, but cannot prevent the mischief of his error. Nay, so easy is it for men to deserve to be punished for their consciences, that there is no nation in the world in which (were government rightly understood and duly managed) mistakes and abuses of religion would not supply the galleys with vastly greater numbers than villany." There is no doubt but that if Phæton get into the chariot of the sun, the world will be sufficiently fired. And if every Absalom, who thinks he understands government and the due management of it better than its present possessors, were enthroned, there would be havoc enough made among mankind. But blessed be God, who in many places hath disposed it into such hands as under whom those who desire to fear and serve him according to his will may yet enjoy a more tolerable condition than such adversaries are pleased withal. That honest and well-meaning men falling into errors about the worship of God, through their own ignorance, wherein their "integrity may expiate their crime, must be punished, must not be pardoned," looks, methinks, with an appearance of more severity than it is the will of God that the world should be governed by, seeing one end of his instituting and appointing government among men is to represent himself in his power, goodness, and wisdom unto them. And he that shall conjoin another assertion of our author, namely, that it is "better and more eligible to tolerate debaucheries and immoralities in conversation than liberty of conscience for men to worship God according to those apprehensions which they have of his will," with the close of this chapter, that "it is so easy for men to deserve to be punished far their consciences, that there is no nation in the world in which (were government rightly understood and duly managed) mistakes and abuses of religion would not supply the galleys with vastly greater numbers than villany," will easily judge with what spirit, from what principles, and with what design, this whole discourse was composed.

But I find myself, utterly beside and beyond my intention, engaged in particular controversies; and finding, by the prospect I have taken of what remains in the treatise under consideration, that it is of the same nature and importance with what is past, and a full continuation of those opprobrious reproaches of them whom he opposeth, and open discoveries of earnest desires after their trouble and ruin, which we have now sufficiently been inured unto, I shall choose rather here to break off this discourse than farther to pursue the ventilation of those differences, wherein I shall not willingly or of choice at any time engage. Besides, what is in the whole discourse of especial and particular controversy may be better handled apart by itself, as probably ere long it will be, if this new representation of old pretences, quickened by invectives, and improved beyond all bounds and measures formerly fixed or given unto them, be judged to deserve a particular consideration. In the meantime, this author is more concerned than I to consider whether those bold incursions that he hath made upon the ancient boundaries and rules of religion and the consciences of men; those contemptuous revilings of his adversaries, which he hath almost filled the pages of his book withal; those discoveries he hath made of the want of a due sense of the weaknesses and infirmities of men, which himself wants not, and of fierce, implacable, sanguinary thoughts against them who appeal to the judgment-seat of God that they do not in any thing dissent from him or others but out of a reverence of the authority of God and for fear of provoking his holy majesty; his incompassionate insulting over men in distresses and sufferings, — will add to the comfort of that account which he must shortly make before his Lord and ours.

To close up this discourse: The principal design of the treatise thus far surveyed is, to persuade or seduce sovereign princes or supreme magistrates unto two evils, that are indeed inseparable, and equally pernicious to themselves and others. The one of these is, to invade or usurp the throne of God; and the other, to behave themselves therein unlike him; — and where the one leads the way, the other will assuredly follow. The empire over religion, the souls and consciences of men in the worship of God, hath hitherto been esteemed to belong unto God alone, to be a peculiar jewel in his glorious diadem; neither can it spring from any other fountain but absolute and infinite supremacy, such as belongs to him, as he hath alone, who is the first cause and last end of all. All attempts to educe it from or resolve it into any other principle are vain, and will prove abortive. But here the sons of men are enticed to say, with him of old, "We will ascend into heaven; we will exalt our throne above the stars of God; we will sit upon also the mount of the congregation, in the sides of the north; we will ascend above the heights of the clouds; we will be like the Most High." For wherein can this be effected? What ladders have men to climb personally into heaven? and who shall attend them in their attempt? It is an assuming of a dominion over the souls and consciences of men in the worship of God wherein and whereby this may be pretended, and therein alone. And all this description of the invasion of the throne of God, whence he who did so is compared to Lucifer, who sought supremacy in heaven, is but the setting up of his power in and over the church in its worship, which was performed in the temple, the mount of the congregation, and in Zion, on the north of the city of Jerusalem, Isa. xiv. 12–14. This now princes are persuaded unto, and can scarce escape without reproaches, where they refuse, or omit the attempting of it. Suppose they be prevailed with to run the hazard and adventure of such an undertaking, what is it that they are thereon persuaded unto? How are they directed to behave themselves after they have assumed a likeness unto the Most High, and exalted themselves to his throne? Plainly, that which is now expected from them is nothing but wrath, fury, indignation, persecution, destructions, banishments, ruin of the persons and families of men innocent, peaceable, fearing God, and useful in their several stations, to satisfy their own wills, or to serve the interests of other men. Is this to act like God, whose power and authority they have assumed, or like to his greatest adversary? Doth God deal thus in this world in his rule over the souls of men? or is not this that which is set out in the fable of Phæton, that he who takes the chariot of the sun will cast the whole world into a combustion? So he who of old is supposed to have affected the throne of God hath ever since acted that cruelty to his power; which manifests what was his design therein, and what would have been the end of his coveted sovereignty. And whoever at any time shall take to himself that power that is peculiar to God, will find himself left, in the exercise of it, to act utterly unlike him, yea, contrary unto him.

Power, they say, is a liquor that, let it be put into what vessel you will, is ready to overflow; and as useful as it is, — as nothing is more to mankind in this world, — yet when it is not accompanied with a due proportion of wisdom and goodness, it is troublesome, if not pernicious, to them concerned in it. The power of God is infinite, and his sovereignty absolute; but the whole exercise of these glorious, dreadful properties of his nature is regulated by wisdom and goodness, no less infinite than themselves. And as he hath all power over the souls and consciences of men, so he exercises it with that goodness, grace, clemency, patience, and forbearance, which I hope we are all sensible of. If there be any like him, equal unto him, in these things, I will readily submit the whole of my religion and conscience unto him, without the least hesitation. And if God, in his dominion and rule over the souls and consciences of men, do exercise all patience, benignity, long-suffering, and mercy, — for "it is of his compassion that we are not consumed," — doth he not declare that none is meet to be intrusted with that power and rule but they who have these things like himself; at least, that in what they are or may be concerned in it, they express and endeavour to answer his example? Indeed, sovereign princes and supreme magistrates are God's vicegerents, and are called gods on the earth, to represent his power and authority unto men in government, within the bounds prefixed by himself unto them, which are the most extensive that the nature of things is capable of; and in so doing, to conform themselves and their actings to him and his, as he is the great monarch, the prototype of all rule and the exercise of it, in justice, goodness, clemency, and benignity, that so the whole of what they do may tend to the relief, comfort, refreshment, and satisfaction of mankind, walking in the ways of peace and innocency, in answer unto the ends of their rule, — is their duty, their honour, and their safety. And to this end doth God usually and ordinarily furnish them with a due proportion of wisdom and understanding; for they also are of God. He gives them an understanding suited and commensurate to their work, that what they have to do shall not ordinarily be too hard for them, nor shall they be tempted to mistakes and miscarriages from the work they are employed about, which he hath made to be their own. But if any of them shall once begin to exceed their bounds, to invade his throne, and to take to themselves the rule of any province belonging peculiarly and solely to the kingdom of heaven, therein a conformity unto God in their actings is not to be expected; for be they never so amply furnished with all abilities of mind and soul for the work and those duties which are their own, which are proper unto them, yet they are not capable of any such stores of wisdom and goodness as should fit them for the work of God, that which peculiarly belongs to his authority and power. His power is infinite; his authority is absolute; so are his wisdom, goodness, and patience. Thus he rules religion, the souls and consciences of men. And when princes partake in these things, *infinite power, infinite wisdom,* and *infinite goodness,* they may assume the same rule and act like him; but to pretend an interest in the one and not in the other will set them in the greatest opposition to him.

Those, therefore, who can prevail with magistrates to take the power of God over religion, and the souls of men in their observance of it, need never fear that when they have so done they will imitate him in his patience, clemency, meekness, forbearance, and benignity; for they are no way capable of these things in a due proportion to that power which is not their own, however they may be eminently furnished for that which is so.

Thus have we known princes (such as Trajan, Adrian, Julian of old), whilst they kept themselves to their proper sphere, ordering and disposing the affairs of this world and all things belonging to public peace, tranquillity, and welfare, to have been renowned for their righteousness, moderation, and clemency, and thereby made dear to mankind, who, when they have fallen into the excess of assuming divine power over the consciences of men and the worship of God, have left behind them such footsteps and remembrances of rage, cruelty, and blood in the world, as make them justly abhorred to all generations. This alone is the seat and posture wherein the powers of the earth are delighted with the sighs and groans of innocent persons, with the fear and dread of them that are and would be at peace, with the punishment of their obedient subjects, and the binding of those hands of industry which would willingly employ themselves for the public good and welfare. Take this occasion out of the way, and there is nothing that should provoke sovereign magistrates to any thing that is grievous, irksome, or troublesome to men peaceable and innocent; nothing that should hinder their subjects from seeing the presence of God with them in their rule, and his image upon them in their authority, causing them to delight in the thoughts of them, and to pray continually for their continuance and prosperity. It may be some may be pleased for a season with severities against dissenters, such as concerning whom we discourse, who falsely suppose their interest to lie therein. It may be they may think meet rather to have all "debaucheries of life and conversation tolerated" than liberty for peaceable men to worship God according to their light and persuasion of his mind and will, as the multitude was pleased of old with the cry of, "Release Barabbas, and let Jesus be crucified." Magistrates themselves will at length perceive how little they are beholden to any who importunately suggest unto them fierce and sanguinary counsels in these matters. It is a saying of Maximilian the emperor, celebrated in many authors: "Nullum," said he, "enormius peccatum dari potest, quam in conscientias imperium exercere velle. Qui enim conscientiis imperare volunt, ii arcem cœli invadunt, et plerumque terræ possessionem perdunt."

Magistrates need not fear but that the open wickedness and bloody crimes of men will supply them with objects to be examples and testimonies of their justice and severity. And methinks it should not be judged an unequal petition by them who rule in the stead and fear of God, that those who are innocent in their lives, useful in their callings and occasions, peaceable in the Lord, might not be exposed to trouble only because they design and endeavour, according to their light, which they are invincibly persuaded to be from God himself, to take care that they perish not eternally. However, I know I can mind them of advice which is ten thousand times more their interest to attend unto than to any that is tendered in the treatise we have had under consideration, and it is that given by a king unto those that should partake of the like royal authority with himself: Ps. ii. 10–12, "Be wise now therefore, O ye kings: be instructed ye judges of the earth. Serve the LORD with fear, and rejoice with trembling. Kiss the Son, lest he be angry, and ye perish from the way, when his wrath is kindled but a little. Blessed are all they that put their trust in him." And he who can inform me how they can render themselves more like unto God, more acceptable unto him, and more the concern and delight of mankind, than by relieving peaceable and innocent persons from their fears, cares, and solicitousness about undeserved evils, or from the suffering of such things, which no mortal man can convince them that they have merited to undergo or suffer, he shall have my thanks for his discovery.

And what is it that we treat about? What is it that a little truce and peace is desired unto and pleaded for? What are the concerns of public good therein? Let a little sedate consideration be exercised about these things, and the causelessness of all the wrath we have been conversing withal will quickly appear. That there is a sad degeneracy of Christianity in the world, amongst the professors of Christian religion, from the rule, spirit, worship, and conversation of the first Christians, who in all things observed and expressed the nature, virtue, and power of the gospel, all must acknowledge and many do complain. Whatever of this kind comes to pass, and by what means soever, it is the interest and design of them who are present gainers by it in the world to keep all things in the posture that yields them their advantage. Hence, upon every appearance of an alteration, or apprehension that any will desert the ways of worship wherein they have been engaged, they are cast into a storm of passion and outrage, like Demetrius and the rest of the silversmiths, pretending divisions, present settlement, ancient veneration, and the like, when their gain and advantage, whether known or unknown to themselves, is that which both influenceth them with such a frame of spirit and animates them to actings suitable thereunto. Thus in the ages past there was so great and universal an apostasy, long before foretold, overspreading Christianity, that by innumerable sober persons it was judged intolerable, and that if men had any regard to the gospel of Christ, their own freedom in the world, or everlasting blessedness, there was a necessity of a reformation, and the reduction of the profession of Christian religion unto some nearer conformity to the primitive times and pattern. Into this design sundry kings, princes, and whole nations, engaged themselves, — namely, what lay in them, and according to the sentiments of truth they had received, to reduce religion unto its pristine glory. What wrath, clamours, fury, indignation, revenge, malice, this occasioned in them whose subsistence, wealth, advantages, honour, and reputation, all lay in preserving things in their state of defection and apostasy, is known to all the world. Hence, therefore, arose bloody persecutions in all, and fierce wars in many nations, where this thing was attempted, stirred up by the craft and cruelty of them who had mastered and managed the former declensions of religion to their own use and advantage; the guilt of which mischiefs and miseries unto mankind is, by a late writer amongst ourselves, contrary to all the monuments of times past, and confessions of the adversaries themselves, endeavoured to be cast on the reformers.

However, a work of reformation was carried on in the world, and succeeded in many places; in none more eminently than in this nation wherein we live. That the end aimed at, which was professedly the reduction of religion to its ancient beauty and glory in truth and worship, is attained amongst us, some perhaps do judge, and absolutely acquiesce therein; and for my part, I wish we had more [who] did so: for, be it spoken, as I hope, without offence on the part of others, so without fear of giving it, or having it taken, on my own, there are among many such evident declensions from the first established reformation towards the old or a new, and it may be worse apostasy, such an apparent weariness of the principal doctrines and practices which enlivened the reformation, as I cannot but be troubled at, and wherewith many are offended; for although I do own a dissent from some present establishments in the church of England, yet I have that honour for the first reformers of it, and reformation itself, that love to the truth declared and established in it, that respect to the work and grace of God in the conversion of the souls of thousands by the ministry of the word in these nations, that I cannot but grieve continually to see the acknowledged doctrines of it deserted, its ancient principles and practices derided, its pristine zeal despised, by some who make advantage of its outward constitution, inheriting the profits, emoluments, and wealth which the bounty of our kings have endowed it withal, but not its spirit, its love, its steadfastness in owning the protestant truth and cause.

But to return, for these things may better elsewhere be complained of, seeing they relate only to particular persons: That what is done in reformation be established, that any farther public work of the same nature attempted, or the retrievement of what is done to its original condition and estate, belongs to the determination of the supreme magistrate, and to that alone. Private persons have no call, no warrant to attempt any thing unto these purposes. However, many there are who dislike some ecclesiastical constitutions and modes of outward worship, which have been the matter of great contests from the first reformation, but much more dislike the degeneracy from the spirit, way, and principles of the first reformers before mentioned, which in some at present they apprehend. And, therefore, though many seem to be at a great distance from the present established forms of the church of England, yet certainly all who are humble and peaceable, when they shall see the ministry of the church, as in former days, in some measure acted rightly and zealously towards the known ends of it, and such as are undeniably by all acknowledged, — namely, the conviction of the world, the conversion of souls, and the edification of them that do believe; and the discipline of it exercised in a conformity at least to the rule of the discipline of the secular powers of the earth, — "Not to be a terror to the good, but to them that do evil;" and in these things a demonstration of the meekness, humility, patience, forbearance, condescension to the weakness, mistakes, errings and wanderings of others, which the gospel doth as plainly and evidently require of us as it doth that we should believe in Jesus Christ, — will continually pray for its prosperity, though they cannot themselves join with it in sundry of its practices and ways. In the meantime, I say, such persons as these, in themselves and for their own concerns, do think it their duty not absolutely to take up in what hath been attained amongst us, much less in what many are degenerated into, but to endeavour the reduction of their practice in the worship of God to what was first appointed by Jesus Christ; as being persuaded that he requires it of them, and being convinced that, in the unspeakable variety that is in human constitutions, rest unto their souls and consciences is not otherwise to be obtained. And if, at the same time, they endeavour not to reduce the manner and course of their conversation to the same rule and example by which they would have their worship of God regulated, they are *hypocrites*. Short enough, no doubt, they come, in both, of perfection, but both they profess to aim equally at; and herein alone can their consciences find rest and peace. In the doctrine of faith, consented on in the first reformation, and declared in the allowed writings of the church of England, they agree with others, and wish with all their hearts they had more to agree withal. Only, they cannot come up to the practice of some things in the worship of God, which being confessedly of human prescription, their obedience in them would lie in a perfect contradiction to their principal design, before mentioned; for those things, being chosen out from a great multitude of things of the same nature, invented by those whose authority was rejected in the first reformation, or reduction of religion from its catholic apostasy, they suppose cannot justly be imposed on them, they are sure cannot be honestly received by them, whilst they design to reduce themselves unto the primitive rules and examples of obedience. In this design they profess themselves ready to be ruled by, and to yield subjection unto, any truth or direction that can or may be given them from the word of God, or any principles lawfully from thence educed. How their conviction is at present attempted, let the book under consideration, and some late unparalleled and illegal acts of violence, conformable to the spirit of it, be a testimony. But, in the management of their design, they proceed on no other principles than those of the liberty of judgment (of discretion, or discerning, they call it), for the determining of themselves and their own practices in what they believe and profess about religion, and the liberty of their consciences from all human impositions, than were owned, pleaded, and contended for by the first reformers, and the most learned defenders of the church of England, in their disputations against the Papists; those they will stand to and abide by: yea, than what are warranted by the principles of our nature and constitution; for no man practiseth any thing, nor can practice it, but according to his own will and choice.

Now, in these things, in their principle, or in their management of it, it may be they are mistaken, it may be they are in an error, or under many mistakes and errors; but from their integrity they know themselves innocent, even in their mistakes. And it is in the nature of men to think strange of sedate violences, that befall them without their demerit, and of suffering by law without any guilt. Their design of reducing themselves in worship and conversation to the primitive pattern, they openly avow; nor dare any directly condemn that design, nor can they be convinced of insincerity in what they profess. And shall they be destroyed if they miss it in some matters of smaller concernment? which, whatever some may boast of, is not hitherto tolerably proved. Shall now their dissent in religious observances on this occasion, and those and that about things mostly and chiefly, if not only, that appear neither name nor thing in the Scripture, be judged a crime not to be expiated but by their ruin? Are immoralities or vicious debaucheries rather to be tolerated, or exempted from punishment, than such a dissent? What place of Scripture in the Old or New Testament, which of the ancient fathers of the church, do speak at this rate? Opinions inconsistent with public tranquillity, with the general rules of moral duties in all relations and conditions, practices of any tendency in themselves to political disturbances, are by none pleaded for. Mere dissent itself, with different observances in the outward worship of God, is by some pretended, indeed, to be a civil disturbance; it hath always been so by some, even by those whose own established ways have been superstitious and idolatrous. But wise men begin to smile when they hear private interest pleaded as public good, and the affections which it begets as the common reason of things. And these pretences have been by all parties, at one time or another, refuted and discarded. Let the merit of the cause be stated and considered, which is truly as above proposed, and no other; set aside prejudices, animosities, advantages from things past and bygone in political disorders and tumults, wherein it hath no concern, — and it will quickly appear how little it is, how much, if possible, less than nothing, that is or can be pleaded for the countenancing of external severity in this case. Doth it suit the spirit of the gospel [of Christ] or his commands, to destroy *good wheat*, for standing, as is supposed, *a little out of order*, who would not have men pluck up the tares, but to let them stand quietly in the field until harvest? Doth it answer his mind to destroy *his disciples*, who profess to love and obey him, from the earth, who blamed his disciples of old for desiring to destroy the Samaritans, his enemies, with fire from heaven? We are told that "he who was born after the flesh persecuted him who was born after the promise;" and a work becoming him it was And if men are sincere disciples of Christ, though they may fall into some mistakes and errors, the outward persecuting of them on that account will be found to be of the works of the flesh. It is certain, that for those in particular who take upon them, in any place or degree, to be ministers of the gospel, there are commands for meekness, patience, and forbearance given unto them; and it is one of the greatest duties incumbent on them to express the Lord Jesus Christ in the frame of his mind and spirit unto men, and that eminently in his *meekness* and *lowliness*, which he calls us all in an especial manner to learn of him. A peculiar conformity also to the gospel, to the holy law of love, self-denial, and condescension, is required of them, that they may not, in their spirits, ways, and actings, make a false representation of him and that which they profess.

I know not, therefore, whence it is come to pass that this sort of men do principally, if not only, stir up magistrates and rulers to laws, severities, penalties, coercions, imprisonments, and the like outward means of fierce and carnal power, against those who in any thing dissent from them in religion. Generally, abroad, throughout Christendom, those in whose hands the civil powers are, and who may be supposed to have inclinations unto the severe exercise of that power which is their own, such as they think, possibly, may become them as men and governors, would be inclinable to moderation towards dissenters, were they not excited, provoked, and wearied, by them who pretend to represent Jesus Christ to the world, — as if any earthly potentate had more patience, mercy, and compassion than he. Look on those Lutheran countries where they persecute the *Calvinists*. It is commonly declared and proved that the magistrates, for the most part, would willingly bear with those dissenters, were they not stirred up continually to severities by them whose duty it were to persuade them to clemency and moderation, if in themselves they were otherwise inclined. And this hath ruined the interest of the protestant religion in Germany, in a great measure. Do men who destroy no more than they can, nor punish more than they are able, and cry out for assistance where their own arm fails them, render themselves hereby like to their heavenly Father? Is this spirit from above? Doth that which is so teach men to harass the consciences of persons, their brethren and fellow-servants, on every little difference in judgment and practice about religious things? Whom will such men fulfil the commands of patience, forbearance, waiting, meekness, condescension, that the gospel abounds with, towards? Is it only towards them who are of the same mind with themselves? They stand in no need of them; they stand upon the same terms of advantage with themselves. And for those that dissent, "Arise, kill and eat," seems to be the only command to be observed towards them. And why all this fierceness and severity? Let men talk what they please, those aimed at are peaceable in the land, and resolve to be so, whatever may befall them. They despise all contrary insinuations. That they are in their stations severally useful to the commonwealth, and collectively, in their industry and trading, of great consideration to public welfare, is now apparent unto all indifferent men. It is, or must be, if it be for any thing (as surely no men delight in troubling others for trouble's sake), for their errors and mistakes in and about the worship of God. All other pleas are mere pretences of passion and interest. But who judgeth them to be guilty of *errors*? Why, those that stir up others to their hurt and disquietment. But is their judgment infallible? How if they should be mistaken themselves in their judgment? If they are, they do not only err, but persecute others for the truth. And this hath been the general issue of this matter in the world. Error hath persecuted truth ten times for truth's once persecuting of error. But suppose the worst, suppose them in errors and under mistakes, let it be proved that God hath appointed that all men who so err should be so punished as they would have Nonconformists, and though I should believe them in the truth, I would never more plead their cause. And would these men be willingly thus dealt withal by those who judge or may judge them to err? It may be some would, because they have a good security that none shall ever judge them so to do who hath power to punish them, for they will be of his mind. But sure none can be so absolutely confined unto themselves, nor so universally, in all their affections and desires, unto their own personal concerns, as not to have a compassion for some or other who, in one place or other, are judged to err by them who have power over them to affix what guilt they please unto that which is not their crime. And will they justify all their oppressors? All men have an equal right in this matter; nothing is required but being uppermost to make a difference. This is that which hath turned Christendom into a shambles, whilst every prevailing party hath judged it their duty and interest to destroy them that do dissent from them.

Once more; what name of sin or wickedness will they find to affix to these errors? "Nullum criminis nomen, nisi nominis crimen." No man errs willingly, nor ought to be thought to tempt or seduce his own will, when his error is to his disadvantage; and he is innocent whose will is not guilty. Moreover, those pretended errors in our case are not in matters of faith; nor, for the most part, in or about the worship of God, or that which is acknowledged so to be; but in or about those things which some think it convenient to add unto it or conjoin with it. And what quietness, what peace is there like to be in the world, whilst the sword of vengeance must be continually drawn about these things? Counsels of peace, patience, and forbearance, would certainly better become professors of the gospel and preachers of everlasting peace than such passionate and furious enterprises for severity as we meet withal.

And I no way doubt but that all generous, noble, and heroic spirits, such as are not concerned in the empaled peculiar interest and advantages of some, and do scorn the pedantic humours of mean and emulous souls, when once a few more clouds of prejudices are scattered, will be willing to give up to God the glory of his sovereignty over the consciences of men, and despise the thought of giving them disquietment for such things as they can no way remedy, and which hinder them not from being servants of God, good subjects to the king, and useful in their respective lots and conditions.

And now, instead of those words of Pilate, "What I have written I have written," — which, though uttered by him maliciously and despitefully, as was also the prophecy of Caiaphas, were, by the holy, wise providence of God, turned into a testimony to the truth, — I shall shut up this discourse with those of our Saviour, which are unspeakably more our concernment to consider, Matt. xxiv. 45–51: "Who then is a faithful and wise servant, whom his lord hath made ruler over his household, to give them meat in due season? blessed is that servant, whom his lord when he cometh shall find so doing. Verily I say unto you, that he shall make him ruler over all his goods. But and if that evil servant shall say in his heart, My lord delayeth his coming; and shall begin to smite his fellow-servants, and to eat and drink with the drunken; the lord of that servant shall come in a day when he looketh not for him, and in an hour that he is not aware of, and shall cut him asunder, and appoint him his portion with the hypocrites: there shall be weeping and gnashing of teeth."